After war service  North West Europe the Salvation Army, more than fifty count years. Later he beca Press Officer of both both travels widely in Latin America and the Caribbean, setting up and advising on welfare programmes for the aged and is a delegate to international conferences on ageing.

His experiences range from membership of the Archbishop of Cape Town's watchdog committee on race relations to hitching a lift with one of Che Guevara's guerillas in the Amazon jungle. He has conducted choirs and massed bands, written and produced musical plays and pageants, performed on the bass trombone, and organized earthquake relief.

By the same author

Tank!

KEN TOUT

Tanks, Advance!

Normandy to the Netherlands, 1944

GRAFTON BOOKS

A Division of the Collins Publishing Group

LONDON GLASGOW
TORONTO SYDNEY AUCKLAND

Grafton Books
A Division of the Collins Publishing Group
8 Grafton Street, London W1X 3LA

Published by Grafton Books 1989

First published in Great Britain by
Robert Hale Ltd 1987

ISBN 0-586-20321-4

Printed and bound in Great Britain by
Collins, Glasgow

Set in Caledonia

Contents

To Arthur Dwight, Eric Good and so many others who happily survived the war and to whom their country owes a cumulative debt of more than forty years during which they cheerfully conquered the disablement which was their own very special sacrifice.

Preface

For those who have already read my first book, *Tank!* – or who may one day be inclined to do so – a brief word of explanation is necessary. As this present book covers my entire journey from Normandy to the Netherlands, it is possible to place in the correct chronological order one or two events which were interjected into the forty-hour timescale of *Tank!* (7–8 August 1944) in order to illustrate what can and does happen in tank battles.

Since *Tank!* was written, we remaining Yeomen have enjoyed a further three tours in Normandy, Belgium and the Netherlands as the guests of those people whom it was our privilege to liberate. We have also met one or two of our former enemies in a more congenial atmosphere. But after all these years our united memories still fail to identify some of those unfortunate lads who were thrust into our ranks as urgent reinforcements when their own regiments broke up, some of whom literally ceased to exist within a day or two of joining.

The reader may therefore like to know that every person in this book to whom a surname is given is or was real. Where we have been totally unable to identify who did what at a certain point, I have used only a fictitious Christian name without surname. Otherwise the record is as correct as can be achieved. It also benefits from memories of some of the liberated villagers, such as the little boy Gazareth in St-Julien who saw us arrive in 1944 and was there again as mayor in 1984 with a massive and emotional demonstration of gratitude planned by the people of the surrounding area.

In addition to all those mentioned in the text who have so freely allowed me to recall their feats and foibles, I would like to thank two 'non-Yeomen'. It was Carmel Elwell who thought that *Tank!* deserved a sequel and who gave invaluable advice, including the inevitable search for a title. And my wife Jai was the person really responsible for it all. She it was who encouraged me, some years ago, to knock on the door of the then unknown Bélenger family in St-Aignan and hazard the statement, *'J'étais soldat anglais ici pendant la guerre . . .'* All the rest just seemed to happen naturally.

K.T.
March 1987

Prelude: *Martial Music*

I marched away
to the glorious trumpets of war,
the haunting horns of ambition,
the laughing trombones of youthfulness,
the pounding tubas of discipline.

I limped back home
to the shivering violins of fear,
the moaning violas of pain,
the sombre cellos of self-knowledge,
the stumbling basses of self-doubt.

Only later
did I discover
that I was my own composer
and my own conductor.

                                        K.T.

1

Have Tank, Will Travel

6 JUNE 1944:

Any story of Normandy, 1944, must begin with D-Day. And the first D-Day found me swinging my arm to bowl: not a Mills bomb but a cricket ball. The scene: not a Normandy beach but a green field near Aldershot.

I was running up to bowl. But the noise of the planes became so loud and insistent that I skidded to a stop. The batsmen, the umpires, the fielders, the few spectators were all looking at the skies.

Like veterans at an Armistice Day parade they came, slowly, in great dignity, formations slightly awry, here and there a lurch of unsteadiness, but proudly all, the great droning planes towing the silent, heavily loaded gliders. Trains of them, echelons of them, armies of them, furrowing and blackening the summer skies. Massed and numerous as the swarms of swallows at summer's end. But slow and ponderous. Having more affinity with traction engines than with Spitfires. Darkening and timeless, as a summer twilight, the tow-planes in drab war colours, and the camouflaged gliders.

All the disappointment, which we had been trying to forget in an impromptu cricket match, surged again. On 6 June 1944 there was only one place to be: on a Normandy beach. Or at least on a tank-landing ship or in a glider hurrying that way. Those of us who knew our Shakespeare remembered Henry V's speech when he rallied his troops with the thought of earning glory on the battlefield, always to be envied by 'gentlemen in England now abed'. For 'now abed' read 'now chasing a maudlin cricket ball', and

that describes our abject shame and bitter disappointment
at missing this latter St Crispin's Day.

For we were tank crews. Spearhead troops. Élite in our
own eyes. The Red Cross of St George blazoned on our
hearts and a tiny White Horse of Hanover fixed to our berets
and lapels. We had trained on Salisbury Plain and Linney
Head and Lulworth and Thetford Heath. For this day. We
had expected to be there, leading among the first waves on
the beaches. Armoured pioneers going ashore in the tradi-
tion of Julius Caesar and Duke William and the boys of
Anzio.

Instead, here we were, playing against a squad of Pay
Corps clerks in a casual match with bat and ball. A match
so casual that we were still garbed in our regulation khaki
and the umpires were neutral fitters from the workshops,
still in their oily denim overalls. A match of so little
consequence that batsmen and umpires and fielders and
the few spectators ignored the bowler and stared longingly
at the infernal pageantry of the airborne invasion.

D-Day, or so the BBC said.

Us – we were élite troops only in our own eyes, and
Monty hadn't bothered to inform us!

7 JUNE 1944:

A bitter day. We had hoped until midnight that movement
orders might come through. But we lost both the cricket
match and the glory of participating in one of history's most
momentous days.

There would be many dressed in khaki, light blue or
navy blue who would be glad to have missed the slaughter
hours of the Normandy beaches. But many more of us
wanted to be there. The element of glorious adventure was
much more potent than the factor of mortal danger.

'Don't know what we bloody well joined up for,' moaned
Johnny, my driver. 'If they didn't want us for D-Day, why

the hell did they bother to call us up? We could have been chasing all that spare skirt from the munitions works at home.'

'Yeah, and all that farce of going on forty-seven hours leave,' growled Bernard, the gunner. 'My girl's family thought I was Bulldog Drummond home from the front when I turned up unannounced with forty-seven hours to go before I, me, myself, landed on the French beaches. Now I'll have to go home and say it was all a bad joke of Monty's.'

'But what buggers me off worst of all,' chimed in the co-driver, Sid, 'is that while all that lot are gathering glory on the Normandy beaches we are still here burning our fingers to the bone with Bostik, waterproofing a bleeding tank. And for what? To land it on some French dockside without wetting the pissing tracks?'

They were enumerating my own complaints. In my case the disillusionment with General Montgomery – to us, God upon Earth – and his High Priest, Major Hank Bevan, had started over a month earlier at Bury St Edmunds. The Regiment had been stationed there, in the woods of a country estate at Fornham Park. The new Sherman tanks were arriving in their full war paint, camouflaged for France. The older Yeomen viewed eventual battle with some doubts and qualms, but most of the younger reinforcements, nineteen- and twenty-year-olds, saw this as an adventure story out of a school magazine, or the *Hotspur* or the *Wizard*. The more literary of us even dreamed of mention on a stained glass window or an oak-and-gold-leaf honours board in some dim school hall.

It was like the naming of the First XI or the First XV at school. No verbal announcements on parade and no special briefing meeting. Simply a typewritten list of the teams, pinned up on the notice-board outside the Squadron Office Nissen hut, by John Pearson, the clerk corporal. Troopers, corporals and sergeants came running from all directions in the Fornham Park woods. The chosen crews had been a well-kept secret. A chattering, seething crowd gathered around the tiny typewritten page. Nineteen Sherman crews. Five men on the 75mm Shermans. Four men on the 'Fireflys' with their larger 17-pounder guns.

'Shout out the names, Tommy. We can't see!' 'Stop pushing, you buggers at the back!' 'Read out 3 Troop first, Dick!' 'Am I on it, Tommy?' 'Who's gunning on Bill Fox's tank, Dick?'

I ran my eye down the list, starting hopefully at the top.

C Squadron, 1st Northamptonshire Yeomanry, Battle Order.
Squadron Leader: Major D. G. Bevan
Driver: Sergeant R. Bates
Operator: Corporal G. Bolton
Gunner: Tpr. P. Pedder
Co-Driver: Tpr. D. Pateman
Then Second-in-Command: Captain W. Fox
   Driver: L/Cpl J. Watkinson . . .
Then Squadron Captain: Captain M. Rathbone
   Driver: L/Cpl H. Hoult . . .

No! No! No! Maybe in 1 Troop . . . or 2 Troop or 3 Troop. Then 4 Troop – Troop Leader: Lt W. Brown; Driver . . . and down to 4 Troop Corporal and 4 Troop Firefly.

But my name not there! No Trooper K. J. Tout!

Banished as to Siberia, to an unknown distant reserve group of whose existence everybody seemed to be in total ignorance. My pals in the HQF barrack hut, Pete and Don and Bruce and Kempy, were sympathetic and wound arms around my drooping shoulders. 'There'll be casualties. Then Hank will have you up.' But it wasn't good enough. I had missed the First Team.

It was Kempy, the Norfolk farmer lad, who brought a ray of hope into my darkened world of frustrated ambitions.

He had been named for fatigues, and his duty that day was to clean the Squadron Leader's office.

'Ken! Ken!' he shouted, coming into the barrack hut later that day. 'I've got news for you. I know why you're going back to reserve. Hank has put you down as a tank commander. You crafty sod! How much did you have to pay him?'

So, on that gloomy day in Aldershot, when I had at last departed to the nether regions of the Reserve Troop, at the back of an odd workshop down a side lane on the outskirts of the camp, there was some glitter left to our war of shining cavalry cap badges and thundering grey-green tanks. And when the Reserve Troop Lieutenant took me down to the tiny tank-park and showed me the new, sleek Stuart light tank, standing alongside three vast Shermans, and said 'Right! That's your tank. Put up a stripe and get the crew working on waterproofing ready for landing in several feet of water' – adventure had returned to the war.

Our 'Honey' – the name by which tank crews called the Stuart light tank – was constructed for speed rather than confrontation, and Johnny the driver could coax it along at up to 15 mph more than a Sherman's top speed. The 37mm gun was a mere pea-shooter alongside the Firefly's 17-pounder (the 37mm being equivalent more or less to a 2-pounder) but it was still a real cannon with real live shiny armour-piercing and high-explosive shells. And we also mounted two Browning machine-guns, one co-axially with the 37mm in the turret and one protruding through a mantle in the co-driver's seat.

So there I was: a fully armed tank and a crew of three other troopers at my command to perform all kinds of deeds of derring-do to compare with the heroes of old, as told in the old bound volumes of *The Captain*, the public school magazine kept in the library of my not-quite-public-school High School. Had my High School been a member of the Headmasters Conference, as the local Cathedral School was, it would probably have had a cadet corps and I would have got a commission fairly quickly. As a High School boy I might some time rise to a commission, but not automatically, as could the Cathedral cadets. And I would have been a Cathedral boy had my parents been Anglicans and not Salvationists. On such slight coincidences hung the fate of the aspiring military hero of the 1940s.

9 JUNE 1944:

'Lance-Corporal Tout! Commanders conference straight away in the Troop Leader's office, please.'

The Troop Leader's office was the tiny cubicle, usually occupied by the Troop Corporal, at the end of the barrack-room to which our Reserve Troop had been banished. The Troop Leader himself was billeted in an officers' mess some minutes walk away from our rear-echelon workshop wilderness. He was a smallish, dark lieutenant, obviously labouring under the same weight of disillusionment as ourselves about finding himself in reserve. Yet as a Troop Leader he held an appointment for which Armoured Corps staff captains would sell their souls and drop their ranks, in order to serve with a 'line regiment'.

The passive little Lieutenant looked around and counted us up. 'Well, as usual it's good news and bad news. The Regiment at last has its marching orders. It is moving to Southampton to board landing ships there. We are definitely going over to Normandy. No doubt about that. However, there is no room at present for Reserve Troop, so we shall be staying on here in Aldershot until further orders. That's it. Tell your lads. Then get back to checking the waterproofing again.'

Back to the tank-park whilst all the while the solemn symphony of war goes on. The deep bass rumbling and crashing of anonymous tanks constantly streaming out towards the coast and the perpetual drone of aircraft of all speeds and dimensions heading out towards Normandy and the innumerable boomings and grindings of 'soft' vehicles forming convoy for the most thrilling of destinations.

A destination known to us, as yet, only from the BBC news bulletins. Arromanches!

11 JUNE 1944 – D + 5 – SUNDAY:

Despite the calendar we still continue with the routine of waterproofing. Inspecting each crack and join in the tank's structure to make sure that the black, rubbery Bostik solution still adheres. Checking the canvas chute which is attached above the engine outlets, to ensure that it is still firmly in place. Cleaning the guns from the dirt of another day. Running the engine and the turret traverse system and the wireless to see that all function as they did yesterday. Driving the tank slowly down the tank-park to try out steering and braking.

'Lance-Corporal Tout. Commanders conference. *Tout de suite*. Troop Leader's office.' And still only 10 A.M. We met for routine orders at 9 A.M. and there was nothing to report then. Could it be . . . ?

The nervous Lieutenant can hardly wait for us all to arrive. 'This is it, lads. We're on the move. Tomorrow. Crack of dawn. Chasing the Hun. Objective: Southampton. Reveille 04.00 hours. Breakfast 05.00. Orders 06.00, with everybody ready to move. Understood?'

'Great!' 'Whack-ho!' 'About time, too, sir!' 'Do we believe it, this time?' 'Shall we be crossing to France tomorrow, sir?' 'Where's the Regiment, sir?'

'One at a time. I doubt if we shall board a ship tomorrow. No definite orders though. I cannot tell you more until tomorrow. 06.00. Meantime everybody ready to move by Lights Out tonight. I will carry out last inspections today.

16.00, all tank kit and spares. Guns stripped. Storage boxes and engine covers open. Then 18.00, all tanks loaded up. And one final inspection closed down. That's it. Good luck.'

I hazard one question from the depths of my junior acting, unpaid, temporary, lance status. 'Do you have maps of the route from here to Southampton, sir?'

'No, Corporal. They will be issued to you and signed for at Orders tomorrow. There may be enemy agents about, and we don't want them to know where Southampton is.' The sergeants laugh, but I am half persuaded that the Lieutenant means it.

I tread soft clouds of warm elation back from the tawdry barrack-room through the oily tank-park and up the front of my gleaming new, armoured-steel charger – the most mobile and virile of tanks.

'Is it *it*?' shouts Sid, with confusing syntax but utter clarity.

'Yes, it's now tomorrow,' I respond in kind. 'Gather round, oh knights in armour, you shoddy lot. We're on our way . . .' and I repeat the Lieutenant's comments.

Bernard, the oldest of my temporary, makeshift crew, is dubious about the map issue. 'I only hope some bugger knows where Southampton is. Otherwise it'll be a typical Yeomanry balls-up,' he growls, having last night told us a story about being left for a day and a night alone and unsheltered on Salisbury Plain, when the Regiment had returned to camp without remembering that he was doing police duty at a lonely gateway on the Plain.

We set about emptying and stripping and opening up everything, every tiniest bit of the tank that is detachable, so that the little Lieutenant can come along and count all the pieces at 16.00 hours. Then we shall have the oily, gruesome, knuckle-scraping, knee-twisting, shoulder-wrenching, back-straining task of putting it all back together again so that it works. Efficiently enough to chase Huns. If we ever see any.

12 JUNE 1944 – D + 6 – MONDAY:

I stand up straight on the turret of my tank. The early sun catches dull gleams from the grey, smooth steel of the turret top. Sid and Johnny sit with their heads out of their individual hatches down in front of the turret. The Browning machine-gun protruding in front of Sid still wears its dustcover. Bernard sits on the turret with his feet dangling inside the turret, like a kid sitting on a low bridge, dangling his legs in a stream.

Bernard is of great age, somewhere about twenty-six or twenty-seven. Sid had his coming-of-age celebration in a Bury St Edmunds pub about three months back. They showered him in best bitter, uniform and all. Johnny and I are twenty. They all come from other squadrons and I did not know them a week ago. But for the time being we are linked together in fate. We have never done a military exercise together. They can see the stitches new on my stripe and have no reason to trust my orders if ever we land in battle.

In this moment of morning exhilaration the sun rises slowly into an empty sky, and the tank-park dust still lies undisturbed in the last few moments before the Lieutenant orders us to start up and move. The papers may talk about Montgomery and Rommel and the 7th Armoured Division and the German Tiger tanks. They do not know. This is my tank and my crew and my D-Day and my War. All my father's yarns about 'the first lot' and all the stories in *The Boy's Own* about the flying men on the Western Front, and all the inspiring reports in the *War Illustrated* about the VCs and DSOs and MMs won at Dunkirk and Alamein and Salerno are subsumed in this moment of standing waiting to order my driver to start up the tank which will finally seal Hitler's doom.

'Corporal, get your men down in front of the tank. Then wait! Wait, I say, until *I* give the word to mount up.' The melancholy Lieutenant is in a bad temper this morning because Brigade has forgotten to provide us with maps. We shall have to ask our way to Southampton. In a Hussar regiment we should expect to form up in front of our tanks and await the Sergeant-Major's bawled order to mount. But in the Reserve Troop of a Yeomanry 'shower' we had expected that our enthusiasm would pass muster instead of the 'bull'. We get down from the tank, and I pretend not to hear Sid's comment: 'The silly little duck-assed twit.' As we land on the tank-park concrete the Lieutenant yells, 'Crews, mount!'

Our first hostile advance of the war takes us 200 yards to the gates, beyond which lies a land as forbidden as Tibet over the last few days. Our exit is still impeded, even at our precise start time, by a vast convoy of trucks, loaded with infantry, which is passing along the road. We wait for the procession to break. As the 'recce' tank I have the privilege of leading our tiny circus towards a clear map reference some sixty or seventy miles away. The only problem is that I have no map. However, the consensus of the infantry convoy seems to be westwards, to the right, so, assuming that the Black Watch would not be retreating, I give Johnny the word: 'Driver, advance, right hand down.' And we sweep with sweet majesty out of the gates and into formation for the embarkation area.

Johnny is impatient to give the new Honey full throttle, but there is little chance for that as, hour after hour, we shunt and shuttle along in a kind of staff officer's nightmare of intertwining, overlapping, intervening convoys. We soon lose the remainder of our tanks and find ourselves in the fairly permanent company of a lorry-load of Highlanders and a field ambulance. After seven days of such martial movement civilians and random soldiers still wave and wonder at the colossal, uninterrupted procession of war machines, like a vast boa-constrictor squirming, day in, day out, along the road towards Southampton.

I solve the problem of the maps. From time to time the boa-constrictor slithers to a stop. We make friends with the Scots in front. One of the 'Scots' is a Hampshire lad who drove a delivery van along these roads in peace-time. He provides us with a running commentary on our progress. 'Oh, no, Mac,' he says to me, another non-Scot, 'we're nowhere near Southampton yet. Not even near Winchester. We're only a mile or two beyond Fleet. You keep behind us. We'll get you there.'

Somewhere just outside Southampton we come, in the late afternoon, to a deep wood screened off by thick barbed wire entanglements. Our Brigade sign (a green and a black triangle point to point) looms large on a pole beside a wide gap in the wire where deep, rutted tracks lead in through splintered trees. A corporal guides the Reserve Troop to a parking area and allocates each crew to a small belltent in the woods.

The Great Adventure has begun. First a pay clerk appears with packets of real French francs. These are colourful notes specially printed for use by the Liberation Armies to distinguish them from currency issued by the Germans. We count up our francs in schoolboy French and laugh to hear the strange numbers.

Then comes the concert party. A continual supper is being served to incoming troops in a large, open marquee. At the doorway of the marquee is a notice to the effect that a late-shift concert party will perform at 22.30 hours. Long before that hour hundreds of soldiers are sitting on chairs in front of a bare platform, or squatting on the long grass, or leaning smoking against trees. Prompt at 22.30 hours a pianist in a dinner jacket and a girl with bare legs and wearing a frilly, fairy skirt climb on to the platform and go into their routine.

This is the very essence of romance. Hundreds of soldiers spending their last night in England before sailing for the hazardous shores of Normandy, many of those soldiers destined never to return, never to see another English girl. Many, like me, without formal female attachments, yet full of dreams of a someday love affair. Above us the fulsome moon illuminates the glades of the woods. Moonbeams sparkle on distant strands of barbed wire. And on the bare stage a tiny, frail but spirited girl with a tearful contralto voice sings the songs of home and of love and of parting and of future return. She sings something about 'But if you can keep her heart, even when you're far apart, then that's not the moon, that's love, my son'. Under the D-Day moon the masses of soldiers claim encore after encore as they sway with the singer's movements and think of wives and sweethearts and romances not yet born.

The rest of the concert party may fade into oblivion like the soldiers' laughing fading into the muted woods around the stage. But the song of the soubrette, pretty and vibrant, will echo on in the moonlit arcades of memory for many of those who paused to listen to a song before setting off to the real war.

In the tents afterwards there is much talking and smoking and playing cards. We savour the last night in England and let sleep come slowly.

'Can't wait to get over that water and see what those French girls are really like,' laughs Sid. 'That was a French girl tonight, wasn't it?'

'No, you idiot,' says Johnny. 'French girls don't have names like Alice Allan.'

'Well, it said she was a soubrette, didn't it? That's not an English word. That's a French word. Even I know that.'

'Soubrette is only a word used for a certain type of female entertainer on the stage,' I explain. 'A comedy singer or somebody like that.'

'Not much comedy about being sent off to your fate,' mutters Bernard.

'Well, I think it was a right good do they gave us tonight. Good scoff in the cookhouse and then that singing girl with all those songs,' Sid insists.

'I enjoyed myself, for one,' agrees Johnny. 'Makes you sort of feel there's something worth bloody fighting for besides bombed houses and snotty-nosed evacuees. England, and love and all that.'

'Silly bugger,' comments Bernard from his wealth of years. 'Fat lot of good England and love and all that will do you when you get a Jerry bayonet up your ass.'

Idle chatter and the clink of coins and the flutter of French francs already being gambled away are my Vespers and my Cradle Song as I drift away into sleep, there upon the grass in my rough blankets. At 01.30 hours I am awakened by Sid. 'There's a corporal bloke here, Ken. Wants you outside on parade. As you are but with boots on, he says.'

I scramble out of the tent wrapped only in denim overalls and clutching the pair of brown shoes which I usually wear and to which the Yeomanry authorities turn a blind eye. A dark, man-shaped mass, enlivened by two well-blancoed stripes on each arm, awaits me. The Corporal shines a hooded torch on a sheet of paper. 'Lance-Corporal Tout? There's a commanders briefing conference. Straight away. Follow me, lad, and watch the stinging nettles.' We plod through the wood in the blind darkness between the trees and tents, some silent, some still alive with muttered speculation. The moon had disappeared behind a thick cloud. The concert platform is bare and chill.

The cookhouse marquee has double exit covers to

preserve the blackout. Inside a group of about twenty
officers and NCOs has gathered. A Staff Colonel, with the
unfamiliar red tabs, stands beside a huge map of Normandy
and calls for silence. We stand under the bleak light of bare
electric bulbs. The grass at our feet is cold with the
midnight air and greasy with the feeding-habits of
hundreds of vagrant soldiers. We listen.

'Well, gentlemen, the 33rd Armoured Brigade is scheduled for immediate action. You are to come under command of the 7th Armoured Division' (the famous Desert
Rats) 'who are engaged in a vital battle to take Villers
Bocage' (pronounced English fashion, we hear for the first
time that awesome name) 'just there!' And the pointer taps
the map beyond a tangle of red contour lines where a
sweep of verdant green suggests thick jungle country. 'The
Bocage!

'If we can capture Villers Bocage, we shall cut off the
Hun in the American sector from the Hun in the British
and Canadian sector.' (Is this a planned morale-booster,
that higher-ranking officers refer to 'the Hun' in the
singular as though there were only one little solitary
German, however terrible, over there beyond No-Man's-
Land?) 'But we shall not win the battle without fierce
resistance from the Hun.' (Is this the anti-American Hun
or the anti-British-Canadian Hun? Or have the two
coalesced into the more customary singular? Or is this yet
another terrible cousin coming up in the centre to reinforce
them?)

'Tomorrow, when you sail, you will be given your orders.
When you land, you will be rushed to the arrow-point of
action. Villers Bocage. You will be face to face with a
formidable foe. Out in the open. Britain and the Free
World will be depending on you.' I notice the Corporal
commanding our petrol lorry and his pal from the ammunition truck looking slightly sick at the thought of their

'soft' and highly inflammable vehicles venturing out into No-Man's-Land at Villers Bocage.

The Staff Colonel jollies along in what must be the umpteenth repeat of his chorus. Do staff colonels and girl soubrettes and camp cooks not get intensely bored and frustrated at having to feed the same course again and again to this voracious boa-constrictor of reinforcements which must continue for days and weeks and maybe even months yet?

I step out into the starlit night – the moon still hidden in a sudden attack of shyness after so many choral references – and square my rather schoolboy shoulders. I have tonight moved up a rung in the hierarchy of heroism. I am more than a superannuated boy-scout. I am a knight released from the vigil.

I am an entire paragraph walking out of the pages of *The Captain*. I am a tank commander charged with a fateful encounter before Villers Bocage.

I am, in fact, a welter of conflicting sentiments for, although I am the lowest possible non-commissioned rank in the army and in command of the smallest tank in the Reserve Troop of an unblooded Regiment just coming under orders, I am surrounded by men, some snoring, some still gaming, who will be dead in two days' time or two weeks' time or two months' time. For a moment of extreme panic I almost wish to be back on that cricket field in Aldershot. Then the moon shines through and stealthy figures move against the lesser darkness of the tents, a match flares and planes drone overhead. I take a deep breath of the vintage country air. Duck into my tent. Realize it's the wrong one. Find the right one. Stumble over Sid's blankets. 'Muck off, mate!' he groans.

13 JUNE 1944:
Am I superstitious? The 13th? Let's say D + 7. Rain on the leaves and the grass and running down the tent flaps.

An immense breakfast for all the condemned men. Blankets rolled. No shouting of 'Crews, mount!' by the rather scared little Lieutenant. We mount up when ready. Switch on engine and wireless. Put on our headsets. Listen for the Lieutenant's word of command to pierce through the 'A' set, audible simultaneously with I/C (Intercom).

'Able 4' (that's us), 'lead on. Follow convoy. Able 4, over.' (Correct battle procedure today.) I press my microphone switch, turn the wireless control box knob to 'A' set and acknowledge: 'Able 4, OK. Off.' (Switch to I/C.) 'Driver, advance!' And the revving engine plays the tremendous tuba music proper to our solemn departure.

In Southampton it is raining. Even on D + 7 people wave us on towards the Normandy shores. But the warmth of human emotion does little to banish the greyness. Grey streets, grey rain, grey skies, grey tanks, grey houses, grey fatigued faces, grey denim overalls, grey guns.

My three crew members, for a few moments heroic and assuming Mussolini poses in the turret and hatches, have now sensibly closed down into the relatively dry tank. I stand, head out of the turret, and shrug down into my gas cape as the rain runs down my neck. Beyond the grey houses and grey warehouses, the grey sea is alive with grey ships. The ships wriggle and bobble and swerve and interlink, like grey maggots in a fisherman's tin.

We are now lined along the docks. We form a queue in order of arrival with no apparent priority – light tanks, Sherman tanks, trucks, recovery vehicles, scout cars, jeeps, ambulances, motor cycles, Bren-carriers, half-tracks, the entire military circus. Out of the mass of shipping, landing-ships detach themselves and form a queue to meet our queue, again without apparent plan. Some of the ships have Royal Navy jacks at their stern, some the stars and stripes, some the French tricolour, others the banners of a dozen allies.

The immense queue shunts forward in the teeming rain. I suddenly realize, having cursed all barrack-rooms, that tonight there will be no warm, dry barrack-room. Only the iron hold of a crude ship. And tomorrow night, the next night, next week, next month – no roof, no walls, no doors, no scalding-red iron stoves, no cookhouse tea after guard. We shall be out in the open, in rain, frost, snow, all weather. Comrades of slugs, snails, snakes, flies, mosquitoes, carrion crows. And the rain will continue to drip down our necks and into our boots and up our sleeves. And the walls of the tank, inside and outside, will be dank and slimy to the touch. Happy war!

A Major with a red armband and a naval Petty Officer in big sea-boots stand at the end of the quay. A cobbled ramp runs down to the sea. An iron ramp, which is the front of the ship, has been lowered to meet the cobbled ramp of the quay. A little grey spume froths and bubbles about the join. The Major waves the queue along. It is the American ship which is now nosed into the quay.

'Driver, start up!' I order. 'Keep close on that Sherman in front.'

'That's it, Johnny,' adds Sid. 'Keep right damn' close, or else we may not get aboard this Yank. There's a Free French boat behind and the Free French have only seaweed to eat.'

We trundle to the head of the ramp. The Sherman ahead slithers perilously down the cobbled section, causes a huge splash of water, then roars up the iron ramp in a cloud of smoke and spray. Its huge bulk fills the entry port. It pauses, wobbles and tilts slowly into the ship, its engine exhausts still showing. The Petty Officer holds up a warning hand against us.

'We've missed the bloody boat,' moans Sid from down below.

American sailors bustle impatiently around the Sherman

which is blocking our way into temporary bliss. The huge
tank moves slowly inwards. The Major beckons us on.
'Yippee!' yells Sid. Our Stuart crunches down the cobbles
as Johnny unleashes his impatience. We gather speed. Hit
the bottom of the ramp with a shuddering impact that
shoots me upwards like a table-tennis ball on a spout of
water. I cling tight to the turret as the Major behind us
mouths inaudible obscenities. Johnny drives up the ship's
ramp like a hill-climber at Shelsley Walsh. Frantic Americans wave at Johnny and look around for a quick exit route.
We brake and settle at the entrance to a vast iron cavern.
Grey. More grey than the skies and the seas. Sullen, war
grey. And crowded with vehicles. Had we been a Sherman,
there would have been no room for us. Our Stuart just fits
the space. A spare three-ton truck follows us and squeezes
in on our left.

'That's it. Let's go. Close up!' shouts an American sailor
with an entire jungle of stripes around his brawny arms.
'Welcome to the US of A, boys. You can sleep in your tank
or under it or up on deck. You eat up aloft on our mess-
deck. No parades aboard this ship. You're in a republic
now.'

The chow on the mess-deck is the best we have tasted in
any man's army. But the grand cavern with its massed
vehicles reeks of diesel oil and stale bilge-water and
slopping latrines. So as evening darkens we grab our
bedding rolls and elect to go up on deck. Up there the
steel plates are rusty and chill, the seas and skies doom-
laden with dark greys and blacks, the wind howling like a
flight of fighter planes in a steep dive, the superstructure
plunging and bucking like a cowboy bronco – even whilst
at anchor. We re-elect to go back down the hatch.

'And to think that when they told me I was joining the
Yeomanry I thought it would be all silver spurs and

chainmail epaulettes and waving flags and blaring trumpets,' groans Sid.

'And galloping white horses and captive maidens shrieking for help and Yeoman Johnny flashing his sword to the rescue,' continues Johnny. 'And all we get is this ruddy great iron tomb stinking of unwiped arses.'

As I make my own decision to sit the night out, wrapped in a blanket in the turret – rather than on that sludge-swamped floor – I hear Sid, ensconced on the engine covers, grumble, 'My Trade Union principles is all against sleeping in a luxury hotel like this!'

I smile to myself: 'Trade Union principles?' And I wonder what principles or lack of principles brought so many of us to this moment of great adventure. Principles had little enough to do with my own presence in this stinking hold.

It was not as a volunteer that I had enlisted way back in 1942. By the time I was 'old enough to go', my age group was being conscripted into service and directed into one corps or another without any personal choice. I had no hand in the first spin of the wheel of my military fate. But I was in no way reluctant to answer the 'calling-up papers' which commanded me to leave my quiet cathedral city in the west of England and report at the Gordon Barracks in Aberdeen, away beyond those Scottish Highlands, whose romantic legends I had once devoured in Scott's novels.

I could have registered as a conscientious objector. My family professed a religious creed of fundamental strictness which produced not a few COs. I had already matriculated as a theological student for 'holy orders', and this could have kept me safely in civilian clothing.

To be honest, it was the spirit of boyish adventure, rather than any immediate concern about Poland or Czechoslovakia or the fate of the persecuted Jews, which made me a not-unwilling recruit. The pages of *Hotspur*

and *The Captain* had more influence on my commitment
than the writings of Moses or St Paul or the foreign
correspondents of *The Times*. In 1942, as in June 1944, we
knew little yet about the sufferings of the Jews in the Nazi
concentration camps. In any case, some of my religious
mentors, devout people whose fundamentalism bordered
on fanaticism, taught that the Jews deserved all they
suffered, for they had crucified the Christ. All Jews were
therefore accursed. Those teachers evidently forgot that
Jesus Himself was a Jew!

As I wriggled around in the tight, damp turret, trying to
find solace in my rough blanket, the Biblical text which
came with most relevance to my mind at that moment was
simply, 'The Son of Man hath no where to lay his head.'

14 JUNE 1944:

Morning finds us slowly nosing out to sea. The huge
'Landing Ship (Tank)', with its collapsible bows, is a
ponderous and slow craft. It turns with a kind of arthritic
limping and skewing. Its path is complicated by the mass
of shipping which lies like the tufts of a continuous carpet
from Southampton out past the Isle of Wight and into the
Channel.

Ships are detaching themselves from the mass and
heading in the same general direction towards the mists of
the sea horizon. The departing ships ease out into a
formation reminiscent of hounds and huntsmen. Somewhere out on the flanks, naval destroyers, minesweepers
and patrol boats ride flank on our main procession. For a
while the incredible multitude of ships fascinates us, and
we search for words: shoals, armadas, swarms, swaths,
hordes – clustered upon the grey-green sea like blackfly on
a leaf.

Then we turn to conversation with the American sailors.
In 1944 Yanks are still strange creatures to most British

people except in southern towns invaded by their new armies. From childhood I have seen Texans bidding for bulls in the market at Hereford, but Yanks in general are still a novelty, a mixture of Edward G. Robinson, Gary Cooper and Bing Crosby. Obviously to them we are an equal novelty – our rough clothes, our primitive armaments, our meagre rations, our pale faces, our stilted speech.

The Stuart is an American-built tank, as is also the Sherman, but it is obviously unknown to the sailors, who clamber over it with interest. One sailor fingers my Sten gun superciliously. 'What's this, son? A toy for your little brother back home?' I too am not impressed by the Sten, which, they say, is patched together in back street garages. It is liable to jam and, when actually firing, sprays its bullets wildly, depending on profusion of bullets rather than accuracy of aim.

'Are you aiming to fight Germans with this, son?' persists the sailor, waving the fragile-looking Sten. 'Aw, don't give me that. Here, come and look at some real guns.'

We go up to the seamen's quarters. My friend pulls out an old blue kitbag. Opens it. Extracts a tommy-gun. The style of the old gangster films. Solid, compact, sinister. 'Accurate!' says my Yank. 'Reliable. That's a real gun. Take it, son. You'll be fighting Fritzies. We won't be meeting any Fritzies in this baked bean tin of a ship. Take it and shoot a few for me and my friends from Tacoma, Washington.'

'You can't mean it,' I say. 'Don't you have to sign for it? Or return it to stores? Or lay it out for kit inspections?'

'Sign for it? Stores? Kit inspections? Where do you think you are? Bucking-Ham Palace? Take it, son. There's plenty more where that came from.'

Sid is also in the seamen's quarters, squatting on a bunk and laying out our forty-eight hours ration pack for the

Yanks to see. We have a small cake of soup powder looking like a solidified version of the scum one finds at the sea's edge. We have tea powder, incorporating coarse tea, lumpy dehydrated milk and grey sugar. We have porridge powder looking similar to, but even more anaemic than, the soup. We have hard biscuit. We have all the luxuries of the Café Royal. Someone has described our powdered soup as 'dehydrated tablecloth'.

One of the seamen snorts in disgust. 'If the Germans don't bump you off, that chow will. You can't go ashore with nothing to eat. Hey, Barney, fetch the Quartermaster. These boys can't starve on those beaches.'

The Quartermaster has an even thicker jungle of stripes than our guide of yesterday. He picks over our pocket-sized rations for forty-eight hours. Looks sad. 'Bloody graveyard food,' he says. 'Wouldn't feed a hundred-year-old corpse. This a joke of that thin beanpole Montgomery? We must do something about this. Follow me, boys.'

We descend a number of iron ladders into a large store-room. Rows and rows of cardboard boxes stand piled around the iron walls. 'Help yourselves, boys. Take what you want. Nothing to pay. A birthday present from your Uncle Sam. Bloody beanpole Montgomery! Take what you want. One thing: don't leave any half-empty boxes. If you open a box, empty it and throw the box over the side. And give the Fritzies hell.'

We tear a box out of the nearest pile. Rip open the cover. Tinned 'Chicken', carol the labels. We reach for another pile. 'Tomato Juice', the labels laugh. We stagger to the other end of the room. 'Corned Beef Hash', the labels chant. And across the room, 'Yellow Cling Peaches', the labels whisper. This is Paradise, Aladdin's Cave and Fortnum & Mason's all in one. Glory, glory, Hallelujah. Hip! Hip! for Uncle Sam! AND his Quartermaster!

Sid, Johnny and I fill two cartons with assorted goods. Lug them up ladders, along gangways past grinning Americans, down into our cavern. Load up the American tank with American luxuries. I see the Sherman behind us, not one of our Regiment, tossing out 75mm shells. Laying the shells on the engine covers. Loading on more American goods.

'What are you going to do with those shells?' I ask the driver of the Sherman. 75mm shells are massive contraptions. Made in one piece, bright brass case and black iron shot joined together, the finished product is about as long as my arm and about as broad as my lower thigh. They take up a lot of room in the turret and in the storage spaces in the hull called 'sponsons'.

'Bugger me if we're going to carry all that lot ashore when we can stock up with Yankee food,' says the driver. 'We'll toss the shells into the sea once it gets dark.'

'They'll get shot at dawn,' says Bernard. 'We're not going to do that are we, Ken?' My disciplined body shudders at the thought. 'If I'm going to get shot,' I reply, 'I leave it to some Jerry at a thousand yards and not a dozen blokes in a firing squad at ten paces, thank you!' But we discard a spare can of water, and Sid throws out an old case from in his compartment, and we grow more like Lipton's without specifically infringing any regimental ordinances.

The evening and night grow squally as Neptune, somewhere underneath us, vents his disgust at the load of 75-mm shells, old clothes, jerrycans and empty US of A Navy boxes discarded overboard as the tanks' crews trim their tanks for tomorrow's landing – with good rations ensured for weeks ahead! As I go to sleep, I feel the tommy-gun lying beside me. Lethal and sleek. A *real* sub-machine gun. So superior to the garage-bench product of primitive tubes called a Sten!

As I am drifting off to sleep, I hear Johnny, snuggled down in his driver's seat, chortle, 'Some Hun will get a shock if that Sherman fires off a tin of corned beef hash in the heat of battle.'

2
Tank in Waiting

15 JUNE 1944 – D + 9 – THURSDAY:
The entire front of the ship slowly falls forward, outwards.
From the huge auditorium in which we sit waiting in
darkness, we see slowly revealed the great stage of the
Normandy beach. A stretch of foaming surf, a slope of
holiday sand, anonymous wreckage, a few shattered
houses, an occasional puff of black smoke, and away to our
right a low cliff which must be the hill above Arromanches.

At dawn, and from a distance still, we had leaned over
the ship's rail and checked our map against the hazy, dimly
perceived coastline – checking where Le Hamel might be.
This was the first time any of us had seen what poets term
'some foreign strand'. All my young life my hopes had
simmered slowly up to this boiling, spilling delight of
foreign adventure. France. The land of William the Con-
queror. And Marcel and Denise of the school textbooks.
And Pétain and Gamelin. And now the 'Nazzi hordes' as
Churchill called them. The schooling, and training, and
drilling, and stamping of steel-rimmed soles on bare
parade-grounds, and slapping of rifle butts, and bruising of
shoulders upon gun recoils, and waterproofing of tanks –
all for this moment of truth. These beaches, the grimy
sunshine, the gun-metal surf, the chill of imminent battle,
the pageant of massing vehicles. Normandy!

We are the first tank to roll off the ship, but in front of
us the single truck must disembark. An American sailor in
black, glistening thighboots ambles down the ship's ramp.
Walks cautiously into the sea. Anti-climax! The surge of
tiny breakers hardly reaches his knees. He walks out a yard

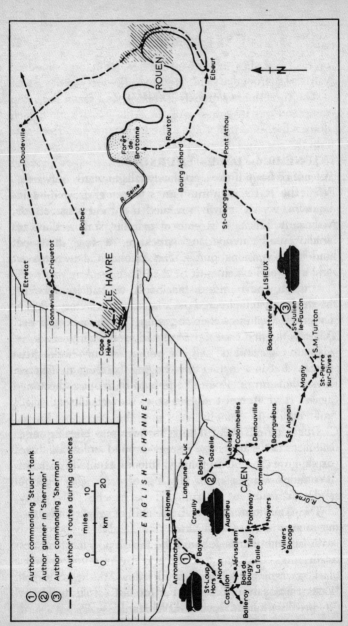

1NY in Normandy, June–September 1944

Legend:
(1) Author commanding 'Stuart' tank
(2) Author gunner in 'Sherman'
(3) Author commanding 'Sherman'
- - - Author's routes during advances

Scale:
miles: 0 10
km: 0 20

or two. Splashes around in the sea, still some hundred yards or so from dry sand. He waves the lorry to descend.

The three-tonner quickly gathers speed down the steep ramp and hits the water with an explosion of spray which douses the American guide. The lorry runs on a few yards into the sea. And disappears!

We sit at the top of the ramp, Johnny's hands about to release our own brakes, my mouth ready to give the order. We gape at the swirling waters where the three-tonner was. Just a yard or two away the American seaman stands, only up to his shins in water which has swallowed a large truck. Two frightened faces appear in the water at his feet and start swimming for life. The American hauls them out and they too stand shin deep in the still rippling water.

The American slides his boots tentatively forward. Moves in a circle, a huge circle around the watery grave of the truck. Comes back up the ramp. 'There's a deep crater. Must be a mine crater,' he yells to me. 'Will go see if the Captain can move off and come in again further along the beach.' But in a moment or two he's back again. 'Captain says tide is turning soon. No time to back out and come in again. Have to try it. Come down slowly. Carefully. It's your skin!'

Our engine is still running, throwing up blue flames in the faces of the tanks and seamen around and behind us. I explain over the I/C to Johnny. 'Bloody Hell!' he exclaims. 'We didn't waterproof for fifty feet of water. Can I get out and walk, mate?'

The American, in his thigh-high, thigh-dry boots, is again standing in the shallow water, indicating ominously with his right hand. Johnny, the fastest and most reckless of drivers, eases the gear sticks with the tenderness of a surgeon assisting a complicated birth. We begin to roll. Faster. Still faster. Too fast. Far too fast. 'Hold it, Johnny! Hold it! Right hand down! NOW! Hard!'

We hit the water crab-wise. Tilt and skid. Swinging right. Not quickly enough. Tilting and swinging. Tilting more and swinging harder. The American seaman backs away frantically. Then we are heading right, heading across the bows of the ship, away from the deep hole, driving for the beach. And the high-booted American guide already turns away from us and fixes his attention on the mighty Sherman sliding down the ramp behind us. In front of us a chain of impatient marshals ('Beach marshals, not field marshals,' I think frivolously) waves and waves and waves us on. 'Don't stop! Hurry! Keep moving! Get off the beach!' Their mouthed words are unheard but the intention is clear.

As we cross the little promenade of Le Hamel and Asnelles, we see our Lieutenant and the other two Shermans waiting on a patch of grass at the roadside. They embarked on a ship behind us (a starving free Polish ship, as we afterwards learned when sharing out our tins of chicken). They disembarked while we were watching the demise of the sunken three-tonner. We line up, my eager Honey leading, and follow the road which arrows straight from the beach towards Bayeux.

And romance and glory await us at the first bend. An old French farmer stands at a gateway, his arms full of roses. And his dark-haired daughter flings a rose to each vehicle as it passes by. She laughs and throws a rose. I laugh and catch the rose. Then a belching, battering gusher of stones, earth, metal, smoke, flame blows up out of the road in front, hovers like an evil genie over our heads and comes showering down to fill turret, mouth, eyes, shirt, nostrils with foul-smelling particles of filth. In fact, the explosion, a large-calibre shell-burst, was some yards ahead of us but Johnny had been accelerating, taking us into the vortex of mess as it disintegrated. In a moment we rumble through into green fields.

'Hullo, Roger 4.' (We are all Rogers today, as dictated by the daily variations of call-signs.) 'Are you fit? Roger 4 over,' calls the Lieutenant somewhat tremulously.

'Hullo, Roger 4. Fit and heavier by one rose and a ton of rubbish. Over.'

'Hullo, Roger 4. Well, the Padre did tell you that the French girls were rather explosive . . .'

'Funny for some!' comments Sid within the private world of our I/C circuit. 'He isn't chewing on minced cobblestones.'

I follow the map and Johnny treads hard on the gas. The slower Shermans are left behind. We come to a junction. I take the straight across road. After a while I realize there are no Shermans behind us. Lorries and miscellaneous vehicles. But none of our Shermans. They must have decided there was a quicker way to Bayeux.

A fifteen-hundredweight truck behind us toots its horn. The driver waves. I wave back. All very jolly. Companions in arms and all that. The truck driver toots again. Waves more emphatically. At a wider, straighter stretch of road the fifteen-hundredweight accelerates and manages to overtake Johnny. The driver points emphatically to the side of our tank nearest the ditch. Not a puncture. We do not have tyres. From my place in the turret I cannot see our tracks. I have to lean far over the side of the tank to look down and then . . .

'Driver, halt! Halt! Pull in to the side. We're picking up miles of telephone wire on our tracks. Dismount. Everybody.' We dismount and contemplate the damage. Wires of various colours, which had been laid at the side of the road, have been spooled up on our tracks. Miles and miles of it.

'We'll get bloody court-martialled for that,' says Sid. 'That must be all Monty's communications, right back to Eisenhower and Churchill's war room and even Franklin

D. Roosevelt in the White House. Enough wire and enough colours.'

'What are we going to do?' says Bernard, removing his black beret and giving the little silver horse badge a random polish on his sleeve.

'Do? Get the cutters, pliers, knives, anything, and chop all this stuff off,' I shout. 'There's no way we'll unwind it all. It's completely fouled up around the tracks and bogeys.'

Like Dickensian grave-robbers we hasten about our nefarious business, furtively chopping and grabbing and slashing and ripping. The road remains strangely still as though the very trees are aghast at our iniquity. We dump armfuls of wire into the capacious French ditch. We pluck and saw the last remnants of tangled wire. Somewhere, somebody with red tabs and even redder cheeks is jiggling a phone up and down on its rest, trying to raise headquarters. The echoes of the jiggling phone dwindle into the depths of the French ditch.

'Mount up! Start up! Advance! Get out of here! Fast!'

At St-Loup Hors, beyond Bayeux, we halt on a field opposite a large church, as near to the map reference as I can calculate. Eventually the Shermans arrive from their explorations of a wrong route. We bed down and set the primus stove going.

Just before dark we are aware of people running in the distance. A crackle of shots. Shouting. There is word that the French Resistance have found a Fifth Columnist. We do not intervene. We stay close to our tanks. I fall asleep easily. At 01.00 I am wakened to prowl for an hour on guard. All ranks share the guard this night. The field is still. Only distant rumblings remind us of war. We might be in a field in England, listening to the bombing.

16 JUNE 1944:
Our tiny Reserve Troop was alone at St-Loup Hors. We did not see the rest of the Regiment. This morning we

move on, nearer the front line. Into Noyon, a little village
with a pottery. Down a side road towards Castillon.

Descending the hill, the road swings suddenly right.
Johnny pulls on his right stick to brake the right track and
swing us to the right. Nothing happens. Johnny, down in
his little tight compartment in front, wrestles with the
lever. 'Driver, swing right. Right! Johnny! Are you awake?'
We are off the road and into the hedge. A horrific steep
drop looms in front. Suddenly, abruptly, with a jarring
jerk, the right track stops and we slew round, skirting the
edge of the drop, one track on the road and the other up in
the hedgerow.

A sweating Johnny looks up at me from his hatch as I
slide down the turret front. 'What happened?'

'My mug. My tea mug.' Johnny's enamel mug had fallen
and lodged behind the brake lever. Now, after Johnny's
desperate lunges, the mug is squashed as flat as a cigarette
case. 'That should teach us to keep everything properly
stowed away,' I observe, without much anger. But with
plenty of relief.

We roll on down the hill to a tiny river running through
lush orchards. A water-tanker is piping water out of the
stream. On up the opposite slope to a church, a crossroads,
an *estaminet*. Down again, past two or three rows of
houses, to a wide field on the left. Woods on the right and
in front. A narrow road leading half right through the
woods. We turn into the field. And are at rest. The
Lieutenant calls a conference of everybody.

'This is where we are, lads,' he says, tapping the map,
'and this is where we stay until the Regiment calls us up.
We are on the divide between the American and British
Armies. About a mile as the crow flies behind the lines. So
we may get strafed. Dig in under your tanks. Remove all
the waterproofing. Clean the guns. Two guards on the gate
and a prowler guard. Keep alert at all times. The Germans

are just over . . .' – he looks up across the woods and calculates carefully – '. . . there!'

Our defence preparations are very simple. The four tanks are parked with their guns facing the four compass points. Under our tank we then dig a deep T-shaped trench. There is room for two of us to sleep in the top of the T and two in the downstroke of the T.

Bernard verbalizes our thoughts: 'If they blow us to Hell, this trench is just the right depth. All they need to do is fill it in.'

Johnny quakes visibly. 'It's deep enough to be safe, ain't it? The Jerries haven't got any bouncing bombs, have they?' It is my turn to shudder. Someone had just walked over my grave. Or the grave of someone near to me.

Outside the trench our valley is green and damp with summer rain. The sunshine smiles out of the buttercup petals and the raindrops. There is no traffic along our little road. The guards stand idly at the gate. The prowler patrol lights a fag and watches a Frenchwoman milk a cow. The war has switched off for the day. We are on a school holiday in happy Normandy. Our most imminent danger, a wandering cow.

17 JUNE 1944:
'So this is war,' intones Johnny at breakfast. 'Give us the medals, then, and let's go home.'

'Did you know the Yanks get medals just for landing in England?' asked Sid.

'Buggers merit a medal, exchanging their food for our ration fodder,' says Bernard, who is raking corned beef hash into one of our mess tins prior to frying it up to serve on dry biscuit.

'Arrgh! Ugh! Horrible!' gasps Johnny. 'Bernard, you sod, you've poisoned my tea!'

'That's the chlorination,' I explain. 'They chlorinate the

water heavily because of dead bodies and flies and bacteria.'

'Do you mean we have to drink that muck all the time we're in Normandy?'

'Till death us do part,' interjects Bernard. The man has an aptitude for flesh-crawling, spine-tingling remarks. But where is the war anyway? I listen hard but cannot hear it for the wind rustling in the grass and the bees busily buzzing and the cows lowing with pleasure after milking and the lads playing cards.

In the afternoon, with the Lieutenant's permission, we walk up the hill to the *estaminet*. A stout woman with a babe in arms is talking to two elderly and mildly dirty French peasants at a dusty table. Before I can air my schoolboy French, Sid triumphantly enunciates his entire French vocabulary, 'Van blong, MAD-'m. Seal voo plate.' The Frenchwoman looks uncomprehendingly. She pours *vin blanc* anyway. We sit and stare at the French. The French sit and stare at us. A peasant says, *'Boche. Kaput.'* We reply, *'Oui, oui. Boche. Kaput.'* Only, we know that the wily, tough *Boche* is nowhere near *Kaput* yet, and we shall have to seek him out, through the woods, over the hills and far away.

We ramble back to our field within the hour allowed. The sentry at the gate shouts 'Halt! Who goes there?' Sid shouts back, 'Use your bloody eyes.'

A little later, squatting on the grass and sucking our fingers after another helping of corned beef hash, we see a singular sight. It is as though, far across the vast field, a giant is beneath the ground throwing up scuttles full of coaldust. A noise slaps at us, like the clatter of a salesman beating an empty tea-chest in Hereford market. That and nothing else. We sit. And stare. And think.

'Jerry shells,' yelps Johnny. 'Bugger me!'

'They nearly did,' growls Bernard. 'Another 300 yards!'

We take our corned beef hash fingers down into our
deep trench and peer out through the tracks of the Honey.
Nothing more happens. No more coaldust. No more empty
tea-chests.

22 JUNE 1944:
We have been sitting here since the 16th, and all this
glorious war has been passing us by. If playing at cricket in
a field in Aldershot was frustrating on D-Day, it is even
more frustrating to play at picnics in a field in France
whilst the 7th Armoured Division and the 50th Division
tear themselves to pieces around Villers Bocage and Tilly-
sur-Seules.

True, we have had some adventures. One day the clip-
clop of a horse's hooves stirred the lazy interest of the
guard at the gate. Down through the woods came a small
dairy cart drawn by a horse. And in the dairy cart were two
Germans in full uniform. They reined in in astonishment
right under the guns (unmanned) of one of our Shermans.
At that, our guard roused from *his* astonishment sufficiently
to shout 'Halt! Who goes there?' The totally disorientated
Germans raised their hands and called '*Kamerad*'. At which
the still astounded guard, prompted only by years of
training, called back, 'Advance, friend, and be recognized.'
Fortunately at that moment the little Lieutenant appeared,
waving a revolver, and concluded that particular armistice,
requisitioning the horse and cart to convey the Germans to
higher authority. This did not encourage our faith in
whatever British or American fortifications might be
erected along that road through the woods.

Another day a tiny plane came hedge-hopping along the
fields – just the type of plane which might take off from a
similar Herefordshire field on Bank Holiday to take trip-
pers up at 5 shillings a time. Only after the plane had
hopped by did we realize that it had black crosses on its

wings. Some less-than-sporting British guns beyond our farthest hedges actually fired tracer at the plane, which whirred like an angry wasp and disappeared into the wooded distances.

This was all great fun. Better than the May Fair at Hereford. Given permission now and again to absent ourselves for up to an hour, we wandered in the woods and, failing to find rabbits or partridges, fired our pistols and my tommy-gun at gateposts and fallen trees. It was on one of these walks that we caught the full stench of the smell which had been with us since landing. A sweet, sickly-sweet smell, leaving a loathsome aftertaste on the palate, like a rotting orange. The smell of death. There were, in the woods, horizontal shapes which were not fallen tree trunks. We stalked closer but not too close. There were several Germans in uniform. Maybe a dozen. Dead. Dead for some time by the smell. We hurried back to the full light and clear air of our field. At the *estaminet*, where they were beginning to understand our schoolboy French, we asked about the bodies. Had there been a battle? Strangely, nobody could now understand our French. One word that was muttered might have been '*Résistance*' and another '*merde*'.

For days it rained as though the heavens had turned all their water cannons upon the rioting populace down on earth. We heard that supplies were held up as ships were unable to come to the beaches. Our little unit had received no more rations, so we fed adequately but fortuitously on our Yankee contraband. Somebody did manage to shoot a rabbit. One of the dirtier peasants brought us two dozen eggs. And the woman milking the cows under the trees filled a jerrycan which the prowler guard carried over to her twice a day. This was indeed luxury camping. But the rain drove us to cower under the great tarpaulin tank sheet which we rigged as a low tent slung from the Honey's tracks.

One day, leaving only a skeleton guard to greet any other German dairymen travelling the lanes, we departed on one of our trucks to carry out beach fatigues. In the event we spent the day sitting in the sand, strewn with rubbish as after a British Bank Holiday, but with grimmer reminders such as a bullet-riddled boot, an exploded Sten gun, a blood-encrusted bandage, the remains of improvised D-Day latrines, rotting food, spent shellcases, dead fish and thickets of barbed wire.

Wandering a little way, we found a demolished German gun emplacement. The gun had been bent and wrenched aside by a giant explosion. The inevitable rags of uniform identified the former tenants. And there were the remnants with which we were to become familiar. Rancid cheese. Empty Calvados bottles. Packets of powdered soup so malodorous as to drive a US Naval quartermaster neurotic. And badges. Swastikas. Eagles. Stripes. Wallets. Photographs of him and his family. Screeds of letters in the strange Gothic script. Bernard knew a little German and could shout *'Heraus! Schnell!'* and such like, but he failed to identify more than a word or two of the scrawled and sprawling Gothic letters traced so finely by wives, parents and lovers back in the Fatherland. This brought us no nearer to understanding our enemies who had so rapidly vacated this evil-smelling place.

So much for six days of flashing spurs and blaring trumpets and fluttering pennants. One of our spare corporals has gone home with chicken-pox. Some kind of notoriety at least!

'Come on, Doug,' grumbled Sid. (Doug Forster is our Colonel.) 'What's keeping you? Send for the lads!'

23 JUNE 1944 – D + 17 – FRIDAY:
A motor-bike skids to a halt outside the field. The rider confers with the guard, starts the bike again, revs up and

comes bouncing over the lush grass and molehills of our field, as far as the Lieutenant's tank. Confers with the Lieutenant. Salutes. Rides bumpily away, swerves through the gate, causes the guard to take quick evasive action, roars away back up the hill.

'Corporal Tout. Report to the Troop Leader, please.'

Now what does destiny, through its intermediaries Montgomery, Doug Forster, Hank Bevan and the anonymous little Lieutenant, ordain for Johnny, Sid, Bernard and me? What kind of Top Secret mission for our dashing, new, gleaming Honey tank? What haste to rescue whom, from what fate, and where?

'Load up. Mount up. Start up. You are wanted at HQ Squadron. Here is the map reference. As soon as you are ready, move out. It's all yours, Corporal. Have a good war.'

I restrain my urge to canter back to the Honey. The crew are watching and guessing and beginning to pile mess tins and 'eating-irons' ready for packing.

'On our way, lads. Johnny, get warmed up, ready to move. Sid, get the packing done. Bernard, check this map reference out with me, will you?'

'Berlin, here I come!' hollers Johnny.

'Is there only a map reference?' asks Bernard. 'Isn't there a wireless frequency? Are we netting in to Regimental frequency or keeping in touch with Reserve Troop?'

'Wireless silence, according to the little man. We're out on our own. Moving up to HQ Squadron. Should be a piece of cake. Here, look! Through Balleroy and then on to that patch of wood. In a wood, the man says.'

'Check,' Bernard replies slowly. 'That is correct. Can't go far wrong on an eight-figure reference. These maps are very clear. You can see every little stream and every tiny orchard, not to mention houses or contours. That's one thing they got right.'

We mount up, the heroes of the hour. The crews of the

three Shermans stand somewhat crestfallen as we rumble by. The odds and sods who ride in the two trucks sense the class distinction as we depart on our mission to HQ Squadron and the counter-attack positions where the Regiment stands. We brush scornfully past the tiny guard at the gate. Turn up the hill. Wave to the woman who milks the cows. Salute the egg man and his friends who seem to spend their days in the *estaminet*. Accelerate through the village. Head for the sector of danger where civilians may not roam. The first mile or two are like a mystery tour, taken through English lanes on a summer evening. Huge hedges, thick orchards, rich pastures, stout cottages, rambling farms, twisting lanes, no people.

Balleroy is still a dead place, its main street, wide and empty, leading up to the gates of the great *château* park. Beyond, the huge *château* speaks of the opulence of dukes and counts and noblemen of this land since the days when William ruled both here and in England.

'Gawd, I didn't know they had moved Windsor Castle out here,' calls Johnny on I/C, slowing down instinctively to take a tourist's look at the luxuriant park, the stately avenue of trees and the magnificent *château* at the end of the drive.

'We go left here, driver,' I explain. 'Heading for the local council estate. This isn't our scene.'

'I bet the owner of that lot claims his rights with all the local brides,' drools Sid.

'From what I've seen of some of the local brides, he's more than welcome,' comments Bernard.

Johnny reluctantly drifts left out of sight of the park and the rattle of our tracks echoes back from tiny shops and cottages. Then we are among country hedges again. Johnny presses the accelerator and we boom down the hill towards our eight-figure map reference. Down the hill, over a brook, round a corner, says the map.

A green figure leaps from a hedge, like Robin Hood accosting a travelling bishop, and waves us to stop. He is American, garbed in a camouflage smock with baggy trousers tucked into sagging gaiters. A latter-day Davy Crockett, brandishing a carbine. Johnny halts and I climb down the front of the tank. The American, face unshaven, scarred and aged by combat strain, looks me up and down with a grimace of surprise. 'Where are you-all headed at, son?' he asks in what must be a Southern or Western drawl, slow and intensely musical and not indigenous to front-line battleposts. 'Where are you headed at?'

I place my map on the sloping tank front and point at my eight-figure reference. A neat red cross near a patch of wood. 'We're headed there: our HQ Squadron,' I explain.

He looks into the distance and declaims, with the dignified omniscience of Parmenides coming to philosophize to Athens in his sixty-fifth year, 'If'n you-all wanna git to that cross, wanna have your guns ready to fight a few hundred wild Apach-ees disguised as German Panzer grenadiers.'

'But we're well behind the front line,' I argue.

'Son, this yer man talkin' at you's Abraham Leroy of the US Army. And in this neck of the woods, Abraham Leroy *is* the front line.'

An American 'lootenant' clambers through the hedge. 'What's the trouble?' he asks in a deliberately casual voice.

'One of our allies looking for his'n headquarters here, Lootenant,' says Abraham Leroy, prodding the map.

'Can I see your map reference?' asks the officer, who is hardly more than my age. He checks the map. 'Looks like you're right, but they're wrong. As Abraham here says, he *is* the front line. Round that bend are the enemy. That wood where you're headed is probably filled with Tiger tanks. You need to take this road all the way back and then run along that other road . . .'

We study the map. I see the light. 'Change the last number but one and that puts HQ Squadron right here in this other wood.'

The lane is too narrow to turn in. Johnny reverses at my instructions. He has no rear vision at all. We crunch back up the lane, waving to the two Americans. The young officer leaps back into the hedge. Abraham Leroy ambles in a more leisurely fashion back to his lodgement in the bushes.

We clatter back into Balleroy in reverse and use the ducal park to turn around. Our route takes us back to Castillon, past the *estaminet* with its permanent complement of drinkers, past our astonished guard at the entrance to our field and up the lane down which the Germans in their milk cart drove. More miles of lovely Norman lanes and then our revised map reference brings us to the Bois de Bougy. Vehicles are nosed in under the trees, here as thick as tropical jungle. It was this density of trees which caused casualties, for Captain Robinson and Captain Grant have been wounded by shellbursts in the tree-tops. A trooper has died and others have been wounded by the same effect of aerial shrapnel. We halt near a wireless truck. We await our fate. Again. Destiny has many quirks in the course of a campaign.

The Regiment needs our Honey. It needs a driver. Johnny can stay. It does not need Sid or Bernard or me. An officer usurps my sleek, sweet-running Honey. Johnny marches triumphantly towards his new charge. We three rejected ones extract our kit and bedding rolls from the Honey and pile them on a jeep. Nobody waves goodbye. Nobody apologizes for the wrong map reference. We head back the way we came 'Unhorsed', in cavalry language.

Back in our field at Castillon, without a tank, we now become odds and sods, although, as a lance-corporal, I am still quite a considerable sod. We live in and around a lorry

filled with miscellaneous stores for the Reserve Troop. Our
shelter, when the occasional shell menaces us, is a rough
trench dug out from the perimeter ditch.

As the HQ Squadron jeep dumps us at our new home, I
say to Sid, 'We've forgotten our last tin of chicken from the
Yankee ship.' Sid grins, 'No mate, I didn't let you down.'
He taps his chest and I realize that his battledress blouse
has swollen considerably. 'Let's give the odds and sods a
treat, then, Sid,' I chuckle.

25 JUNE 1944:
Rain. In a sodden field in Normandy we have done nothing
for two whole days except stand guard at the gate and then
crawl back under the tarpaulin which we have extended
from the side of the lorry. Even on guard we have no
German milk carts to enliven our hours of soaking misery.

Bernard, usually the pessimist, concedes, 'At least we've
got a decent green field to camp in. And no bloody fighting
like those poor devils at Tilly. Even if we do now have to
ask permission to listen to BBC on one of the Shermans.'

Yesterday we heard a BBC reporter describing the
Normandy bridgehead, jammed with troops and tanks and
guns and store depots. Not an inch to move in. Not an acre
where the sound of battle did not burst upon his ears. Not
a furlong before some grim tragedy of war was revealed to
his eyes. He had not visited Castillon. Here one woman
milks her cows in the orchards, and another serves her
customers in the *estaminet*. About thirty of us sit in a field
and wait. Maybe the Post Corporal will call. Maybe a water
wagon will descend to the river. Otherwise the mighty tide
of war has slopped us to one side. Maybe the British staff
planners think our lane is in the American sector. And the
Americans don't consider our lane wide enough for their
tumultuous passage. And even the French children lack

the curiosity to come down from the village and watch us as we moulder and grumble and curse the rain. Maybe we are in quarantine?

26 JUNE 1944 – D + 20 – TUESDAY:

The Post Corporal called and brought us pulsating news. C Squadron is going into action. My Squadron. Today. At last. We were half afraid that the war would be over, that the German Army would have retreated and surrendered before the 1NY got a look in. Five years some of my mates have been training for this day. More than twenty years RSM Jelley and some of the sergeants have been preparing. Even I, the newest recruit, have been on the way for nearly two years.

The Post Corporal had no details about time or location or strength of battle. I find myself hoping that someone will be wounded so that I can go up to the Squadron. Then I realize that whoever is wounded will most likely be one of my pals. So I try to do a deal with Fate. Negotiate with God. Let somebody be wounded, but let it be just a minor scratch. Perhaps one of the married men with a family would like a 'nice cushy Blighty One'. Or else, God, if it has to be bad, let it be Sergeant X or Corporal Z. Above all, divert the bullets from Hank and old Bill Fox and, of course, Don and Pete. And then there are all those friendly blokes in other Troops – Frank Hickson, always smiling, and Tommy Madelaine, so debonair, and George Valentine and . . . and . . . but in C Squadron one had to recite virtually the entire Squadron battle state in order to include all the nice blokes and pals.

So we sat and waited through Tuesday, each with our thoughts. Each escaping into silence. Listening for the echoes of battle from the front line which was still only just beyond our wooded hill. For the Germans had not yet retreated to Berlin or even to Paris. They had not even evacuated Caen. They had lost and retaken Villers and

Tilly. The war was not going to end just yet. *My* Squadron and *My* Regiment will have found a moment of glory to compensate for the waiting and the 'bull' and the 'balls-ups' and the Normandy rain.

27 JUNE 1944:

I spent the night tossing and turning on the ground, between exhilaration and misery. Our Squadron had been blooded but I had not been there. I had dreamed of coming back home to my parents and friends with a row of bright medals on my chest, and stripes on my arms or maybe even stars on my shoulders. But it seemed harder to get into battle than into a royal garden party. My most heroic deed yet has been to reach the American front line entirely by accident, the wrong place at the wrong time and even in the wrong army!

'Up! Up! Everybody up! Wakey-wakey! Up and ready to move!' 05.00 hours and we are to reinforce C Squadron. There have been casualties. Nobody knows how many. The Lieutenant calls us out of our beds and into our tanks and lorries. We frantically roll our bedding and button our trousers. We leave the lacing of footwear until we are mounted up ready to go. We sit thus, unmoving, for five hours.

10.00 hours and the Lieutenant stands us down to get breakfast. While we are still eating, he comes round with a list of those who are to go up to C Squadron. My name is on it. At last. I am going to be a real soldier. Now let the Germans do their worst!

The Lieutenant tells us that we are to rendezvous with the Squadron at Jérusalem crossroads. I resist the temptation to ask whether that is on the Calvary side of Jérusalem. It could be too flippant. Or it could be terribly relevant.

We trundle through the narrow Normandy lanes between the high, fortress hedges. From time to time the

sun bursts through the leaves and branches to make our
badges glint and sparkle, the little silver horses on their
patches of sky blue on our black berets. We sing contented
little songs in low key, not the brash strains of 'Roll out the
barrel' or the poignant wistfulness of 'We'll meet again' or
tne martial pace of 'Tipperary' but the softer songs like
'Nelly Dean' and 'Danny Boy'. For we are rolling through
the quaint, shell-battered villages with exotic saints' names
on the way to our pre-ordained destiny. And that knowledge leads to contentment.

There is nothing sensational about the winding lane
leading from Folliott to Jérusalem. There are a thousand
orchards in Herefordshire which are almost identical to
this orchard in France. An old orchard where the trees are
spaced by the vagaries of nature, gnarled, ancient, prolific
trees. Not the sheared, regimented, crowded young trees
of the modern orchard. This is a place for chickens to peck
and pigs to chunter and horses to champ. What makes it
different are the huge, turreted Sherman tanks standing
between the trees. And the crowd of tired, ashen-faced
men in oily overalls who work on the tanks or converse
mechanically in the orchard or sit dejected on the grassy
bank which runs along the edge of the trees.

Nobody pays attention to us at first, so we accost the first
person we see and ask the inevitable questions: 'What
happened? Did we win? Was anybody hurt?' The first
Yeoman I encounter happens to be Michael Hunt, a driver
in 4 Troop. 'What happened, Mike? We've just arrived.
They haven't told us a thing. Only that the Squadron was
in action. What was it like? Tell us about it.' Two or three
of us new arrivals listen for Mike's first words. Other
reinforcements gather around others of the returned
warriors.

'Bloody awful,' says Mike. I am disappointed. I wanted
to hear heroic words. I wanted to know that C Squadron

had conquered. I wanted to shake hands with victors. 'We got clobbered. It's the *Bocage*, you see. The fields are so small. You go through one great hedge into a field and within fifty yards you have to crash through another hedge even thicker. And the orchards. And farm buildings. Ideal places for the Jerry tanks to hide. And hide they did. Waiting for us.'

'Did we lose any tanks? Did we knock any out?'

'Of course we lost some, in that kind of country. Tanks popping up at fifty yards range. But we got some of them too. Harry Graham knocked out a Panther at fifty yards with his first shot.'

'Great! Good old Harry! Knocking out the Panthers. They're bigger than Shermans, aren't they?'

'Who cares? What's more important is: Frank Hickson's dead.' Oh, no, not Frank, that big, hearty, smiling fellow whom everybody liked. A corporal, commander of a Sherman. Never raised his voice to give an order. Always so friendly and happy that he seemed to bring sunshine into the barrack-room, even on the darkest winter day. He's gone. 'And Tommy Madelaine's had it . . .' No, not Tommy. Tell us it's not true! Tommy, young, slim, upright, intelligent, popular. Tommy as well as Frank. 'And George Valentine . . .' The gods have been unkind to the Squadron. George, Tommy, Frank. A trio to liven up an evening in a pub or in a dull NAAFI canteen. A trio to rely upon for one's life in an emergency. 'And three of Frank's crew. Brewed up. They didn't have a chance. And Len Wright with a wound in his skull, and tanks going up on mines, and Jerry tanks with their great guns waiting behind the hedges . . .'

I notice that my two reinforcement companions have wandered away. The medicine is too strong for them. Mike continues to tell his story almost oblivious of me, letting out the horrors of yesterday, exorcizing the ghosts of the

German guns behind the hedges. Trooper Martyn G. stayed in his tank and gave covering fire whilst his commander was being dragged away wounded. They say Hank will recommend Martyn for a medal. Not all the story was glorious. One driver stalled his engine, said he had run out of petrol. Only after the battle was it realized that he had funked. The infantry, D-Day people, were exhausted and did not support the tanks. One of our corporals is still missing, thought to have been blown right over one of these immense hedges.

Mike's story runs down like an old-fashioned gramophone needing winding. The Squadron Sergeant-Major comes looking for his reinforcements. SSM Sidney Turton, a dapper, humorous but sometimes supercilious little man. I sometimes crewed on his tank in England as reserve.

'Right, lad. You're back in the big league. Glad to be home? Not nice malingering about in the Reserve, you know. Here we are. You are in 3 Troop. Gunner on the Troop Corporal's tank. Corporal Snowdon just made up to commander. Look after yourself, lad.'

'What about my stripe, sir? Do I drop that now?'

'Ah, yes. You've been playing with the infants class. Now you're with the men. Take your stripe off. For the time being at any rate. Many more days like yesterday and you'll all be sergeant-majors before you're finished.'

I report to Ken Snowdon, who had the grisly experience of evacuating a very badly wounded commander yesterday. Our operator, Tommy Tucker, who will share the Sherman turret with me, is one of the characters of the Squadron. He has the most voracious appetite for all delights. He eats enormous amounts of food but is the thinnest man in the Squadron. The front compartment of our Sherman is shared by the driver, 'Hickey' Hicken, who looks a mere schoolboy and is of a very sunny, easy-going disposition;

and the co-driver, Rex Jackson, who wears glasses, chubbier than Hickey, a very quiet, thoughtful chap.

Looking at the four men who will be my companions in battle and at rest, morning, noon and night for as long as death or wounding stay away from us, I am again impressed by the level of intelligence in most tank crews – as also, I suppose, in air crews – for the tank, in addition to being immense in dimension, is a complex machine, and its battle equipment requires most delicate control.

I get a razor blade out of my small pack and carefully pick the stitches from behind my one lonely stripe. I manage to draw blood in one finger before I successfully reduce myself to the rank of trooper again. Not that that matters very much, for German shells are not equipped with sensors able to detect and punish rank.

I toss my bedding roll up on to the engine covers of my new home, one of the four Shermans of 3 Troop, C Squadron, 1st Northamptonshire Yeomanry. There is a Troop Leader (Lieutenant Bobby McColl), a Troop Sergeant (Chris Wilkins), a Troop Corporal (our tank), each commanding a five-man Sherman mounting the normal 75-mm gun. Another sergeant (Jack Ginns) commands our fourth tank, which is the Firefly, a Sherman with an immense 17-pounder gun. It is able to carry only four crew members because of the interior fittings of the gun which protrudes – or seems to – a couple of yards beyond the front of the tank.

The flaps covering the engine and forming the slightly sloping rear deck, are on a level with my eye. I have to clamber up there before I can continue my climb into the domed turret. The Sherman is a high tank compared with British Churchills and German Mark IVs. My gunner's seat is a cramped little niche on the right of the turret, hunched up between the great, shining gun breech and the rough, curving armoured turret wall.

Some wireless-operators (I am trained as an operator) consider themselves the élite of the crew. In fact, each member has to be expert at a demanding trade. The gunner must have a quick eye, steady hand and cool nerve to traverse the massive turret in which the gun is fixed, and to elevate and depress the gun within its mounting, so that a hairline cross on the gun telescope rests precisely on a target a thousand yards away, even whilst the tank is bucking and rolling across country. The driver has to be able to maintain and pamper an engine complex and powerful enough to move the mighty mass of armoured steel weighing over thirty tons at speeds up to 30 mph (although the official speed of the Sherman is quoted at around 25 mph). The co-driver must also be a competent mechanic. In addition he has his own machine-gun to handle in the front compartment and must be able, at a moment's notice, to take over any other task in the crew.

As I stand by the turret I catch an overpowering dose of battlefield stench as the breeze swings from west towards south. This testimony of decomposition has come to us faintly in the remote fields of Castillon but here at Jérusalem it is more potent and persistent. It is the increasingly familiar odour of open latrines spiced with lilies and rotting oranges. Sweet but abominably putrid. We have encountered it in the destroyed gun-emplacements near the beaches and we have savoured it along the Norman lanes. But then it was from dead Germans, aliens from a field-grey culture. And from the swelling, sun-bloated carcasses of cows and horses. Now the treacherous breeze blows from the orchards and fields where some of our own mates still lie, dead hostages to the enemy guns beyond them. And either the nose or the mind descries a hint of charred flesh on the breeze, from the tanks which burned out yesterday.

I seek the company of my living comrades, crouching

around a primus stove: Rex pumping energetically at the stove, Hickey wrestling the tin-opener around a can labelled 'Haricot Oxtail', Corporal Snowdon applying oily French farm butter to hard biscuits, and Tommy already chewing a dry biscuit as he collects our mugs together for tea.

Bobby McColl, bareheaded and in shirt sleeves, with cloth stars on his epaulettes, saunters from his tank beyond the next venerable apple tree. He is a tiny but efficient man, younger than any of us. 'No more action today, lads. Tomorrow we have to be ready to move into counter-attack positions. But B Squadron will be first on call. So there will be no reveille. Get up when you like. If we need you earlier, we'll call you in good time. *Bon appétit.*'

'*Bon appétit!*' snorts co-driver Rex, looking at the swilling excrescence which Hickey has concocted for supper, one tin each of 'Haricot Oxtail', 'Pork & Veg' and 'Irish Stew' all mixed into one. 'No wonder they call them messtins.'

When we have finished supper, we wander down through the trees. I don't know how it will be with regular cavalry regiments, or whether they have formal parades, morning and evening, even in Normandy. Maybe they even polish their brasses and their boots. I don't know. What I do know is that in this regiment the discipline is relaxed when there is no urgent need for action. Given general orders by the Troop Leader, each tank commander is left to organize the programme of his crew as he thinks fit. As long as every working part of the tank gleams with efficiency, we can spend the rest of our day in idle pursuits.

Today those of the Squadron who bore the brunt of yesterday's horrors have been sleeping for long periods. Some of them drowning in the deepest reaches of unconsciousness. Others half-waking and fighting yesterday's battles, suffering their comrades' wounds, all over again. A number bed down after eating supper. Some bring out the inevitable pack of cards. Others scribble on field postcards which have ready-printed messages so that the writer simply scratches out the inapplicable words such as 'I am in hospital' or 'I am coming on leave'.

A few of us amble down the gentle orchard slope to the road. There being no dens of vice locally to which we can gravitate, Tommy begs my ration of cigarettes and we go door-to-door shopping in the tiny hamlet. Tommy knocks at a cottage door. A tired, bedraggled Frenchwoman of uncertain age opens the door.

'Avez-vous des oovs, Mad'm?' One or two of us speak reasonable French, enough to carry on a simple barter conversation. But it is much more amusing to watch Tommy's theatre show. 'Des oovs. Des oovs. You no comprenez my French, mad'm?' he asks. 'Oovs and pool-etts?' Then follows the inevitable flapping of elbows and crowing like a cockerel, followed by 'Pork-o? Le bacon?' accompanied by scurrying on all fours, snorting vigorously, followed by 'Let, then?' and a great charade of adjusting a milking-stool, pulling the udders, passing on to churning the butter and, with fingers gripping the nostrils in disgust, making the cheese. The Frenchwoman shakes her head sadly and closes the door.

At the next house there is no answer. A shell or bomb has extracted the interior of the house so neatly that we do not notice it until we have knocked at the door in a wall still standing intact. At another house we swop four English cigarettes for half-a-dozen eggs and a hunk of some dark sawdusty bread. And next door to that we are invited in by an elderly Frenchman who has a bottle of wine to share with the liberators.

In the gloaming we dawdle back to our orchard, spread our blankets on the thyme-scented grass and look up at the flame-irritated sky. Somewhere a night battle is developing. Just a mile or so away the country is devastated. Yesterday we won back 500 yards of France. At the price of Frank, the other Tommy, George, so many: all dead. A blood price. Tonight the old Frenchman regaled us with the blood of the French vine. We are heroes to him. He is only an infinitely small segment of world opinion but . . . we are heroes to him. And although I was not there yesterday, my cigarettes bought the eggs and the bread and I am accepted by my crew as a blood brother, sharing their achievements of yesterday for '*liberté*'. In these villages '*liberté*' is a tangible experience. We can understand this clearly although our knowledge of Nazism is minimal.

Liberté: the liberty to lie here and think whatever thoughts one will. And then expound and dissect them freely with our Corporal and Rex and Hickey tomorrow. And the liberty to own the patch of sky above one's head. The hope that one day each one of us will select his own patch of sky and dwell safely beneath it.

Tonight that sky is irritated by flames.

3
Tank at War

30 JUNE TO 1 JULY 1944 – D + 24:
After the high point of C Squadron's first battle at La Taille
(a place on the map but only a farm and one or two
labourers' cottages in the hedgerows), we have relapsed
into what seems to be our fate: sitting and waiting while
the D-Day troops waste themselves to destruction.

Our orchard at Jérusalem is pleasant enough but, as with
cricket pitches at Aldershot and green fields in Castillon,
this is no place to be when the horrific battles around Tilly
and Villers are being fought out. Hank says we are just as
important, sitting here in reserve and menacing the Germans, as if we were up at Villers Bocage, losing dozens of
tanks and knocking out the odd Jerry Mark IV or Tiger.
But sitting in reserve doesn't win any medals or earn any
stripes. If I had merely wanted to go camping I could have
done that with the Boy Scouts.

From this side of the hill we can see a wide expanse of
lower country which is the killing-ground between the
armies. According to Montgomery, this is the area where
we have to hold the German armoured divisions so that the
more mobile American troops can speed away up the
peninsula to Cherbourg, and then round behind the Germans. During the day this area of front line reveals itself as
an innocent stretch of fertile countryside with the occasional slow, indistinct rise of smoke, a smoke which is no
more ominous visually than the smoking of fields in which
harvest stubble is being burned. Except that this stubble is
human flesh.

At night every distant light shows distinctly. The remote

flashes illumine our faces under the apple trees. And tonight a full-scale battle has erupted. We are not tired, so we sit and watch as one day passes into another D-Day plus day. We have few duties to do now that our lost tanks are replaced and our guns cleaned and our ammunition replenished.

Down in the valley, beyond our immediate darkness, the battle is like one of those long-exposure photographs taken of a busy road junction at night, with intricate patterns of headlights and sidelights and rearlights and neon signs and traffic signals, all frozen into a kind of tartan woven of coloured streaks and patches of light. This battle is like that, except that it is a flaming tartan pattern fed into a giant kaleidoscope and then run through a high speed ciné camera. The effect is of all the firework displays that ever happened, laid one over the other and interspersing and frantically changing, blooming and disappearing. Up here it is fascinating, awe-inspiring, hypnotic. Down there scared infantrymen are clawing their way through the roots of the hedges. Machine-gunners and artillerymen and air bombers of both sides hurl flaming packages of pain and destruction over the heads of the chosen few who close up to the enemy in actual mortal combat.

We are not tired, but thrilled, excited, committed. And pretending not to be fearful.

5 JULY 1944:
Almost a month gone by since D-Day. And what have we done? Except for La Taille, we have sat in counter-attack positions. Called by higher authority, we have dashed off across one of the wide, dusty tank lanes now criss-crossing the Normandy countryside. We have arrived at a map reference. We have sat. Eaten. Slept. Been called away in another dash, to position ourselves, sit, wait, eat, sleep.

'Don't worry, lads,' says Harry, one of our wits, lying

naked except for a pair of shorts, and sunbathing on the rear engine covers, 'we are menacing the enemy. We are scaring the balls off Rommel. We have got silly old Hitler guessing this time. And he says to von Rundstedt, "What are those bloody Northamptonshire Yeomen up to now?" And von Rundstedt says, "Who bloody well cares?" We're winning the war, boys. Pass me the sun-tan oil.'

'Well, at least we can almost see Caen, now,' Tommy comments. 'And we were supposed to have captured Caen on D-Day. I don't know what all this fuss is about. Why is Caen so important? I reckon it's just like any other town: houses, railway station, churches and schools, butchers' shops and brothels. Why should Jerry get so excited over it? I bloody well wouldn't if I lived as far away as Berlin.'

'Ah,' intervenes one of the sergeants who, by dint of his three stripes, considers himself an expert in the Grand Strategy of War. 'A front line is like a door. There's the bit that is the hinge. And there's the bit by the knob that swings in when you push it. But if the swinging bit is locked and bolted, then the best bet is to bash in the hinges. And Caen is the hinge. So Monty says.'

'Ignorant sods, these generals,' answers Tommy. 'Me, I'd go in by the window. At night!'

We are now at Fontaine-Henry, strung out along a hedge on a rising slope which rolls up behind us to a stretch of woods. In front, a wide panorama is closed off on the horizon by the Lebisey Woods on the outskirts of Caen. There is word that we may be advancing in a day or two. Meanwhile we clean guns, maintain engines, check tracks, cook and eat, sunbathe or shelter from the rain.

So we wait on these pleasant slopes, their natural scents of clover and mint and dung faintly desecrated by the encroaching stench of battlefields. And in our minds the Technicolor pictures of knights in shining armour and prancing steeds and waving *guidons*, acquired from the

Saturday morning cinema, are strangely confused with the vision of the vast, mauling tracks and the huge, blasting gun of a Tiger tank, a monstrous steel fortress and a gun that can shatter a Sherman turret at 2,000 yards. When a British tank is 'brewed up' in the bridgehead it is quickly recovered by workshops and either repaired or discreetly hidden away. The British bodies are decently interred and marked with a cross. When a German tank is destroyed, it is left where it stands. And sometimes the bodies are buried and sometimes they are not.

It was only curiosity which induced us to explore the burned-out German tank near Creully. We did not expect to intrude on the privacy of the crew still seated inside, charred to the size of wizened monkeys and to the consistency of burned sausages. The roasting of human flesh and the combustion of ammunition and the defecation of a million voracious flies created an aura of such sense-assaulting horror that we recoiled. We retreated even before our minds could aspire to the pity and loathing which would have sent us hurrying from the presence of those incinerated mummies.

Then there was our encounter with a dead German near that same place. We had smelled the presence of death. And we had found him sleeping undisturbed from some previous battle. Bobby McColl had ordered us to bury him where he lay. We were used to digging slit trenches for our own shelter and, in the soft Norman earth, it was no great toil to dig an enduring shelter for this alien in a strange uniform. We dug deep, not out of respect for the dead but because we must continue to eat and sleep nearby. With some reluctance, but hurried on by our own revulsion, we grabbed his limbs to swing him into the trench. The arm which I seized disintegrated under my fingers, and the clumsy body slumped to the grass again. We vomited into the handkerchiefs which we had tied over our noses. Then, taking our spades, we unceremoniously shovelled the decomposing pieces of human residuum into the deep pit.

Such thoughts as these cause dissonance in our dreams of silver trumpets and charging cavalry as we sit and watch from Fontaine-Henry.

7 JULY 1944:

Rumour has it that we are about to advance on Caen. Perhaps 'rumour' is an inaccurate word for it suggests a tale which had its origins at a distance. 'Speculation' is a more appropriate term, for we have discussed endlessly the strategy of the High Command and the tactics of the immediate neighbourhood. The exhausted D-Day troops must now be requiring the infusion of fresh blood which we represent. And Caen is still the sore thumb sticking in Montgomery's eye.

It is a surprise, however, when the bombers begin to arrive. At first just a distant droning, then a louder booming, a noise which should indicate great bombers above our heads. But no planes are yet visible. The noise increases until the sound of planes reverberates inside our skulls, the very bones of our heads setting up fresh echoes to torment us, until we become scared that we are hearing ghost planes, the ghosts of all the dead planes since the war began, for the sky above our head is clear of both planes and clouds.

At first in the distance a few specks above the horizon hardly justify the ferocity of noise. The specks accumulate and spread and advance and accelerate. The noise becomes, unbelievably, even greater. The planes are near enough to quantify as flights and squadrons and wings and groups and even higher massed formations. They are near enough to identify – the wide wings, the four engines, the smooth lines, the gun turrets, the RAF roundels – as

Lancasters. They are overhead, high but linked to us by the noise which laps about us as an invisible ocean. We are counting them, scanning back through the formations to spot the tail of the armada, but they extend back to the farthest horizon as out of the far sea mists more and more specks appear in continuing squadrons. Dozens. Scores. Hundreds. Thousands of planes.

Down the slope from Fontaine-Henry, behind the trees of Lebisey, in front of Caen, we now witness an extraordinary sight. It is as though someone in the sky were drawing up from earth a wide latticed curtain reaching almost into heaven. Or rather one of those curtains consisting of vertical strings of beads. But these beads are sparks of tracer and series of anti-aircraft shells merging into an impregnable blazing wall against which the air armada must dash itself to pieces in its hundreds and thousands.

The first Lancasters drone majestically over Caen, maintaining height and formation and speed. From leading planes soundless flares descend, like warning messages to the people beneath. We line the hedgerow at Fontaine-Henry and cheer. This is the real war, at last. Massed movement and united valour and overwhelming noise and ourselves lining the touchlines ready to assist. From the succeeding Lancasters we see, or we imagine we see, clusters of tiny black bombs detaching and winging, rather than falling, diagonally towards the target area. Whether we actually see the bombs or not is immaterial because we hear their concussion and in a moment we feel the shock waves. We cheer again. 'Give 'm Hell, boys!'

The endless succession of heavy bombers rolls on. The anger of their bomb-flashes surges above the trees like a swelling, fiery sea. The impregnable curtain of anti-aircraft fire begins to waver, to droop in places, to thin, to descend, to splutter, to disappear. The planes continue to come. One or two swing away, smoking suspiciously. None is seen to explode in the air. The anti-aircraft response has ended. The marker flares have merged into dense smoke. The distant concussions continue to pummel our faces like the punches of a light-weight boxer. And finally the inevitable smell, compounded of cordite and burning buildings and disembowelled streets and singeing flesh.

'Are we going in now, sir?' someone asks Lieutenant McColl, who is standing amongst us at the hedge. 'Not tonight, lads. We would need prior notice of a night attack. Tomorrow morning, perhaps. There's a Troop Leaders conference in half an hour.'

We bed down in a darkness painted over with a red scumble of flame from the burning beyond Lebisey Woods. We can see the Troop Leaders conference taking place behind the Squadron Leader's tank. Hank, as imperturbable as ever, sitting upright on a camp stool; the others leaning on the tank or squatting on the grass. After a while they break up, and Bobby McColl comes back to our group of four tanks. Our Corporal and Troop Sergeant Wilkins move to meet him. They huddle around their maps and make careful marks on the perspex covers, lines and arrows and circles and code-names. Corporal Snowdon detaches from the group and ambles back to us as we sit in our blankets.

'Operation Charnwood. That means capture Caen. At last. We go in with the Shropshires. 3rd Division. Second wave.'

We groan. 'What, bloody second wave again!'

'Hold it, my lads. Wait for it. Two good things about the second wave. Firstly: reveille is not until 06.00 hours and we don't move off until 10.00 hours at the earliest. Plenty of time for breakfast. Secondly: the leading wave will only try to take those woods – they're still in the German lines. It'll be the second wave, that's us, the good old NY, who actually liberate Caen.'

Tommy guffaws. 'That's it, then. All the other buggers in the British and Canadian Armies have had a go. Now it's the NY that has to liberate Caen.'

Hickey says, 'Hope the Jerries have gone home before we get there.'

Our commander's face, as he stands looking down at us, is flushed the colour of damson wine in the reflection of the fires still burning through the night.

8 JULY 1944 – SATURDAY – D + 32:

It is late morning before we trundle down the lanes and across the main Caen-to-coast road and on towards Lebisey Woods. Here I see for the first time a scene reminiscent of a Great War photograph of troops massing for a 'Big Push'. 'Big Push' is not of this war's terminology. The Germans have implanted the word 'Blitz' on all vocabularies. The Blitzkrieg: the Lightning War. But today's scene is more like the opening day of the Somme Big Push in 1916. A couple of thousand infantry, an entire brigade, assembled in open order across a wide parkland on the safe side of the woods – platoons and companies and battalions of men in khaki, all loaded with equipment for the advance. In open ranks they stand, waiting attentively.

Except for one man. A motor cyclist. He hangs sideways against a tall hedge as though crucified there. His motor cycle has been flung up even higher, into the top branches of the hedge, by some high explosive blast. Today's first sacrifice. If I could get out of my tank and touch him, his body would still be warm. But dead. Discarded. Evacuated by his spirit in search of safer realms. The searing blast wrenched the very life force out of his body but left no visible mark.

And the others leave him hanging there, with less compunction than a herd of deer abandoning a wounded stag and with less interest than the soldiers guarding the crucified Jesus. In a more civilized setting, how different it would have been. The priest mumbling holy prayers, the women keening and sobbing, the men sitting round in solemn vigil, the children peeping scared through a crack in the door, an elder placing a sprig of evergreen in a jar of holy water between the flickering candles. But here, their backs turned, the men stand about, laughing and smoking and cursing the delay. The officers study their maps one final time, checking anxiously on landmarks. The women and children, if they exist, hide in cellars.

Untouched by his puny sacrifice, we roll immensely on, my tiny periscope scanning distant views of marching companies, and close-ups of bored, sullen light infantry-men. The motor cyclist totally forgotten, as though he had never existed. I have a momentary vision of a vast score-board somewhere in Hell, which rolls on to 13,567,456, remains flickering for a moment, then jerks on again to 13,567,457. Maybe in some eternal Records Office they have inscribed his name. And in a day or two, in a small terraced house in Shrewsbury or a farm cottage by Clun, a yellow telegraph envelope will drop softly on to the mat . . .

'Operator, load 75 with AP' (armour-piercing shot), snaps the commander's voice as we pass between the woods. The infantry open out into single files on either side of the road and a Sherman ponderously fills our horizon.

At my feet are two buttons. If I now tread on the right-hand button, the 75mm gun will belch and bellow into flame, leaping back on its spring haunches inside the turret and flinging from its barrel at thousands of feet per second a spinning shot of iron, weighing six pounds or more, primed to rip through armour plate, exploding that armour plate as steel splinters into the interior of an enemy tank. If I tread on the other button, the Browning .300 machine-gun linked up to the 75mm cannon will chatter out a stream of tracer bullets on Tommy's side of the cannon. Tommy sits invisible on the other side of the guns, ready to reload and tap my leg as a signal to fire again.

We continue to advance, not so much the galloping glamour of yesteryear yeomanry as a country tour aboard a steamroller. The woods fall behind us and we are turning along a wider road with a view over the valley to our left.

'Hill 60,' says the commander on I/C. 'The objective is just ahead. The river is down there in the dip, by that huge factory. Colombelles!' I am not sure whether Colombelles is the river, the area or the factory. Then I remember that the river is the Orne and the factory, with its sky-searching chimneys, must be at Colombelles. 'Driver, slow down. Left-hand down. Come alongside 3 Able and halt.' In our radio jargon, 3 is Bobby McColl's tank, 3 Able is Sergeant Wilkins, 3 Baker is our tank and 3 Charlie is Jack Ginns' Firefly. Each day we are given a new call-sign to tack on the front of our individual sign. Today we are Yoke 3 Baker, tomorrow we may be Mike 3 Baker, and the next day Baker 3 Baker. Each letter of the alphabet has its own code-name.

'Hullo, all stations, Yoke,' – that is Hank's voice speaking on the 'A'-set frequency but audible on our internal I/C set. 'All stations Yoke. There are undesirable elements somewhere amongst those chimneys. See if you can knock them down. Range about 2,000 yards. Open fire as you are ready. Stations Yoke, over.'

I nestle down into my seat, my left shoulder brushing the gun shield, my right shoulder brushing the hard turret wall, my forehead rammed into the rubber shield on the front wall, my eye to the telescope, my right hand subtly touching the twist grip which sends the turret hissing around to left or right, my left hand delicately raising the gun so that the hairlines meet the target chimney, my back aware that the commander's knees are pressing into it as, in the confined space, he stands with head and shoulder out of the turret top.

'Loader, reload with HE' – high-explosive shells now to wreak their damage on bricks and mortar and possibly human bodies.

I have the gun aligned. I am ready to fire my first shot. This is too easy. But this is the reality. This is the front line. Those chimneys are the enemy's post. Men down there are observing us up here and adjusting their sights, reloading with HE. This is the moment when the champions wheel their horses at the far ends of the jousting ground and begin to trot; this, in days gone by, would have been the moment for the silver trumpet call, now superseded by Hank's cool, Eton voice; this is the moment for which I was born; for which my father's Last War tales at suppertime prepared me; for which my schoolmaster's reminiscences of the Somme honed me; for which the Gordon Highlanders' sergeants, marching me round and round the paradeground, disciplined me; for which the Training Regiment trade-tested me; to which the 1NY has transported me. Now let it begin.

It begins with Tommy slapping my leg. And the firing instruction: 'A shot or two. Get the range. Then we'll try some Browning as well. In your own time.' My own time. My own gun. My own decision. My own war.

The polished steel button under my foot hardly sends a message back to my brain as I tread, hard, firmly, once! The entire tank shudders. A winter's ration of blazing fire burns from the muzzle of the gun barrel. A thunderstorm rolls back up the barrel, out of the automatically opening breech, and through the tiny cracks in telescope and periscope mountings. A thunderstorm wrapped in black clouds of stinking, blinding smoke which, outside my telescope, for a moment blinds me to the flight of my shot.

Then, as smoke and flame clear, I identify my own tiny

spark of tracer racing away from me, straight at the chimney, but dipping, dying away, falling into dead ground somewhere near the unseen river.

'Short! Up 200,' I hear.

I ignore the traverse grip and touch the elevating controls. Up 200. Tommy slaps, I tread, the 75 crashes, the smoke clears, and out of the ground just down the slope a fountain of mess, laced with raging flame, flings a roaring challenge back at me. A dud, I think. My shell was a dud. But in the distance *my* tracer is still speeding. Sparks low on the chimney. Other fountains of flame and noise leap at us, along the slope left and right of our own tank's tracks. Then I realize that it was no dud. It was a real live enemy shell, from Colombelles or thereabouts, fired *at* us by unseen gunners under control of observers in those self-same chimneys. The unholy gun music swells, like Zulu drums beating out the challenge, beating out the warning of death, beating out a distorted, shattering, maniacal rhythm.

Our guns, battering at our own ears even within our protective headphones, but inflicting only tiny, distant sparks of wrath on the immovable, gargantuan chimneys of the Colombelles factory. Their guns, ploughing up the slopes about us, tearing the very daylight with gaping wounds which pour fiery blood. Bruising the wide landscape with blue-black swellings of smoke and dirt and iron shards. Fatal messengers hammering for admission on the turret of our tank, so that the commander ducks inwards and closes his turret flaps and concentrates his gaze through the upper periscope.

'Why don't we pull back out of sight, Corp?' I query in a moment of reloading.

'Not to fear,' he replies calmly, with all the experience of two or three hours of earlier battle. 'They obviously have no armour-piercing shot down there. Those are mortars,

HE shells. No danger to us as long as we stay tucked up inside. Keep shooting.'

We continue shooting. The replying fire from the other side is more sporadic. I wonder why the Germans do not bring some 88mm guns to bear on us. We are in high profile here at the top of Hill 60. But their fire gradually dies down. The massive chimneys remain erect, for all our pounding. The 75mm shells bounce off those reinforced layers of brickwork. But others of our shells are falling in the surrounding area of factory buildings. A steady cloud of smoke, distinct from the individual, evanescent goblins of smoke emitted by single shells, begins to form over the factory.

'All stations, Yoke. Hold your fire. Watch for movement. Fire at your own discretion. All stations, Yoke, over.'

We relax one twist on the ratchet of intensity. We have as yet seen no identifiable movement down the long slopes, although we have heard our Reconnaissance Troop on the wireless, reporting movement of enemy vehicles and men, somewhere down there. But not advancing in our direction, yet!

'Aw, my Gawd!' yelps Tommy's voice. 'I'm in agony!'

'What's the matter? Are you hurt?'

'Hurt, yes! I'll never recover from this hole in my stomach. Do you know we haven't eaten a thing for hours and hours. Ain't there any food anywhere?'

'Don't be such a damn fool, Tommy' – commander irritated. 'For all I know you might have been sitting there with a real hole in your stomach, from a German AP.' He is once more up aloft with his head out of the turret. 'Pass some biscuits around and open that tin of corned beef. Rex, there are one or two others out back of their tanks, brewing up tea. Would you like to have a try?'

'Sounds quieter out there. I'll give it a try' – Rex.

'As quiet as the Cathedral Close on a Sunday night,' I comment.

'That tea tastes as though it's been brewed in the swimming bath after all the mothers' meeting has been for a swim,' moans Tommy.

'Chlorination keeps the germs away,' explains our commander rather superfluously.

'Keeps your bowels open and your teeth shining white,' chirps Hickey.

Rex and other lads from other tanks will now be performing their most hazardous duty yet – making tea. For the German mortar bombs fall indiscriminately and at random intervals. The next one might just as well fall on an unprotected tea-maker as on the front of a closed-up Sherman. However, our tea is brewed safely and our slice of corned beef consumed upon a hard biscuit. And still we watch, scanning the slopes down to where the increasing pall of smoke continues to rise up the outside of Colombelles chimneys.

The major movement in front of us now is the gentle lengthening of the shadow of our tank as the sun begins to descend. We yawn and rub our aching necks and rest our eyes from the insistent demands of the periscopes as one after another takes turns to watch. Wireless silence portrays the lull in the battle.

'Gunner and co-driver, come up! The ammunition lorry is coming along the road. Driver, keep a good look-out.'

Rex and I thankfully climb out into the evening air. At the same moment the Germans begin another visitation of mortar bombs. Our thankfulness turns to reluctant obedience. We stand close to the tank and watch the progress of the ammo truck along the back of the other Squadron tanks.

Usually the truck is staffed by an NCO, the driver and one or two reserve troops to handle the chores. Today the manual labourers are, to our surprise, Bill Fox and the RSM. Captain Bill, our second-in-command, is a tough yet tender old-stager. He is some years older than Hank, who is a major. Legend has it that he has 'knocked about the world a bit', although he comes from a privileged background. He is a harshly spoken man, yet most thoughtful in his care of the youngest troopers. Beside him works the RSM, George Jelley, a bigger man physically but not unlike Bill in temperament. Legend again has it that George falsified his age in order to join up and fight on the Somme in the Great War. He received his first promotion before I was born. Now, as Regimental Sergeant-Major near maximum age for overseas service, he could well sit back in the supply echelon and send others up to the front.

The ammo truck comes level with the back of our tank. Mortar shells continue to spatter the wide fields and slopes as well as the road on which the lorry stands.

'Eff-ing Huns!' snarls Bill Fox. 'Don't they know we can't paste them back until we've filled up with ammunition?'

'Come along there, my lads. Get all the work done before knocking-off time,' shouts George. 'Catch!'

And he and Captain Bill throw huge 75mm shells to Rex and me as though we were playing at beach-ball at Weston-super-Mare. I clutch at the first flying shell, potent enough to shatter the turret of a Sherman, and think to myself that Bill and George are more of a danger to us than the German mortar crews. Corporal Snowdon looks on in horror and visibly prepares to dive for safety if we drop a shell. I throw my shiny, slippery 75mm shell up to the Corporal, who slides it into the turret where Tommy is stocking up and counting. The Corporal turns to make a frantic goalkeeper dive for another shell diverted by Rex.

'Enough!' we hear Tommy's voice faintly from inside the turret.

'Enough!' Rex and I shout with the eagerness of messenger boys.

'Enough's enough, then, my lads,' smiles RSM George. 'And be sure you're still here safe and sound when I come by tomorrow.'

'And now get in your tank and give those bloody Jerry mortars what for!' yells Bill Fox as the ammo truck draws up by Sergeant Wilkins' tank, which is the extreme right flank of our line.

But as we pile and squeeze into the tank again, the mortar bombs cease to fall. Perhaps the movement of the ammo truck attracted their attention. Peace descends over the wide hillside, and nothing moves within the segments of country under our periscope vision.

It is rapidly becoming dark when the commander taps me on the shoulder. We have shut off our engine to conserve fuel, although we must switch on from time to time to recharge the batteries which supply the power for the wireless and the turret traversing machinery.

'Come up, Ken, and keep watch. There is a commanders conference by the Troop Leader's tank. Call me there if you need me.'

I nod and haul myself up from the gunner's seat which is immediately under the single turret hatch where the commander reigns. I inhale the pure air, as I think, then recoil violently for the air outside is more polluted than our hot, rank iron den inside. The wind is now blowing from the direction of Caen and bringing with it an overpowering version of the stench to which we think ourselves accustomed. After that tremendous bomber raid last night there must be thousands of bodies down in the outskirts of Caen, lying unburied all through this hot July day.

In ten minutes or so our commander is back. He calls us out of the tank, and we stamp our feet on the welcome turf. Feet become soft and sensitive after a day within an iron monster.

'We're going in,' he says. 'We're going into Caen. Our Squadron has been ordered to probe through the ruins left by the bombing. Our Troop has been given the job. Our tank is to lead the way. We are to be first into Caen. The Canadians are still fighting their way in across the airfield from the west. Against the SS. So we are going in from the north.'

'When? At first light?' someone asks.

'No, now. In half an hour. We advance down this road. Turn half-right. Down a street that leads into the centre of Caen.'

'In the dark?'

'Well, it looks dark to me. The rest of the Troop will be keeping close up. And the Ulster Rifles will follow us down. So empty your waterworks. Have a smoke. Then do a quick check on the guns. Load up with HE. You won't be able to see much, Ken, down there. But a 75mm gun blasting away in the dark should scare off any ghosts.'

'If the ghosts are wearing field-grey uniforms, they may not scare all that easily,' I mutter to Rex, who looks grim. Tommy opens a tin of cold 'Pork and Veg'. Corporal Snowdon lights his pipe. We sit silently on the edge of the tank and try to think of things to say. The night is ominously silent.

Bobby McColl speaks to us before we lead off. 'If it's any encouragement to you, Sergeant Jack from the Recce Troop has already walked into the centre of Caen on foot. But there was no road through for tanks the way he went. Now we must have another try by a higher route. Take it easy, and I'll be close behind you.'

We move off in the darkness, easing away from the protective grouping of the Squadron. Somewhere in the distance westwards another battle is continuing. The flashes from that battle are our guiding light but a very fickle light at that. Like the light from a flickering coal fire seen whilst blinking one's eyes rapidly. An irritating view of the world. But the succession of snapshot views available to the eyes enables the mind to form an approximate picture of what lies ahead.

We recognize the outskirts of Caen not by the houses but by the ruins. At one moment we are running through grassy open slopes, the next moment the slopes have become uneven and mounded with rubble. Within fifty yards the rubble grows into mountainous proportions. Our progress changes into a series of thuds and crashes and tumbles as we climb over fallen houses and descend into interlinked craters.

'For what it's worth,' comes the commander's voice. 'We are now in Caen.' The wireless clicks and the atmospherics die away as he switches to transmit on 'A' set.

'Hullo, Yoke 3 Baker. Code sign Ranter now. 3 Baker, over.' (Tonight our code signs for objectives are the names of John Peel's dogs. 'John Peel' is our regimental song.)

'Hullo, Yoke 3 Baker.' (Troop Leader replying; the higher authority always using the lower station's call sign.) 'Am in sight of you. Off.'

As we have swung down the hill, the street gap between the houses has become rapidly more distorted by piled rubble until now it has disappeared. There is no more street. There are no houses. There is no Caen. Only a towering wilderness of indescribable ruins pervaded by the worst stench we have yet encountered. There is no escape from it. I tie a handkerchief over my nose but the foul, almost tangible odour desecrates my sinuses. The weird flashing battle reflections turn this ruined world into a bogyland, fit for hobgoblins and fiends and ogres. Surely no German soldier would remain in this uncharted chaos. Yet a wonderful site for ambushes! Behind any mound may be a Panzer grenadier waiting to pounce. The ruins have no form, no symmetry, no recognizable architectural traits to enable us to discern a foreign shape. The place may well be haunted not by hobgoblins but by human werewolves.

Now we are grinding up Everests of pounded rubble. And sliding and rocking down Wookey Holes of RAF excavation. I cling to my gun handles and jam my head firmly into the rubber pad in order to try to keep my eye close to the telescope of a gun whose sights I cannot distinguish in this light. The continual shocks jar my forehead, whiplash effect rips at my neck, my nostrils are soured but not anaesthetized by the reek of death, my eyes are alternately dazzled and blinded by the fluctuations of light, and my heart is squeezed by fear of what may be lurking out there. And an inner voice whispers through it all, 'You wanted the glory, boyo, and this is it. The first tank into Caen. Reeking, stinking Caen. Glory, Hallelujah, and tell it to your grandchildren, if you come out of this lot at all.'

I put my feelings into a message through the mike. 'Commander, I cannot see to aim the gun. Visibility is nil down here.'

'That's OK. It's just as bad up here. If we need to, just blast away regardless with the 75 and hope it scares them more than they scare us.'

'Whoa!' shouts driver Hickey. 'Hey up! Hold tight! Can't hold her!'

We have topped another peak of rubble, and before us lies a black void, blacker even than the momentary pauses of blackness that are the night. And even with tracks braked and halted the Sherman is toppling and sliding down into what seems an underground cavern. Hickey plays the brakes and gears off against the slope and we crash safely but with bone-shaking violence to the floor of the ultimate pit in a system of interlinked craters. This must have been the very epicentre of the earthquake unloaded by the RAF last night. There is silence for a moment. The engine has stalled. The only sound is Tommy singing faintly, from 'The Grand Old Duke of York', the refrain

> And when they were up, they were up;
> And when they were down, they were . . .

'Oh, shut up, Tommy, you ass,' growls the commander through the headphones.

'My view is absolutely blocked down here,' I report, but, touching the traverse gear, 'the gun seems to be working OK – for what that's worth.'

'It's dead stop ahead,' reports Hickey.

'Just a blank wall, like a blinking quarry,' adds Rex.

'For your information,' says our commander, 'it's no better up here. Come up a minute, Ken, and keep watch. I'll see if I can find the Ulsters and Bobby.'

As the commander's feet, thighs and stomach – my own visible impression of him – ease up through the turret hatch, I follow him up, expecting to find a whole world outside. As he said, it's no better up here. The incessant repetition of thousand-pounder bombs falling over an area half the size of a football pitch has hollowed out a massive abyss with its own high and irregular parapet of rubble. I stand on the turret of a Sherman, my feet nine feet from the ground, but the parapet of rubble is still above my eyes. I see no world.

Corporal Snowdon is a tall blob of black detaching himself from the side of the tank and intermittently flicking alight into a ruddy apparition as the Canadian guns continue to grumble not so far away. Another tall blob, too tall for Bobby, not tall enough for Hank, materializes – almost certainly an Ulster officer. A smaller blob, apparition, blob is our own Troop Leader scrambling down through the glacis of mess behind us, like a mountaineer losing his footing on a steep scree in Bobby's own Highlands. The three indistinct figures consult and move slowly around our roofless dungeon. I watch the dim skyline between our premature grave and the less dark living world. No further figures, friendly or enemy, appear. I listen for movement, the engine still silent. Tommy wriggles up beside me in the tight turret hatch where I am once again sitting.

'Pretty hopeless situation,' says I, the budding strategist.

'Bloody scandal there ain't any foodstalls here. A whelk stall. And jellied eels. That's what I fancy.'

'Lord, man, don't you know there might be Jerries up there and we might all be bazooka'd in a minute?'

'At least let me die with me stomach full,' he groans and subsides back into the turret, no doubt searching for the odd dry 'dog biscuit' or a cider apple filched from an orchard.

The corporal blob attaches itself to the tank again and climbs up to the turret. 'No way forward. Bobby agrees. Ulsters say no use staying here. We came. We saw. We conquered. And a fat lot of use it was.'

Back down in the turret I clip my headphones over my beret in time to hear Bobby calling: 'Hullo, Yoke 3. Total. I repeat, total destruction here. No street visible. Craters deeper than the biggest hornet. Our little friends agreed we do no good here. Propose we pull back. Yoke 3, over.'

Hank's midday voice, as cool and fresh as ever, responds immediately: 'Yoke 3. Understood. Wait . . .'

We do. In silence. Down here the sounds on distant earth, even the Canadian battle, seem muffled. We prefer the engine switched off for the moment. This is the eternal problem of the halted tank. If the engine is running, there is no possibility of hearing those first faint noises which may herald the approach of an enemy, close at hand on foot or farther away in armour. Yet if there is a sudden need to reverse and get away, the second's delay in switching on the engine may be fatal. Tonight at the very arrow-point of advance the ability to hear takes priority.

'Yoke 3. Permission granted. Come back to Ruby. Over.'

(Tommy: 'I'll come to Ruby any day.')

'Yoke 3. Thank you. Off to you. Hullo, 3 Baker. You heard? I'll wait and watch you out. Then follow me. Over.'

'Yoke 3 Baker,' responds our commander gratefully. 'OK. Off.' He switches to I/C. 'Driver, start up and reverse. Better take a good running jump. We can't see very much, so come back straight as you go and hope for the best. In your own time.'

The Sherman engine roars into life. Echoes batter back from every direction. We have a spotlight but this is a hazardous place, so near to a possible enemy, and we elect to take our chance in the darkness. Hickey reverses. Fast! We run level for a moment. Then the Sherman tail lifts like a plane taking off backwards. Lifts and lifts until we feel we are falling forward. Lifts and topples . . . backwards! Levels. Crashes down on to what is comparatively solid earth. We scrunch around in the ruins of people's lives and homes and follow the great shadowy bulk of the Troop Leader's tank approximately back the way we came, compass direction still being more relevant than street names.

'Ruby' is our start point, and we swing back into our former resting place, up the slope from the factory, still noticeable as a red glow down the slope. The rest of the Squadron has already gone to bed, except for prowler guards. Four of us wearily drag our blanket rolls from where they are lashed to the engine covers. Tommy scouts around for some supper. We do not dig a trench. We throw our groundsheets down and collapse.

At some time in the night a big German Panzer grenadier

in his coal-scuttle tin hat raises his head above a lip in the ground down the slope and sees me lying, rolled up in my blankets, on the open grass. There is nothing between us except 500 yards of sloping grassland and the occasional prowler guard walking amongst our tanks. The German eases himself slowly out of his trench and equally slowly and cautiously begins to crawl up the slope. I watch in horror. He is crawling directly towards me and I am lodged the farthest away from our tank. He comes nearer, crawling carefully, body pressed to the ground, no weapon in his hands. Huge hands. Staring eyes. Hate personified. I try to move but have wound myself so tightly into my cocoon of blankets that I cannot even loosen my arms. I try to shout but my dry throat emits no sound. He is near. I can hear his breathing. I can smell his breath. I can feel the warmth of his nostrils on my face. He extends his hands to throttle me as I feverishly wriggle. 'Where are the prowler guards?' His hands clutch my throat and begin to squeeze. Those huge hands. That rancid breath. Those hateful eyes. My last thought as I drown is 'Of course! He wouldn't fire a weapon for fear of attracting attention.' The steel fingers give a last squeeze.

I wake up. Shivering. Hot with fever. Cold with running sweat. Arms trapped in blankets. Petrified.

After hours I go to sleep again. Again he slithers out of his trench, crawls up the slope. Again my arms are pinioned, his hands reach out. The hands. The breath. The eyes. The drowning.

I wake and wrestle with the blankets. Stare at the sky. Fearfully look down the slope. I can see no more than about ten yards of grass. But I know that at the bottom of the slope . . . I sink into a terrible, mind-lacerating sleep, and he comes again the third time, crawling up on me the third time, breathing and staring and reaching out and I kick and struggle and fight with the hands, and my pal, the prowler guard, holds on to my hands and says, 'It's all right, mate. It's not Jerry. It's John Peel getting up early for the hounds. It's yer old mate Jim. Settle down. Get some kip. Soon be dawn.'

'No, mate. It's young Ken there . . . bin dreaming . . . bin down in Caen . . . bin doing a bit o' conquering, like . . .'

9 JULY 1944:
They let us sleep on this morning. When we finally roused, the Squadron had shuffled along somewhat so that, although we were still in the front line, we were not at an exposed angle. Down the slope B Squadron was putting a bulldozer into what was left of the streets of Caen. A Squadron was closing the gap with the Canadians. All this we could hear on the radio.

When we had eaten breakfast, we mounted up again and took our normal places in the tank. There was still a war on. At moments during the day the Germans remembered us and sent us a few bombs and shells to keep us alert.

At one moment of the day we were surprised to see a naval officer appear in his navy blue uniform. Later he was perched on Hank's tank, using a pair of outsize binoculars. From time to time an invisible presence sounding like a vast express train rushed through the air above us and, after what seemed minutes, a related thud echoed back to us from beyond Caen. The naval officer was ranging the guns of a battleship on the German lines beyond the city. After a month of attacks and untold spilling of British and Canadian blood the front line was still within the range of the naval guns out in the sea off the beaches where we landed. Yet our Regiment must have clocked up hundreds of miles rushing from one emergency area to another in our former reserve role.

Later in the day there was news that the Canadians had

arrived in Caen after battling across Carpiquet aerodrome. It seems that for this battle we had in fact been under command of the Canadian Army although surrounded by Ulsters and Shropshires of a British division.

Later still Hank came strolling along, his pace no more hurried than when scheming on Salisbury Plain. 'Sorry it was impossible for you to get through last night,' he commiserated. 'At least you can tell your grandchildren you were the first tank into Caen.' Tommy, never afraid of authority, replied, 'I haven't got any grandchildren, sir.' Hank smiled. 'Knowing you, Tucker, you'll probably have 500 one day.' We credit Hank with one winner on that remark.

Now much later, the rations come up, with RSM George Jelley once more delivering the goods. The Germans infuriate Tommy by choosing that moment to open up another barrage which almost succeeds in pulverizing our next two days' food. 'Bloody Huns,' yells Tommy, waving his fist to points vaguely southwards, 'always bombing non-military targets!' and he grabs a pile of tins and sprints for the tank, like a rugby scrum-half sneaking for the line.

We learn that both the Padre and the Medical Officer have been hit by that barrage and themselves have had to be treated after treating other shrapnel casualties.

Smoke is still rising, though now only faintly, from an area of the Colombelles factory. Whatever we had hit down there must have been highly inflammable. But the two immense chimneys still stand up straight, somehow symbolic of the bold, solid defensive strategy waged by the Germans with such success.

It is evening before a thought strikes me. 'Do you realize,' I say to Rex, 'that in all our conquering advance into Caen, we didn't fire a single shot?'

'That's the best kind of war,' he observes.

4
Tank Among the Hedges

10 JULY 1944:

Back among the hedges near Basly (Fontaine-Henry area).
A day of cleaning and maintaining the tank and bathing and
shaving ourselves. Writing letters. Reading post. Listening
to the BBC news account of the capture of Caen by the
Canadians. No mention of us. Perhaps it was too dark for
the war correspondents to see us go by on the road to
Caen. Perhaps we were too far ahead to be noticed. No
mention of us in the news. No place for us in history.

Our ack-ack Troop today covered themselves with glory,
claiming 'half a German plane'. The plane came sweeping
over at dangerously low height, to be met by a spray of fire
from our Regiment and from artillery gunners nearby. The
plane crashed in flames but the pilot managed to survive.
By all accounts he was the most arrogant type of German
pilot and was most angry and resentful at having been shot
down and captured by mere tank gunners. So the Regiment
laid undisputed claim to the prisoner, but the artillery
gunners claimed they had fired the shot which brought
down the plane. The dispute was settled in friendly fashion
by the award of 'half a plane' each to the artillery and to
the Regiment.

12 JULY 1944:

Being located only a few miles from the sea, we were today
able to take a truckload of 'other ranks', selected by lot,
down to the beach at Luc-sur-Mer. Bathing was inhibited
by the presence of underwater iron obstacles, and the sea
was still awash with barbed wire in places, but Tommy and

some others flipped around happily in the water like seals in the silvery sun. I stayed with the majority, stretched out on the beach where the sea had completed a satisfactory job of cleansing. Now the hedges and fields of Normandy are associated with shellbursts and festering bodies and inescapable stench. The beach, adjacent to those fields, seems a different environment, and the saline air wages a successful war against the worst of the land-borne odours.

So I lie with nothing to do, no trenches to dig, no guns to strip, no shrapnel to duck, no officers to salute. In the balmy midday of sea, sun, bracing air and laughing youths on a French beach, I listen again to the remembered echoes of those silver cavalry trumpets of my schoolday books and, ear to the sand, seem to hear the thundering hooves of an earlier day, the swords, the mail, the breast-plates, the plumes. Tank warfare, by comparison, is garage business.

The SSM, that sardonic man Turton, has the last laugh of the day. All the sunburned heroes who spent the day on the beach are appointed to do the night guard.

14 JULY 1944:

We are parked in the idyllic grounds of the Château d'Audrieu, an elegant U-shaped building with an imposing front drive guarded by a regiment of neatly trimmed shrubs (carefully tended even in wartime for the *château* had been a German headquarters). At the back of the *château* rows of immensely old trees form a small wood protecting a wide green park from prying eyes. Our tanks are spread out across the grass and under the trees. It is still very much like scout camp in the grounds of the *château* in the high summer sun. It is still very much like holiday times as Rex and I sit swinging our legs on the back of the tank with not a care in the world.

At this moment a plane hops over the trees, dips towards

us, comes racing at us emitting a ripping noise and, before we can even gasp or gulp, zooms away over the *château* roof. Gone!

'That was a Jerry!' I gurgle at last.

'And the beggar was firing at us!' says Rex. 'Don't nod your head too hard. It may fall off.'

I try nodding my head gently. It stays put. We dive off the tank, like two more planes descending, grab spades and begin to deepen our half-dug shelter trench. The plane does not return.

Night. They say we go into action again tomorrow. I am unlucky enough to be on night guard again. I do not complain. I am not tired. And the park is a very pleasant place in which to prowl around. We have not yet had the problems of Germans trying to infiltrate into our camps at night. There is no reason why they should try it tonight. So I pad silently around the lovely grounds of this stately mansion. The moon shines through the trees, and there is hardly a grumble of battle on the breeze. Even bomber pilots and artillerymen must sleep at times.

In the early hours of the morning I hear tanks approaching. Not from our Regiment. The track sounds are the more clattering, rusty noise of Churchill tanks. Another Regiment moving up in the night. I look down the long drive as the noise gets louder and wait to identify the tanks at a distance. No tanks appear.

Again I hear the mysterious tanks approaching. This time it is the smoother, muted rattle of Shermans with engines booming at full cruising speed. This time they really must pass the end of my drive. The noise builds up to a crescendo of sound and then gradually goes away. Yet there is nowhere for tanks to go away without my seeing them. The noise swells and dims. I hurry, as slowly as may be decent, to the guard hiding in the hedge by the main entrance.

'Can you hear that noise?'

'Course I can bloody well hear it. But I can't see it, can I? Can't see a bloody thing.'

'It's a bit spooky. You hear about haunted houses. And this looks a very old *château*. But tanks?'

'There's been a lot of tanks knocked out and crews killed in these parts. Bugger me if it isn't the ghosts coming back to haunt the place at midnight. *You* can hear them. *I* can hear them. But not a bloody thing to *see*. It scares me more than a great Tiger coming in through the entrance.'

The tank noise again swells to fortissimo, and we both cower back nearer to the hedge. A large van, with loudspeakers projecting from it, brakes on the road, backs into our drive and then drives away in the direction from which it came, its loudspeakers still blaring tank noises into the still hours before dawn. We look at each other's scared faces. And burst out laughing.

'Next thing,' says he, 'they'll have magic lantern slides of Shermans to shine over on to the Jerry front line. Make 'em think we're advancing.'

15 JULY 1944:

Next morning Corporal Snowdon comes back from a commanders conference.

'Young Ken was right,' he says. 'We're doing a feint attack. Not only have they had loudspeaker vans on the road playing tank noises, they have rubber tanks blown up under the trees to swell our numbers when the German recce planes come over. Make them think our attack is the real thing.'

'Which it isn't?' suggests Tommy.

'Which it is, but it isn't. In other words, we do have a real job to do. Cut the main road from Caen to Villers Bocage at a place called Noyers. Then Jerry will move his armour over opposite us. Then the Armoured Divisions will break out from Caen. The end of the Normandy battle. Our second line (the 2nd Northamptonshire Yeomanry with the 11th Armoured Division) will probably be in Paris in a day or two.'

'While we stay here and play balloons with the rubber tanks?' asks Tommy.

'And Ken goes ghost-watching at night,' says Hickey.

16 JULY 1944:

First light: Our Troop is lined up in a lonely stretch of French lane, totally anonymous – no houses, no signposts, no animals, no people. And no outlook. Both sides of the lane are obscured by hedges taller than our tank. Hedges, for what we can see, wider and deeper than our tank. All about us the fury of an artillery barrage crashes and whistles and flashes. We can see nothing of it except the brightening of the early light with each hidden flash. But none of it touches us. We are in a tiny, leafy asylum for psychotic youths who leave their ploughing and baking and clerking to go hunting men as though beasts of the jungle.

Our engine is switched off. The Troop Leader mounts the turret behind us. 'Setting off in five minutes,' he says. 'Just turn your tank like a damn' hunter and take that fence on your right. God knows what you'll find but probably a tiny field. If you can't see me, report in at every hedge and wait for the rest of the Troop to move into line in their own little fields. You know the form. Good hunting.'

Corporal Snowdon passes on the orders to Hickey: 'Start up. When I say, come right and go over the hedge. Slowly. There's a damn' high bank under that hedge. Straight through the hedge, but be ready to reverse out if there's a Jerry gun the other side. Operator, load with AP. Gunner, ready with the 75 for any tanks or guns. Co-driver, sing out if you can see anything before I do. You're well up front.

Right, driver, start swinging. But don't stick your nose through the hedge until I tell you.'

Hickey swings the Sherman round until I lose sight of my gun in the hedge in front of me. I have a close-up of a square yard of prolific bramble. Our rear end must be crushing the other hedge. We stay there, engine idling, waiting to crash up and over. Wondering what waits on the other side – 'over the top,' as they said in 1914–18.

'Driver, advance!' The Sherman climbs up the bank. I get a view of the tree-tops above the hedge. We level off and stay perched on the bank. This is the evil moment when the Sherman shows its thinly plated bottom to any gunner or bazooka man sitting out in the field beyond. It is a naked, unprotected feeling. Hickey revs the engine a little, we begin to topple, a giant hand seems to rip the hedge aside, we crash down to earth, and are through!

We come looking for guns, for flame, for smoke, for the frantic sudden movement of mechanical monsters behind hedges. Or the solitary field-grey hero nursing a bazooka and challenging us to move our big gun more swiftly than his modest iron tube. But this is an empty field. A tiny field. Not big enough to kick a football in. Certainly not the space for a game of cricket. A tiny grazing area defended by high ramparts of hedgerow. And nothing to see. Another tiny private world of our own. Conquered by us. And nobody the wiser.

We roll up to the opposite hedge, merely a couple of rotations of our tracks and we are again pressing into the greenery. The commander must be able to see something from up above. I return to my botany studies. I should end this campaign an expert on privet, hawthorn, bramble and such. Troop Corporal reports to Troop Leader. I sit and wonder whether the end of our barrel is projecting through the hedge to the amusement of a crew of German anti-tank

gunners the other side. My continued existence suggests
that this is a fallacy.

We get the word to move again. Presumably 3 and 3
Able and 3 Charlie are also forsaking their little conquered
fields to brave another hedge. We crawl towards the sky,
tip, balance, wait for the crash of anti-tank shots through
our exposed bottom plates, then crash down frontwards
into a new green world – as tiny as the previous one.
Behind us the infantry will be moving up and peeping
through the horrendous hole we have just made in a
farmer's hedge.

Across the field. This farthest hedge is not so high. Not
so thick. We nuzzle into the hedge and the gun prods
through. 'Can you see yet, gunner?' The leaves fall away
from the periscope and I can see. Germans! By the next
hedge. But dead. Lying in a group face downwards as
though thrown there by some mighty blast. I point my
guns at them, then traverse away towards more ominous
areas.

As we begin to cross this further field, Rex calls 'Those
Jerries aren't dead!' I swing the guns, see the Germans,
leaping to their feet, hands held high and empty, mouths
expressing the desperate words *'Kamerad! Kamerad!'* and
trembling into incontinence as my gun almost grazes their
faces in its onward swing. Corporal Snowdon, up above,
and Rex, opening up his lower hatch cover, by dint of
much waving and kameradly grinning, manage to persuade
our petrified enemies to work their nether limbs back
towards our Staffordshire cousins in the hedgerow
behind us.

Again we probe through a hedge. This time the opposite
hedge is penetrated by a wide gateway – which causes me
to wonder how the farmer obtains access to those previous
fields where I did not notice gates! A German hops across
the gate space like a scared rabbit. I am too astonished to

react. Another German runs across the space, left to right.
I douse the right-hand hedge with machine-gun bullets. A
third German takes the leap. Again I press the floor button,
and tracer spits into the hedge on the right of the gate. I
am waiting for the fourth German, with his basin-shaped
helmet, his wide, neat tunic, his sloppy, baggy trousers,
his carbine in hand. As he sprints across the gate, I fire
into the hedge, his destination. He keeps running. I am
totally perplexed.

'Gunner, there's obviously a trench behind that hedge!
Or a deep ditch to give them cover. Operator, reload with
HE. Gunner, fire three rounds of HE in your own time!'

Obvious! But not to me. Tommy slaps my leg. I tread
hard. The flame at the gun and the flame at the hedge are
almost simultaneous. The hedge is so near that the tempes-
tuous concussion against the hedge rebounds and slams the
turret whilst the gun is still recoiling from its own dis-
charge. For a moment we have the sensation of a small
ship hitting a big rock in stormy seas. A hurricane of noise,
flame, smoke, sods, leaves, burning air, wraps us round.
The gate space is twice the size it was. Tommy slaps. I
tread. Another tornado. Slap. Tread. Blast. The hedge,
what is left of it, begins to burn. No more Germans leap
the gap.

Until now my main fear has been the elephantine shape
of a heavy German tank, a Tiger, Panther, Royal Tiger or
Self-Propelled Gun (SP) suddenly appearing downwind of
us, its all-destroying gun pointing at us and its armour plate
impervious to our 75mm shot. Now a new peril is evident.
If single German infantrymen can pop in and out of ditches
within fifty yards of our tank, single German infantrymen
may be crawling through the hedges alongside us or
through the long grass behind us. And some of those
infantrymen carry the notorious Panzerfaust, a simple,
throwaway bomb-projector, known to us as a bazooka and

looking something like an outsize bassoon, an innocuous-looking instrument but one which, at fifty yards range, can blow our turret to smithereens. The cosy little fields darken into a tight, ugly death-trap, as though a vast, black cloud had come over the summer sun. We sit and watch the burning of the hedge and wonder about Panzerfausts.

We have now learned to distinguish various kinds of projectiles which are aimed at us. Artillery shells tend to descend in 'stonks' of irregularly spaced bangs preceded by rushing noises. The lighter but equally horrific 'Moaning Minnie', a multi-barrelled mortar, arrives in precise rhythmic batches of six, each preceded by something between a howl and a whistle. Tank and anti-tank guns, firing over a level trajectory at very high velocity, do not descend: they rush direct from muzzle to target and at close range the crash of firing and crash of impact are almost simultaneous.

At this moment we hear such a CRASH-CRASH that the day again seems to chill several degrees. Somewhere close at hand a gun larger than ours is roaming invisible behind these infernal hedges. I traverse the gun back and forward and pry through my periscope with murderous intent but can see nothing which is not natural to this quiet sylvan picture. No square shapes or straight lines which denote man's intrusion into nature's extravagant art.

The commander has heard something on 'A' set which I did not catch. 'Gunner, aim through the gate at those hedges beyond and put three rounds of AP over there, spaced out, in your own time . . . fire!'

I aim through the gateway at a mess of more distant hedges, seen through a cluster of apple trees. Aim and tread the button. Three successive tracers leap at the hedge and pierce it in various places with no apparent reaction. The commander orders me to follow up with three HE shots. These explode in or behind the hedges, causing eruptions of smoke, earth and branches which only intensify the impression of indecipherable mess in the distance. For some long time we wait, wondering, watching and repressing our thoughts about Panzerfausts. Then men appear. Khaki men. The South Staffs, moving forward slowly, well dispersed, into the gateway and through the gaps which we have caused in our hedge.

Corporal Snowdon orders Hickey: 'Driver, move up and take position in the gateway. Ready to reverse if necessary.'

Beyond the gateway, among the apple trees, is a small black-and-white timbered farm. The windows are shattered. Smoke drifts lazily from an outbuilding with a galvanized iron roof. More smoke oozes from behind a hedge, behind the farm. Otherwise stillness. Another Sherman rolls up to the farm. Infantrymen run into the farm and outbuildings. Nearer us a South Staffs captain stands with two or three soldiers and nonchalantly lights up a cigarette. He notices us watching him, waves and deliberately gives us a thumbs-up signal. Objective gained! Another 500 yards of France liberated. A day's war done. And, instead of the trumpet sounding recall, an infantry captain giving the thumbs up and Bobby McColl's voice on the wireless, 'All stations 3, keep a good look-out, over.' On that same wireless frequency the more distant voices of A and B Squadrons tell of more dramatic opposition, a tank brewing up, an anti-tank gun destroyed, 'sticky' moments, dangerous isolation at the spearhead of advance. Here the smoke from the outbuilding is hardly more dramatic than that coiling up from the captain's cigarette.

'Anything to eat?' asks Tommy.

17 JULY 1944:
Today we have an even more exposed feeling. Having spent yesterday milling around in some of the smallest fields on earth, so small that it seemed that our tank could

not do an about-turn without knocking down all the hedges of the field, the generals now seem to have found for us the largest field on earth. And instead of sitting behind it, we are arrayed in a long line in *front* of the hedge. Not one tank or the Troop but the entire Squadron, maybe the whole Regiment.

At dawn we advanced along another French lane and then turned right into an endless field whose far side is bounded by a hedge and the main Caen–Villers road. That road is now effectively cut. Nobody can use that road without being blasted away by our guns. Beyond the road is an area of country with only narrow lanes which fall away to the ravine of the River Odon. So this road has been one of the arterial ways for the enemy.

'God, I feel like a sitting duck,' grumbles Tommy. 'What a marvellous target for any Jerry Tiger out hunting. He could pop us off, one by one, pop-pop-pop, just like that.'

'We've got a few guns of our own to bring to bear,' I respond.

'And what odds will you give me on a Sherman against a Tiger at this range?' argues Tommy with considerable justification. 'Give some Jerry tank commander a bloody good birthday present. Twenty Shermans in the bag and the Iron Cross with Oak Leaves on his chest.'

'Oh, go and stick an Iron Cross up your backside, Tommy,' answers Hickey. 'You're getting us all scared.'

'Take pity on him,' Rex intervenes. 'He hasn't had any breakfast yet.'

'Speaking of which,' continues the commander's voice (for we have the engine still running and are chatting on I/C), 'will you get out, Rex, and brew up tea behind the tank? Then we can have breakfast.'

'What? Get out here? I thought we were in the face of the enemy?'

'Hank thinks we shall be safe enough if we keep round

the back of the tank. In case of snipers. You can even get out to pee today.'

'I'm flipping well not getting out to pee,' declares Tommy. 'I'm quite happy enough with a nice warm 75 shell case.'

'You need an 88 shell case,' laughs Hickey. 'Size 75 isn't big enough for you.'

Rex makes our breakfast in safety. We descend down the back of the tank, one by one, to commune with nature. I look along the line of tanks and think again how ridiculous a formation it seems. Still, Hank must know what he's doing, and also the Colonel. But we don't have all that much faith in some of the more elevated ranks, never seen in our mortal world. The myth, if it is, lives on from the First World War, of generals who never came to see how the cannon fodder existed in the real front line.

All in the afternoon, hot and drowsy, in the world of droning bees and shimmering squadrons of gnats in the still air: a black object, like the head of a seal in a harbour, scythes through the heads of the corn across our front. A puff of smoke arises from beyond our distant hedge. One rending howl, like a dog in pain, rushes past the left shoulder of our tank. A noise like a huge door slamming comes from across the main road.

'SP!' shouts the commander, who has been dreaming on the turret. 'Gunner, traverse left and fire. Fire! Traverse!'

I saw it all and grab at my power traverse grip. Hickey saw it all and tried to start the engine, which was still. The power traverse fails to respond. The tank's engine fails to start. Our batteries are flat. Nothing works. A German gunner across there is adjusting his sights. Touching the traverse gear. Squeezing his hand-trigger . . . The electric power system spins our turret, weighing many tons of solid armour plate, right through 360 degrees in thirteen seconds. But when the power fails, the only alternative is to winch it round by hand on its ratchet system – a frustrating, long and muscle-wearying business. Like a maniac I throw my weight on the controls and spin the reluctant turret slowly round. Edging inch by inch when we need yards!

Over there the gunner must be squeezing his trigger . . .

Hickey has started the engine at last but no power comes through the turret system yet. Another black object scythes the corn again, slightly to the right of the last, scything, screaming, howling – instinctively I duck – and the rush of wind misses the right-hand side of the tank. They don't miss twice. That one did. The Germans must be getting short of gunners. He won't miss the third time. I drive the turret round harder. The crossed hairlines on the sight move slowly to the place in the hedge where . . . move slowly to the place where . . . he won't miss the third time . . . move slowly . . .

As my hairline sights meet the smoke in the hedge, a new flame lashes up out of the hedge – but it is one of our shots landing, not one of theirs emerging. I tread button, and tracer shoots for the hedge. Other tracers arrow in as other gunners along our line of tanks waken and sight and fire. The hedge becomes a blazing beacon, and whatever was lodged there, crewed by suicidal idiots or inveterate heroes, has retreated or been blasted to Valhalla, while above the hedge in the gentle breeze there writhes a grotesque shape of smoke like a human being suffering pain *in extremis*.

'He missed us twice,' I babble.

'Correction. He missed us three times. I saw the third,' says Rex, with an excellent but perilous view down below.

'Hullo, all stations Fox,' comes the gruff voice of Bill Fox, standing in for Hank (and the Squadron's call-sign today is, coincidentally, F for Fox). 'Let that be a lesson to you. Keep your eyes open as well as your bowels. And keep your batteries charged. This happens to be a war not a bloody Sunday School picnic. Off.'

'Do I get any credit for brewing up that Jerry?' I ask.

'Judging by the reaction of the rest of the Squadron, I expect you will get credit for one nineteenth of a Jerry.'

'Cheer up, Ken,' Hickey calls to me. 'Even if it's only a nineteenth, if that was a Tiger, it means three whole tons of tank to your credit, that you can brag to the girls about when you get home.'

'Thank God for that,' concludes Tommy. 'We've fired the bloody gun at last. Now I've got a nice, new, shiny, warm shell case to pee into.'

We settle down to contemplating the unchanging panorama again. As the tank is halted but we are constantly running our engines to keep the batteries charged, the temperature rises to baking heat. Inside the tank it might well be a ceramic oven, and we are pieces of china statuettes being baked to a shiny gloss. The occasional well-spaced brews of tea take us along our weary, drowsy path towards evening.

'Hullo, all stations Queen.' (Queen is B Squadron.) 'Air reports of thirty repeat thirty Tigers heading this way at 2,000 yards. Keep good look-out. All stations Queen, over.'

'Well, that's it, then,' says Hickey. 'Over and goodnight!'

'All stations Fox,' Hank's voice this time. 'Did you hear? Thirty Tigers suspected heading this way. All stations Fox, over.'

We forget our mugs of tea standing on the floor of the turret or driving compartment, and press our eyes against our periscopes. Thirty Tigers, I think. If they line up behind their hedge as we are lined up in front of our hedge, their commander can give the word and they can fire in unison, brewing us all up in one foul blast. But nothing looms in the periscope. I switch to the telescope for a magnified view. Traverse left and right along their hedge. See no movement.

I duck abruptly as something screams. Like the scream of a shell. But this scream goes on and on. Over the enemy hedge, beyond the road, above the trees, a slim, winged shape comes hurtling earthwards. I have just time to identify it – 'Typhoon!' – when what appears to be fizzing flame shoots from its wings. The plane swoops upwards out of the dive and is chased by an immense cauldron of flame and smoke bubbling up from its target area.

'Rockets!' screams Tommy. 'Bloody hooray! Typhoons with rockets!'

The second Typhoon dives and scatters fire beneath it. A third Typhoon. A fourth and fifth. The boiling concussions sweep across the field like a veritable China Seas typhoon and rock our tank back on its springs.

'Pity the poor sods under that lot, Jerries or not!' gulps someone.

'Make the bastards squirm,' cries a voice over the wireless – someone pressing their microphone switch without changing from 'A' set to I/C.

'Unknown station. Use your bloody I/C,' commands Bill Fox's voice.

'All stations Fox,' Bill continues. 'Forget the cheering. Keep your damn eyes peeled. Off.'

'That little twit, Monty, will be pissing himself with delight for having brought all those Tigers over this way,' adds Tommy. 'Wish the bugger were sitting in my seat and I was sitting in his just now.'

So we watch the patch in front, now sprouting a sky-high crop of black vegetation as unexplained infernos of fire rage where the rockets hit. Are they Tigers on fire? Are there Tigers still advancing on us? Were there ever Tigers? Will they take fright and hide in case the 'Tiffies' come back with more rockets? We watch, our eyes to the rubber pads of periscopes and our fingers curled, white-knuckled around the mechanisms of our instruments of retaliation. Hickey keeps the engine running. I continually give the traverse gear a swish right and a swish left to make sure that the gun is fully mobile. Ready to flash into action . . .

I can almost hear my pulse beating in my neck. The fear is still fever-hot there and behind my eyes, and under my heart. My arms feel heavy and leaden when they should be nimble and lithe. My mouth tastes of stale fish.

Like tadpoles diving through water the Typhoons sweep down the sky again. Fiery death rages away from their rocket nozzles. They become flying fish, leaping up out of the turbulent lower element of smoking war and into the clear sky where the sunlight glints on their wings. And the winds of their descent whip the woods into a stormy sea of fire and smoke. We sit and watch, our fingers and foreheads soldered into the metal of the tank. Fear begins to run down in my heart like sand in an egg-timer.

We watch through the twilight. We prowl night watches around our laagered tanks. We watch another day through. The sun imitates the rage of the Typhoons and heats our tank again to torture point. We drowse and watch. Nothing ventures along the road. There are no roars from hidden Tigers.

19 JULY 1944:
Back from our field at nightfall to replenish and maintain engines and weapons, we switch the wireless to BBC wavelength. The armoured divisions have broken out from Caen. The German line is broken. The way to Paris is open.

20 JULY 1944:
Still in the Noyers field, watching the main road which nobody uses, and the distant hedges from which no

German response emerges. Hank has told Bill Fox, who has told Bobby McColl, who has told Ken Snowdon, who has told us in strict confidence, so that whoever might be sitting out in a Noyers field listening should not hear, that the break-out from Caen has been another 'bloody balls-up' (undoubtedly Bill Fox's paraphrase of Hank's more technical description). The armoured divisions did *not* break out, the Germans did *not* break up; in fact, *nothing* broke except an exaggerated Press story.

The Germans are still holed up, behind lines of 88mm guns, on some ridge or other called Bourguébus, still overlooking Caen and still able to annihilate anything that creeps on all those slopes. And our Second Regiment has lost God-knows-how-many men dead, dozens of tanks and a whole squadron disappeared. Or so they say. And the Canadians walked head first into bloody slaughter like the Somme in 1916. Or so they say. I wonder whether this trumpets and banners thing is such fun after all. Some A and B Squadron lads are staying when we leave Noyers. The only flags they will get will be on their coffins when they are reburied after the war.

21 JULY 1944:
Last night a flight of German bombers picked us out for delivery of airborne hate. One of the Recce Troop corporals was killed. To add insult to injury, the German bombers also unloaded showers of propaganda leaflets, telling us how the traitor Churchill had hoodwinked us into fighting the good Nazis and how the German secret weapons were still winning the war. We were in no mood to pay heed to these badly presented, badly written, badly printed messages. Normally we would have laughed at them. Today we only growled.

We are back a mile or two farther from Noyers at what might once have been a pretty village, before the war came, Fontenay-le-Pesnel. A hard name for English tongues. Fontenay-le-Pisshole is the popular rendering. Tommy has even more vulgar versions.

22 JULY 1944:
We move off tomorrow from this pleasant little place of bombed ruins and orchards. Rex and I wandered into a deserted cottage garden, luxuriant with summer flowers and herbs. We found some fresh mint to boil with the potatoes Hickey had dug up in a field. 'Real food!' chortled Tommy. But we move tomorrow. We don't know where and are not going to ask. We don't like the answer we think we'll get.

23 JULY 1944:
Our immediate destiny is disclosed. The seaside! Langrune-sur-Mer, the summer retreat of pre-war opulent Parisians. We are apparently moving from one corps to another. So we are parked out of the way for a day or two. At the seaside. True, it is raining. 'Just like bloody Blackpool on Bank Holiday,' says Harry Graham from Liverpool. But who cares? We explore the beach, swim in the sea under the gentle Normandy rain. 'I see no battleships,' says Hickey. The host of fighting ships which was once mustered off the beaches is no longer in evidence off Langrune.

Our Squadron is in laager near the railway line. We make friends with the man in the signal-box. We have not yet had much opportunity to talk to French people. The signalman invites us into his box and later into his house. He brings out some wine which the Germans did not know about. He tells us stories about the Atlantic Wall (Hitler's famed coastal defences) and about the doings of the French Resistance and about D-Day itself.

'Should have gone straight through to Caen. Could have

gone straight through to Caen, your troops,' he says. 'I could have sent them down the line into Caen. Didn't even need to walk or ride in a tank. Could have gone in by train. But somebody was too nervous. Never had a chance after that.'

We tell him about our descent into Caen, our narrations made more complicated because one or two comedians like Tommy insist on interrupting our painful flow of schoolboy French in order to enact charades supported by incoherent babblings of music-hall *patois*. The signalman and his wife and the old grandfather understand and join the frivolity. And the old grandfather rattles away in his thick Norman dialect, telling stories to which nobody listens – until he shuffles off to find another bottle of white wine, when his stories suddenly become most popular, even if uncomprehended.

The fun and the civilian company and the swimming have already cleansed from our minds some of the strain of those days of feinting and waiting out in the open at Noyers. The old grandfather even has a First War bugle on which we tootle and blow 'retreats' and 'cookhouses'. Not quite silver trumpets but a youthful regression to less mechanized days.

5

Night of the Tanks

26 JULY 1944:

We drove up from the beaches, along our route of some weeks ago to Hill 60. Then down the hill to the factory which we shelled, Colombelles. Past the spot where the German in my dream had left his trench and crawled up the slope. At last we saw the River Orne and crossed it by means of a temporary Bailey bridge. We were now in the narrow corridor of liberated territory beyond the Orne through which the armoured divisions had passed so hopefully just over a week ago. We halted at a place called Demouville.

Along our route were notices – 'Dust costs lives', 'Dust brings shells', 'Go slow: stay alive!' Discouraging signs for speedy motorists. Demouville was a flat plain of dust, a veritable Valley of Death. Even a boot scraped in the ground caused a small hover of dust. Lorries crawling slowly along the road raised young cyclones of dust. A tank turning round in its own length threw up a veritable cumulus of dust. And the Germans could oversee everything along that plain. Our view was blocked by far-distant woods and hedges and the ruins of Troarn, but somewhere up the slopes high-magnification field-glasses charted our every move and brought artillery fire down on precisely registered target points. So we sat tight. We carefully hollowed out our trenches in the barren soil under our tanks and lived either inside the tanks or under them. Even so, shells and mortar bombs came crashing down at random intervals and with varying frequency. One of A

Squadron's sergeants was killed and several other crew were wounded.

But the menace of the guns soon diminished in comparison with the Demouville mosquitoes. These mosquitoes must be to the insect world what piranha are to the fish world. Whereas ordinary mosquitoes are content to feed off the blood in a human being's veins, the Demouville breed appeared to take a sadistic delight in sinking the teeth into skin, veins, cheeks, ears, arms, ankles, out of sheer rabid animosity towards mankind. Or perhaps they had absorbed some of the belligerence of the German artillery gunners and considered that this was the required treatment for a British soldier, wounding morning, noon and night. No escape with darkness and no escape with daylight.

Someone suggested a wood fire to keep the mosquitoes at bay. The fire seemed to achieve this but immediately brought a sustained stonk from those other predators in field-grey in their observation posts beyond our view. Within hours faces and limbs began to swell with an affliction like an itching, paining dropsy.

'Hello,' says Hickey to Tommy. 'Who are you?'

'Bloody funny,' says Tommy. 'But your own face is like a football. Lie down and I'll kick a goal.'

'First time any part of Tommy has ever been fat,' I say.

'You look like you've got scarlet fever, smallpox, cholera and flaming shingles, all in one,' retorts Tommy.

All is not lost. The Medical Officer provides an antidote. It is a repellent ointment. We smear ourselves with it and look as though we have bathed in motor grease. The mosquitoes settle on us in droves, in armies, in myriads.

'Jumping Jehoshaphat,' says Tommy the glutton. 'They're effing well eating the ruddy stuff. It's mosquito bait, not mosquito repellent. I can't stand it. I'm going to throw myself in front of a low-flying Moaning Minnie. Death, where is thy sting?'

For some reason the Luftwaffe are not as reticent to strafe this area as they appeared to be in the Bocage. Gloaming and midnight and dawn seem to be their favourite times for vying with the pestilential mosquitoes for the honour of bringing most annoyance and hurt to the troops. At least when the low-flying aircraft appear we can give vent to our fury by loosing off belt after belt of fiery machine-gun bullets in their direction. As for the mosquitoes, the draught of the bullets seems to blow them out of the path of the bullets, and they keep coming in their multitudes long after the Luftwaffe have gone home.

Corporal McKenzie and a pal manage to extract a few moments of grim humour from the situation. From some deposit they discover two German SS uniforms, so that they dress up and come strutting past the tanks, giving the Nazi salute and bawling out fantastic German words like 'Donner und Blitzen' or 'Sie mussen mein Backside kissen'. They climb on to the backs of several tanks and cause consternation and, they say, more than one instant surrender. The pantomime ends when another commander, who is not in on the joke, turns a Sten gun on them whilst they are 'capturing' a nearby tank. Fortunately the commander's aim is as unreliable as his weapon, and McKenzie & Co live to enjoy the joke – until the Sergeant-Major has reason to be harassed by the idea of mistaken identities. We have not yet heard what he knows.

Although there is a screen of infantry out in front of us, our fear is that enemy tanks may break through that screen and come charging upon us, guns blazing. That is what we are here to counteract. So we take it in turns to keep a good watch through the long days. We heard on the wireless that one of our corporals out on the flank was astonished to see what he took to be a Tiger tank making such a charge from the German lines directly at him.

He gave the orders to fire and his gunner fired. As he reported in by wireless, he revised his assessment to 'an enemy SP' (self-propelled gun: a vehicle with less gun traverse than a tank but still mounted with a gun much bigger than ours) rather than a Tiger. The corporal's gunner hit the stranger first shot, but the SP kept coming. A second shot from the Sherman hit the SP before the bigger gun could fire back. The corporal had just wirelessed, 'They must be fanatical heroes in that tank. They are still firing, even after being hit', when both vehicles went up in flames. The Sherman crew escaped but the corporal himself died in the last flurry of shots. The SP also was reduced to burning wreckage with all its crew dead.

We had listened in horror to all this on the wireless. What we did not yet know, and what the Sergeant-Major now knew, was that the SP was in fact British. It was a new type of tank which .none of us had seen before. This particular·vehicle had got lost and was, or so its commander thought, advancing on the enemy when our corporal's well-hidden and disguised tank opened fire. The two heroic Britishers thereupon fought their duel to the death.

4 AUGUST 1944:
It is doubtful if one member of the 1st Northamptonshire Yeomanry felt the slightest grain of regret about leaving Demouville. Especially when our next destination proved to be well behind the lines and within the smell of sea air. There were plenty of flies but few mosquitoes at Gazelle, our new lodging place, not far from Fontaine-Henry, where we watched the RAF raid on Caen.

6 AUGUST 1944:
For two days and two nights they have been teaching us to march in columns of four – not on foot but in tanks.

'Bloody drill,' said Tommy when we were first given our instructions. 'These effing officers have got nothing better to do than think up new sorts of bull to entertain the troops. Why don't they let us get on with the war? Bloody drill in the front line. It's worse than the Guards.'

When they sent us advancing in fours, we thought of the marvellous target we would make for the German gunners – better than in our single-line formation at Noyers. When the practice continued into the night and it was obvious this was to be a night affair, we forgot our fear of close formations but began to worry how we might defend ourselves in the dark. Our gun-sights are useless at night. But there were no answers to our questions. The entire Regiment simply drilled up and down the gentle slopes of the open fields near Gazelle.

Now we have crossed the River Orne again, bypassed Demouville with its mosquitoes and gone 'into harbour' at a place called Cormelles on the far side of Caen. Above us are the infamous slopes of the Bourguébus Ridge. All this area is the scene of the slaughter of the armoured divisions after our feint at Noyers. From here the slopes look unimpressive, just a gentle upward roll of cornfields. The maps tell us that those slopes continue rolling up to places like St-Aignan-de-Cramesnil and Cintheaux. And the contour lines tell us that everything that happens along those slopes will be visible to the gunners at the top.

However, here outside Cormelles there is a final dip in the slopes which gives us cover from observation, and here the entire Regiment is harboured, spread out across the grass at the city's edge like the vehicles of a circus before the grand marquee is raised. Quite what *our* circus is to be we have not yet been told, but it is to be performed in columns of four at night. And a skirl of bagpipes tells us that our infantry colleagues will be from the 51st Highland Division, the Scots known in the last war as 'the ladies from Hell'. Somebody says glumly, 'Élite infantry equals bloody battles to come.'

7 AUGUST 1944 – MONDAY, AUGUST BANK HOLIDAY:

We are enjoying something of a holiday on this hot August Monday for we are to move off tonight. We are now officially Canadians. The 51st Highland Division and our 33rd Armoured Brigade have been posted as reinforcements to the battered Canadian Army.

Tonight four columns of the Canadian Army will assault these slopes which have proved impregnable in daylight. Four columns. The Germans have fortified all the villages on the slopes. So we shall bypass the villages, taking a twisting course across country in the dark. In four columns. In columns of four. And our column will be the left-hand column. With nobody on our left.

The official war photographer comes to take pictures of us for the daily papers and for posterity. We pose as heroes for a few moments. But nagging in our minds are the thoughts: columns of four; in the dark; a twisting course; fortified villages.

The Colonel and Hank come around the tanks giving us friendly little pep talks. Captain Tom Boardman has gone out to 'recce' and will be leading us tonight on a compass bearing, like a ship's captain. The Colonel and Hank are cool and reassuring. But the thoughts nag our minds. All those slopes dominated by the German 88mm guns. Advancing across country. Across railway lines. Across sunken roads. Across trackless cornfields. And nobody on our left. On the slopes where the uncounted dead of our Second Regiment still lie unburied.

We finish our maintenance. We lie and sunbathe. The Sergeant-Major and Quartermaster-Sergeant bring round the rum ration. They trot out the hoary old jokes. Serve us the rum. Cheer us up. And the thoughts continue to nag. The rum ration. The last rite for the cannon-fodder about to go over the top. In columns of fours. All neatly dressed in files by the left. But nobody on the left. And the 88s and the Tigers and the SS waiting at the top of the hill.

Corporal Snowdon shows us the map with the battle details neatly marked in fine ciphers. Sometimes it is worse to know. God ordained for each man an hour in which to die but softened the blow by keeping that hour an eternal secret. Here they tell us the hour and the place when the 88mm tools of destruction will be turned upon us. Whilst we are on a compass bearing in the trackless dark. Perhaps it was better, like Wellington's or Haig's men, not to know, simply to march to the sound of bugle or drum . . .

8–9 AUGUST 1944 – TUESDAY/WEDNESDAY:

02.00 hours. Still I cannot sleep. One would have thought that, after forty hours of sleeplessness, strain and frequent frantic activity in the face of imminent destruction, sleep would have come as surely as night after day. But sleep, I cannot.

The Night March is over, and the inevitable counter-attack. We and the Black Watch established our armed camp miles behind the enemy's front lines and then held that camp against the onslaught of the SS veterans from the Steppes of Russia. Half the Squadron has been written off. Half the Regiment. The Colonel wounded. The dead unburied.

Now in the grumbling silence of the second night we lie still hemmed in on two sides by the haunted unknown. On the other two sides we have insecure links with our equally beleaguered comrades of other units. It is not the fear or the haunting of the phantom enemy which keeps me awake. In a strange way those elements are stimulating, challenging, exhilarating in the cool, gun-trembled night under a sky whose stars flicker militantly with the flashes from Earth. The planet Venus blushes into an impersonation of Mars, blushes not with love but with bloodshed. The silver disc of moon transmutes into a blood-orange with every surge of terrestrial flame.

It is the human tragedy which holds back sleep. Today again we have not been able to bury our dead. Ken Snowdon and Rex, Tommy and Hickey and I have sat nearest to the open tombs of our comrades, tombs that were blazing tanks or holes scooped by the fatal shell-bursts. We have sat nearest, in our own tank, and held each our own secret vigils. But after dark we were ordered to withdraw to a place of security for replenishment and maintenance and sleep. And we left them there, our mates, lying untended. Now death will go about its grisly business of decomposition before our hands can offer the final tribute to comradeship and affection.

Young Wellbelove knocked out three German tanks in that isolated arrow-point of advance beyond the gully, before he himself died. Soldiers won VCs for less than that in the last war. He will win no medal nor even the courtesy of a timely burial, for the ground beyond the gully is still contested country, No-Man's-Land. 'No Go' area.

This last forty hours we have been asked to accomplish three tasks not normally asked of human beings: first, to face appalling wounds, burning and possible fearful death at fifty yards range; second, to destroy other human beings; and third, to leave our own dead unburied. Lying here in the cool, reasoning void of the anonymous hours (was it not T. E. Lawrence who held that the thought waves are less trammelled and more lucid at this hour?), I realize that, for me, those tasks were costliest in reverse order.

To sit in a vehicle and drive deliberately towards a known power of death, each yard making the certainty of incineration or dismemberment more real, is a dread undertaking. The mind suffers acute and agonizing qualms. But there are inducements which make the act almost automatic – the ingrained discipline of army life; loyalty to Hickey, Rex and the others; confidence in Hank and Bobby McColl; the conviction that the Nazi occupation of Europe is evil; the natural pride of the young *macho* in the face of the charging bull; and, somewhere behind all that, the echoes of silver trumpets faintly discerned in Father's First War tales and still echoing through the genes, the grim music of Waterloo and Crécy and Hastings.

All these considerations make the second task, that of elimination of fellow human beings, similarly automatic, especially when the action is mechanized through elevating wheels and traversing systems and foot buttons and telescopic lens. From time to time the telescope catches the pallor of a German's face or even the supremely human factor of baggy trousers. The mind revolts, the stomach heaves, as the foot-propelled shell impacts on another Nazi cipher.

But it is the leaving of one's own dead unburied which is the task for which no training has prepared us. It is the act whose unique agony Jesus recognized – 'Let the dead bury their dead, and come . . .' It is often easier to walk to death oneself – millions of men are doing this in August 1944 in Normandy, Italy, Russia, Burma, the Pacific Islands – than to leave unserved good, earthy pals who have suddenly passed into the ultimate priesthood of death. He cannot appreciate this fully who has never been compelled to retreat from his own personal St-Aignan-de-Cramesnil.

And I remember the survivors of that more terrible slaughter on the Somme in 1916 – looking out towards their own St-Aignans. Not so much pained by the futility of their attack, or the failure of their arms, or their own wounds and fatigue, but grieved beyond comprehension or description by the sight of their comrades left hanging on the enemy wire. To the photographer mere human husks, hung by the rags of bullet-tattered uniforms on a forest of rusty spikes. To their watching comrades a failure in the most basic of human and eternal decencies.

I was privileged to accompany heroes to St-Aignan-de-Cramesnil – Hank Bevan and Tom Boardman, Colonel Doug and Bill Fox, young Wellbelove and short-sighted Corporal Stanley, and those German infantrymen who braved the burning cornfield, and the Black Watch who must remain at the gully all night. I sat and watched and pressed a few buttons. Now, in the comparative security of our tank laager, I lie but cannot sleep.

The history of our forty hours is simple. We formed up at Cormelles in our ranks of four tanks, Captain Tom Boardman in the leading tank and Captain Ken Todd in the second, navigating across the unknown, unseen landscape which had been blasted and moonscaped by the earlier battles. A Squadron following and our C Squadron just behind the Colonel, Doug Forster. Then the Black Watch in their new armoured carriers and B Squadron watching the rear. Like a vast compact centipede, we wriggled through the night.

The sinister profile of the old battlefield was made more hellish by the green tracer bullets being fired overhead as a guide to our route, by the green shellbursts serving also as markers and by the 'artificial moonlight' of searchlights shining on clouds. The scene was further bedevilled by the proximity of an RAF raid only a thousand yards away on our unprotected left, whose immense and continuing volcanoes of fires, punctuated by the brief blackness of original night between bomb-bursts, revealed us as clumsy, blind dinosaurs stumbling across a primeval landscape against a background of bleeding skies.

Held up and scattered by crashed vehicles or anti-tank

explosions or banked railway tracks or towering hedgerows, we followed Tom Boardman in his apparently vacuous quest across a lost countryside, our neat centipede disintegrating into a slow-motion buffalo stampede. And precisely on time, at another anonymous midnight hour, we found ourselves at the hedge code-named 'Fly-by-Night' which was our objective.

At dawn the stone cottages of St-Aignan-de-Cramesnil slowly became visible through the thick mists. Our line of tanks laced and interlaced the village with machine-gun fire while the Black Watch scurried into a brief fight and an early victory. Passing through the empty village, we paused in the green fields beyond. As the early morning sun strengthened, our crew breakfasted in the shade of a belt of woodland in a sudden silence which prompted the thought that this was all a mock exercise: that we were still practising at Gazelle and had not yet joined battle.

By midday the Germans, aware of our presence, had gathered their resources and launched tanks and infantry in a counter-attack. Tigers advanced down the main Falaise road, but Tom Boardman again led a tiny mobile hunting party of ostensibly inferior Shermans through the orchards. The four Tigers, product of history's most efficient mobilization of technology and military ability, were destroyed within minutes by the unprofessional tactics of Yeomen who came from a long inheritance of shooting gentry and poaching peasants.

Bruce, in Bill Fox's tank, and I shared credit for one German SP which, in brewing up Ken Todd's tank, indiscreetly showed a couple of inches of square armour beyond its leafy hide. Rex and I poured hundreds of machine-gun bullets promiscuously into cornfields where German Panzer grenadiers advanced by their hundreds and were grilled alive by their scores.

Our 2 Troop, after inflicting losses on the enemy,

disappeared into oblivion from the wireless network like a Roman legion marching into the forests of an earlier-day Germany or like an aircraft disappearing over the Antarctic. Except that 2 Troop was only about three minutes' walk from where we sat on the open hillside, looking over the gully and the orchards and the woods towards the farm at Robertmesnil. Somewhere in those woods beyond the gully 2 Troop perished. We counted their survivors as they trudged back from the gully, but there were not enough survivors. Count them how many times we would, the mathematics of our sadness and desperation still failed to tally with our hopes.

And we shared, in our minds, the bodily suffering of our badly wounded friends, like Eric Good and Phil Monkman and the Colonel himself. And all in among the fiery Hell, Hank Bevan took a casual stroll to reassure us who lived on. In the afternoon and evening our tank sat almost at the lip of the gully and we watched the German Red Cross orderlies looking for their surviving wounded. Like us, they carried away their stretchers but left their dead, many more than ours, lying along the gully slopes.

So I survive, and tomorrow the Regiment, reduced to two Squadrons, returns to the gully at St-Aignan at first light. And I cannot sleep, except for macabre snatches of snake-infested semi-consciousness, in which I 'listen out' for some voice from those human souls of my pals, carried on the unceasing radio waves of the universe, out beyond our ability to think, and spilling into some far maelstrom of fate, horrific or sublime.

The day of yesterday and its yesternight remain with me in memory flashes so like the shell flashes, brief, brilliant and appalling: the pale German in a trench in the night, paralysed and unmoving as our gun almost brushes his grey face – just a kid like ourselves; the crumpled waxwork that was a German motor-cyclist riding round a corner of a remote, stinking farmyard, driving into a Black Watch bullet, falling grasping frantically at the new sun; tiny figures of crewmen squirming out of a burning Sherman turret like maggots out of a ripe Camembert cheese; a knocked-out Sherman emerging from, and merging into, the mists of the broken land, like a parody from *Swan Lake* – a lonely, empty, iron monster, a high point of a former tide of enthusiasm, a roosting place for rats and shadows; where 2 Troop should be, two towers of flame gushing to the sky, spilling out foul black smoke; the rugby scrum of cooks, fitters, clerks greeting us on our return; RSM George Jelley, bombed by the American Air Force, seeing the blast which killed lads behind the lines – 'No trace of 'em. Not even a hand to shake goodbye to, like you found in the old trenches.' And always, night and day, until they are tumoured onto our eardrums, the thunderous concussions of tank engines and our gun-blasts and their shell-bursts; and always, until it is saturated into our nostrils, the stench of chemical obscenities and animal putrescence; and always, until they are stencilled into the very brain matter, the incessant atmospherics of the wireless whose tentacles reach out beyond the cool voice of Hank and the frenzied messages of neighbouring battles and into the mysterious whisperings of the upper ionosphere and beyond, where the voices call of those who are trying to keep in touch . . . through the gloom . . . past innumerable worlds . . . everlasting night . . . ?

9 AUGUST 1944:

In a sleeping daze we rose at 04.00 hours, scalded our fingers trying to make a hurried mug of tea, piled clumsily on to our tanks. Now we are on the road back to St-Aignan before the light has conquered the darkness.

By some dispensation of fortune our Troop appears to be the only Troop in A and C Squadrons, and one of only three Troops in the entire Regiment, which is numerically intact. This morning A and C Squadrons combined to form one unit, so heavy were our casualties during the Night March and St-Aignan battle. Hank has moved up to Second-in-Command of the Regiment, for the Colonel has been evacuated with a serious wound. Bill Fox is our new Squadron Leader, a major now, with Ken Todd as his second. There is no spare officer, so the Squadron Sergeant-Major, that perky, humorous, sardonic man, will be coming up to take the Squadron Captain's tank when that is replaced.

The modest cottages, the tall Norman church, the rambling farm buildings, the fruitful orchards of St-Aignan all present a holiday brochure picture in the summer sun. Only a closer examination reveals smashed walls and bullet-pitted trees, yellowing bodies of man and beast and blackened, burned-out tanks of yesterday's strife. Today the Black Watch stand boldly about the village street where yesterday they ducked and sprinted. Their cooks tend roaring fires where yesterday the shells of both sides spewed flame. Even in front of St-Aignan, towards Robertmesnil, they rest easily in their slit trenches under the apple trees and hedgerows, confident that the SS will not wish to renew yesterday's experience, which left an untimely harvest of field-grey bodies in the still-smoking cornfields across the gully.

We take our place among the trees on the slope of the gully, yesterday a veritable race-track for German tanks and forbidden territory for us. The green gully winds away in both directions, its slopes dense with woodland. The day blurs into unreality as a few artillery shells and mortar bombs fall, but no mass activity of enemy troops is to be seen. Eventually we are confident enough to allow one or two of the crew out behind the tank for natural purposes and to brew more tea than we were able to enjoy yesterday.

Our tank still smells of smoke where a direct hit set our camouflage on fire yesterday and convinced us that we were about to explode into flames, as we had seen Ken Todd's tank brew up a few yards away. My head still aches and my forehead is swollen from a wasp sting which was my only injury amid the confusion of battle. Our store bins are full of food because we received full rations for an entire Squadron when only half a Squadron remained.

As I loiter aimlessly about at the back of the tank, gulping in fresh air after the oven atmosphere of the turret, and as quickly revolting against the evil odours with which the air is tainted, Bobby McColl, the Troop Leader, approaches.

'How is the wasp wound today? Dangerous game, wandering around the French countryside.' He switches on that rather shy, reticent sixth-form smile. 'Have you still got that stripe you wore on the way over? Put it up again, will you, please? Your promotion will be in orders this evening. Hank wants you to be ready to do a commanding job in an emergency. We are running short of commanders after yesterday.'

I get the stripes and the needle and cotton out of my small pack and have a vision of John Pearson, the Corporal Clerk, sitting somewhere in the orchards, faithfully typing out Part II Orders for this evening – 'to be Lance-Corporal, 147 Tpr Tout, K.J.' – and maybe ducking out of the way of a mortar bomb or a stray aeroplane bullet between typing the K and the J. As we heard from the RSM last night, the lottery of danger is only slightly weighted in favour of the Troop Corporal's tank as compared with the Quartermaster's truck. And when death strikes, it is as final for the clerk as for the gunner.

10 AUGUST 1944:

Len Wright, wounded at La Taille, breezed back into the Squadron today. Together with other reinforcements, tanks and humans, he helps restore our Squadron to size, except for the shortage of captains and lieutenants.

Someone has discovered from somewhere a huge Nazi banner. We display it on the back of a tank. Somebody else produces a clandestine camera with which to take a quick snap. We all give the Nazi salute, the camera clicks and we laugh with the pent-up fury of psychiatric casualties from St-Aignan. Some German gunner, telepathically aware of our imbecilities and resenting the slur on the swastika, sends over a few random shells, random in timing but precisely aimed at our gully. We disperse and grovel before the gods of cordite and TNT. Or whatever gods inhabit those flailing clouds of shrapnel fury, for our schooling in the theoretical aspects of gunnery is elementary in the extreme.

Tonight we shall not withdraw from the gully. The Black Watch are permanently dug in around and in front of us. The Poles and the Canadians have drawn a tight half-moon of guns across the slopes where for a while we camped alone. So we shall sleep in our own trenches under the tanks, and our 'soft' vehicles will creep up through St-Aignan in the twilight and replenish us where we stand.

Ossie Porter, Tom Rushton and one or two others have heard there is a Promenade Concert on the BBC wavelength tonight. We decide to take over our tank and form an impromptu audience for the Prom. 'Bugger that,' says Tommy heatedly. 'All music is a bore. Symphonies or Glenn flooding Miller. All I ever wanted out of a Saturday evening hop was the floozie with the red hair. You can switch off the band, for me.' We bribe Tommy with a spare tin of corned beef to go off and sit in another tank.

Outside a single prowler guard plods among our tanks, very much a formality with the Black Watch night guard alert in their slit trenches a few yards away. Into a five-man tank a dozen of us push and squeeze as though playing at sardines. I have a reserved seat, the luxury of the operator's perch, seeing that Tommy does not want to attend. In the driver's compartment half-a-dozen lads sit on the laps of those occupying the available seats. Outside another batch of Moaning Minnies screams and thunders down. Somebody closes the turret hatches. There are not enough headsets to go round. We could, of course, spread ourselves around several tanks with ample supplies of headsets. But that would not be such fun. It would not be in the spirit of the Proms.

As the owner, I tune our wireless to BBC – quite legitimate if the Squadron is not on wireless watch – and net into the descending buzz of the signal. There is conversation and coughing in a distant concert hall, discreet shuffling; somebody says, 'Get off my ferking fingers' (within the tank); the plaintive far-away note of an oboe to which reply violins being tuned, as well as one of our troopers who releases his own windy signal from a nether region of the anatomy with a certain tunefulness and says, 'A bit flat, I'm afraid.' Applause, repeated enthusiastically in the turret, for both leader and conductor. 'Arggh! Bugger!' says Ossie, who has tried to imitate the conductor's opening bow and caught his skull on a projecting smoke-bomb discharger. The applause and coughing pass into the appropriate diminuendo. Into silence. The scrape of a chair. Tap of a baton on a stand.

The first notes of Tchaikovsky's wistful Sixth Symphony drift in through the ether. We cluster around the earphones, which are packed into two mess-tins to form a home-made loudspeaker. Cellos and violas sigh as though in sympathy with the pathetic human emotion which has filled our air waves these last few days. The bass clarinet reminds us of an approaching aeroplane. The tank rocks slightly as our own artillery behind us blasts into action to scare away the author of the Moaning Minnies which continue falling at random, dulling the impact of the orchestral tympani. And when at last the trumpets sound, they are not silver with the ephemeral glory of ancient battle but golden with the heroism of a personal confrontation with the Inevitable. And the descending cadences of the last movement, the most tragic in orchestral repertoire, remind us of the burying party which went across the gully to look for Wellbelove and Jim Stanley and the others.

We open up the turret and emerge in unaccustomed serenity and pensiveness. Outside the tank the SSM stands chatting to one of the sergeants, unsublimated by Tchaikovsky's music. He goggles at us as we give an imitation of one of those comic films where an inordinate number of people emerge from a tiny automobile. 'What's this then?' he yelps. 'A bloody secret caucus of the revolutionary IRA?'

13 AUGUST 1944:
We have moved from St-Aignan-de-Cramesnil and are lodged at an even higher contour point near St-Sylvain. From these woods we can see the view which the German 88mm gunners have had down the long, undulating slopes towards Caen.

Some of our people have been touring the battlefield and peering into knocked-out tanks. I risked a glimpse into one German Mark IV, thinking to examine its mechanical equipment. But death had posted a grisly guard inside in the form of a decapitated and already mouldering driver. The lords of the flies, entire nations of them, held sway there. I lost my enthusiasm for German mechanical ingenuity.

They say the offensive has run into problems. The incredible achievements of the first day of Operation Totalize, the epic Night March and the devastating St-

Aignan battle were followed by routine daylight attacks on either flank. The Poles and Canadians suffered the inevitable punishment from the last thin screen of German 88s. So the drive to close the circle on the German 7th Army falters, not on the loyalty of the common soldier or the inefficiency of his immediate superiors but on the madness of consigning marching armies, on foot or in armoured vehicles, to open country dominated by higher ridges occupied by an enemy with superior guns. In broad daylight!

I have spent three days telling myself that I should write home and say that I am safe. Although our battles have been announced by the BBC as a Canadian operation, my parents must guess that somewhere amid all this carnage this tank is carrying their only son. They saw our Sherman tanks parked in the streets of Gloucester, and every photograph of a Sherman tank in the *Daily Sketch* or *News Chronicle*, whatever the caption, will be their son's tank. Even after a twelve-hour day at his shoe-repairing business, with hundreds of pairs of military boots to renovate, my father will study the two newspapers from cover to cover for clues as to my whereabouts. I could write home but am still in a daze of green, luminous skies and boiling crimson-flame woods, and shuddering concussions and screaming wireless messages and long, empty forenoons and hideous, sweat-soured, stench-saturated afternoons and sleepless, ghost-haunted nights. I get my notepad and pen to write home but my wrist is petrified. My fingers clasp the pen but no message arrives from the brain.

Ken Lyke, from B Squadron echelon (all the Regiment's trucks form one continuous supply train in an emergency), delivers petrol to our tank. Ken was at school with me. He says he will write and tell his parents to let my parents know I am safe and well. Then I can postpone the letter-writing for another day or two.

15 AUGUST 1944:

We cross a tiny river, the Laison, on a Bailey bridge. The Germans had blown the bridge just before A Squadron arrived. We advance like zombies across fairly open country. Fortunately this is a weak place in the German lines, and they fail to take advantage of our torpor. We travel on to another anonymous hedgerow and halt, as much for lack of adrenalin to advance farther as from the realization that we have reached our limited objective. The Germans retaliate by dousing us with artillery fire from various angles and, when darkness at last falls, send in one of their infrequent air raids. We do not realize that we have penetrated ahead of other units on our flanks. All we know is that the infernal noises continue: if not mortar bombs, artillery shells; if not artillery shells, aerial bombs; if not aerial bombs, tank engines running to maintain batteries; and then back to mortar bombs again.

I am sitting on the turret top, involved like the others in some routine chores of the night, in spite of the heavy aeroplane engines droning overhead. Somewhere a bomb drops. Near or far, I am not sure. Then something wet hits my hand. Another drop. Liquid. Heavy, wet, sticky.

'Gas!' I think. 'Mustard gas!' The final dread of this war's soldiers, that the Germans, in their extremity of despair, may use chemical weapons.

The scant anti-gas training we have received has served more to inculcate fear of gas than to prepare us to meet the danger. We have worn our gas capes as occasional raincoats so that they are ripped and battered. Our gask masks are stowed away somewhere at the bottom of one of our storage bins. We never really thought . . . 'Gas!' Raising huge blisters on the skin, burning the lungs, leaving a strong man a pitiful invalid for life or burning him up inside as surely as a brewing tank burns him up externally.

I try to shout 'Gas!' but my dry mouth and throat emit only a faint croak amid the noises of the night attack. Another drop hits my hand. No sensation of burning. No pain. No agony in the throat or lungs. Another large drop. And the drops gather into showers of cool rain. I stick my tongue out and suck at the life-giving rain. Another bomb drops, somewhere near or far. One of our tanks lets loose with a machine-gun, tracer bullets racing up at a black, clouded sky.

'Stop that bloody gunner,' shouts an authoritative voice. 'The idiot will do more damage to us than to the damn' Jerries.'

In the ultimate rite of the day, I take a spade from the rack at the side of the tank. I trudge towards outer darkness, counting the paces. In a wasted land, desecrated with human and animal waste and flagellated by shards of metal and explosives, our Squadron insists on the gentlemanly niceties of life, prohibiting what is known to the troops as 'crapping at close range'. Twenty-five yards from the nearest tank is the order. Twenty-five yards at least before you dig your little private latrine.

We are near a minefield. The engineers have done a quick survey and laid white tapes at the limits of our safety. At twenty yards I hit a white tape. I have no desire to die a hero's death by treading on a mine, much less court a 'Blighty One' by squatting on a mine. So I begin to dig.

My reverie is broken by the high, squeaking voice of the Squadron's most aggressive sergeant, god-damning and blasting me for effing squatting at less than figures twenty-five yards and 'crapping right in your comrades' flooding mess-tins'. I argue about the white tape and he accuses me of funk, yellow-liver, thoughtless creep. We both vent our battle agonies in a squabble about squatting over a tiny hole in a remote Norman field.

A rasping, irritated voice cuts into our argument. 'What the bloody hell's going on here? Troopers can't sleep for your squabbling. Isn't there enough war around without you two acting like a couple of screeching cats on heat? If I were at home I'd throw a damned great hunting boot out of the window at you.'

The well-known voice of Bill Fox precedes him as he moves into our tiny vision of starlight, deftly pulling up his own trousers. He too has been squatting within the white tape limit. We thrust our arguments at him. 'Bloody insolent, insubordinate brat still at school when I was a corporal . . . it was a white tape, and orders say white tapes should not be crossed . . . young whippersnapper . . . a bit exaggerated, sir . . . told 'im, sah!'

'Aha, yes, Sergeant. Very good, Sergeant. You go off to bed now, Sergeant. I'll deal with this, aha, whippersnapper.' The irate Sergeant salutes with Aldershot intentions but drunken effect as he stumbles tiredly back into the darkness of the laager. Bill Fox, buttoning his braces, says calmly, 'Not good enough. Squatting at less than twenty-five yards. Don't let it happen again, Corporal. Offensive to the lads eating their supper.'

'It *was* a white tape, sir,' I insist.

'Damn' dangerous things, white tapes,' growls Bill. 'Get mixed up with your bootlaces. Well, there you are. Don't cross white tapes. And don't squat before twenty-five yards. And don't do as I do. Do as I say.'

'And how do I sort all that lot out, sir?' I ask again, knowing that old Bill is infallibly good-tempered.

'If you could sort that lot out, you'd be a general not a corporal, lad,' he grins, shouldering his own shovel. 'Give you a bit of advice anyway. Get digging quickly. It's a long way to the nearest laundry.'

And with that he too merges into blackness and leaves me to my own unmilitary devices.

6
Tank Command

16 AUGUST 1944:

SSM Turton is the messenger who ends my service with 3
Troop and commands me to say farewell to my good friends
Ken Snowdon, Rex, Hickey and Tommy – a very solid and
loyal crew on 3 Baker. The SSM himself has taken over the
third tank in HQF (Squadron Fighting Headquarters)
Troop. That tank is usually commanded by a captain,
termed the Squadron Captain. But we are now short of
officers and so SSM Sid is acting Squadron Captain.

'Right, get your gear, lad. You're moving,' chirps the
irrepressible Turton. 'I'll whistle up a pantechnicon while
you get your grand piano and euphonium out of the old
homestead.'

'Where am I going, Sergeant-Major? Not back to
Reserve Troop, I hope.'

'No more bloody reserves for you in this war, lad. You're
first team now. International class. Test batsman. Might
even play for Northamptonshire if you're lucky.' (Northants
had been bottom of the counties cricket league when the
war terminated cricket.) 'No. You're for the really big
posting. A 17-pounder gun for you, sonny. We haven't
enough 17-pounder gunners. Only a few of you got trained
at Bury before D-Day hit us between the eyes.'

'On whose tank, sir?'

'Another commander bit the dust. So Corporal
McKenzie is commanding his own tank today, and there is
nobody to replace him as the gunner. 17-pounder. 1 Troop.
Go and report to Mac. Don't need me to hold your hand.
Give Jerry Hell with that bloody great gun!'

I report to McKenzie. He is the comedian who dressed up as an SS Panzer grenadier at Demouville and nearly got strafed by one of our own tanks. 'Hello, Mac,' I shout up to him as he stands on the turret. 'Which country's uniforms are we wearing today?'

'Wear any uniform you want, kid, as long as you fire this 'orrible gun on target. Get in and try it out. We are advancing in an hour's time.'

The Firefly tank is an ordinary Sherman but, in order to accommodate the immense breech of the 17-pounder and to store its massive shells, the co-driver has been eliminated and his little den has been used as storage space. The electrical traversing gear makes it easy to swing the gun around but heaven help me if I ever have to traverse the 17-pounder by hand, as with the 75 at Noyers. The flash is so brilliant that both gunner and commander need to blink at the moment of firing. Otherwise they will be blinded for so long that they will not see the shot hit target. The muzzle flash spurts out so much flame that, after a shot or two, the hedge or undergrowth in front of the tank is likely to start burning. When moving, the gun's overlap in front or, if traversed, to the side is so long that driver, gunner and commander have to be constantly alert to avoid wrapping the barrel around some apparently distant tree, defenceless lamp-post or inoffensive house.

St-Pierre-sur-Dives is our first objective. Before leaving 3 Baker I had heard lustful Tommy chortle, 'Dives! Real French dives at last. And "Peer soor Dives" – does that mean the dives have little peep-holes where you can peep through?' Possibly because of Tommy's presence in the Squadron, we are not routed through the town. We pass around and set our sights on the hill beyond.

The road rises steeply through orchards and woods. We advance so slowly that the Black Watch infantry alongside us have to halt and wait, before plodding on again at something much less hearty than a Highland fling. There are three or four tanks in front of us, and files of infantry beside and behind them in the road. The first intimation of problems is the sight of Sergeant Wilkins' crew from 3 Troop, walking back down the road. All of them grin and wave but with that pallid, zombie attitude which tells that their tank is somewhere up ahead, 'brewed up'. Several A Squadron lads also walk back down the road, more than one of them bandaged or limping.

Bill Fox's rasping voice breaks into the atmospherics in our earphones. 'Howe 2. Break off to the right and find a way around the bottom of the hill. Howe 1, follow and support Howe 2 on his right. Howe 2 and Howe 1, over.' A 2 Troop tank ahead turns politely through a wide gate into a field but, with little room to move, the driver demolishes the gate and the surrounding hedge. Another 2 Troop tank blatantly swings and charges straight through the hedge.

'Driver, follow through that gateway,' says McKenzie, now no longer the comedian but a sensible, level-headed NCO. 'Loader, make sure there is an AP up the spout. Obviously there are enemy tanks about. Gunner, keep a good watch on that piece of road, down through the orchard.'

On the right of our road the hillside falls away through an open field and an orchard beyond which a short stretch of another road shows through the trees. Away to the left are more trees, thickening into a wood or orchard. To the right, the outskirts of St-Pierre. We descend the hill behind and to the right of 2 Troop. As 2 Troop move in and out of trees, they begin to fire machine-gun and 75mm tracer. We cannot see the reason for their firing.

'Hullo, Howe 2. Parties of enemy infantry with bazookas. Am scaring them off. Howe 2, over.'

'Hullo, Howe 2. Take care. Off.'

McKenzie's voice breaks through on the I/C set: 'Driver, watch where you are going. The ground looks very swampy. 2 Troop seems to be having trouble. Keep well to the right.'

'Hullo, Howe 2 Able.' (It's my aggressive Sergeant of last night, now commanding 2 Troop, speaking to his second tank and using, as required, the code-sign of the lesser authority.) 'Hullo, Howe 2 Able. I'm bloody stuck in the mud. Come over and pull me out. You'll need the tow-rope. Over.'

'Howe 2 Able. Will do. Off.'

We pull out from behind a row of apple trees and see the scene set: Howe 2 partly sunk in a stretch of brilliant green boggy ground alongside a small stream. Howe 2 Able backing gingerly towards Howe 2, the tracks of Howe 2 Able beginning to slither and churn mud alarmingly. A figure in denim overalls between the two tanks, dragging a tow-rope from Howe 2 Able and waiting to link up to Howe 2. The head of the aggressive little Sergeant poking out of the turret of Howe 2, watching the tow-rope, looking right and left, jerking suddenly left, staring horrified to the left.

A thick hedge, tall trees above the hedge, pleasant pastureland, a great gap in the hedge. A mighty armoured steel machine in the gap. Huge gun pointing away from Howe 2 but beginning to traverse. A Tiger tank!

Mac sees it. 'Gunner, fire 17-pounder. Can't traverse it because of the trees. But fire! Scare the bugger away! Fire anywhere! Driver, advance.'

I fire the 17-pounder and the world goes black with flame, raging, blinding, terrifying flame. I wait for my sight to return. The loader slaps my leg after the hefty job of reloading. We have lurched forward into a clear view of the hedge. I traverse hard. The gap in the hedge is there, wide and blank. The Tiger has disappeared. Howe 2 and How 2 Able are still struggling to link the tow-rope.

'Put another round into that hole in the hedge,' says Mac. 'Looks as though we scared the bugger.'

I fire again, closing my eyes. And open them to see the tracer speed precisely through the centre of the gap and into oblivion. There is no explosion. No reaction. One round of 17-pounder flying on and on and on, I think, up the road to Paris. Maybe five or six miles further on some poor German headquarters or echelon trooper will get a tremendous surprise when that lands on his foot. It has to land somewhere. But there is no solid armour behind that hedge. We shiver, nevertheless!

Our burst of speed has brought us level with the stretch of road, about a hundred yards away. We can now see that it peters out at the edge of our field. There are houses down one side of the road. About fifty yards further along it bends to the left and disappears. Tracer comes from the right and sprinkles the first house.

'There are Jerries in that house,' says Mac. 'Knock it down!'

'There's an AP up the spout,' I say. (In theory, armour-piercing solid shot should go right through a house leaving a neat hole front and back. High-explosive shell is needed to blow a wall down.)

'Shoot it off. Don't wait to reload. Then load with HE,' commands McKenzie. Ricochet, I think. A ricochet shot will bounce and spin (remembering a ricochet shot we sent over the gully at St-Aignan).

I fire again. Blink. The solid black mass slams across the field, hits ground just short of the house, whirls upwards, brick dust explodes like an imitation bomb burst, and the wall disintegrates.

The house is left like a doll's house with one side neatly removed. Kitchen and bedroom revealed to the world. Clouds of brick dust rising over the roof like fire-tinged smoke. Men in field-grey scurrying from the bedroom. I fire the machine-gun to encourage them on their way.

We sit and watch the empty house. A vehicle pulls into the road from the right. Heads towards us. A half-track troop-carrier. Full of field-grey troops. Sees us. Spins around in its own length. Scuttles down the road. White faces above green armour-plating. I fire both guns instinctively. Too high! Lower the guns. Drag them down. Still firing machine-gun. A body lurches. The half-track swings to left. At end of road. Gone! My 75 HE shot follows it. Gone! Leaving me with a vision of coal-scuttle helmets all in a row. White faces turned towards us. All in a row. A dozen or twenty men still sitting upright. All in a row. Two rows. Paralysed! and one body jerked . . .

'Driver, advance. Left hand down.' While we have been firing, I have been vaguely conscious of voices on the wireless reporting snipers in trees. The trees are there in my periscope. I see nothing unusual. I move my eye to the gun telescope. Greater magnification. Ropes dangling. 'The snipers must be up in the trees, using those ropes to shin down,' says Mac, who is up above me looking out of the open turret through his field-glasses, oblivious to the real danger from snipers. 'Can't see 'em. So try and knock those trees down by the roots. HE, loader. HE, please!'

The 17-pounder is mainly a tank-versus-tank weapon, using armour-piercing shot. So we carry less HE than in a 75mm Sherman. And loading with HE involves struggling with huge shells stored in racks way down in front of us. And no room for manoeuvre. Seconds pass as we get loaded with HE. Mac obstinately keeps his head above the turret opening. The loader slaps my leg. I aim at the foot of one of the trees. Fire! Blink. Watch.

An immediate furnace of red-hot steel seems to flare at the tree's base. The tree, killed instantly, takes a tired leap, like a shot deer, topples and crashes flat.

'And the next one!' orders Mac. As I aim at the second tree, I see at the margin of my vision a field-grey figure swarming down his rope. Then muzzle flame breeds another grossly distending furnace. The second tree splits apart. The smoke clouds clear. There is no tree. No rope. No field-grey figure.

We shrug back into the trees and skulk behind a hedge as though ashamed of our own ferocious deeds. We wait for darkness to cover us. The wireless is crackling with reports of enemy infantry prowling in the orchards, dug-in Tiger tanks on the hill-top, anti-tank guns on the flanks, unidentified armoured vehicles moving beyond the hedge. We seem to have wandered into a seething hotbed of enemy activity. As darkness comes, the human beings hiding from us out there become bogeys invested with supernatural powers of speed and destruction. Sitting behind guns whose sights are now useless, in a great tank whose armour will not resist the Tiger's 88mm shot, we feel vulnerable, scared, haunted.

Mac has a brief conversation with the Troop Leader outside the tank. 'Right, lads,' he reports on his return, 'they say it's too dangerous to withdraw. Anti-tank guns and bazookas that way. So we're going through the orchards the long way home. All hatches closed down. Periscope vision only. Follow our leader. And Bill Fox will be at the front, on foot, guiding the entire Squadron through the orchards. Right. Close down. Driver, start up. Ready to advance.'

Now begins an experience compared with which the Night March of 7–8 August was child's play. Admittedly then we were attacking one of the strongest German defence lines of the war. But then we were marshalled into close, impregnable ranks and files, as compact and reassuring as the centre men of an ancient Greek phalanx. Then we had an RAF raid scourging the enemy on our left flank.

Then we had more solid columns of armoured colleagues on our right flank. Then the land in front of us was open and we had only to choose a stealthy path between the villages. Then we had artillery guiding us along the route as we watched their green tracer sailing overhead. Now we are lonely wanderers in a dense night. Now we are lost in meandering orchards, bounded by intricate and vast hedges, lapped by troublesome brooks and invisible swamps. Now we are strung out in single file through the trees, our flanks unguarded and the fragile link of sight with the tank in front and behind us likely to be broken by the slightest interruption, such as a hedge or a ditch or a stalled engine or a German mine or a sleepy tank commander.

So I sit at my periscope and watch an oblong patch of blank void and know that Mac, with his hatches closed for fear of snipers or maverick enemy infantry leaping on the back of the tank, has no more vision, and that the driver is equally impeded, and that our vast proboscis of a gun may at any moment foul an obstacle and either explode the round up the breech or cause us to crash with little hope of extraction.

So I sit and watch whilst my mind supplies the vacant dark with gliding armies of bogeys and ghouls. All the horrors of my childhood dreams come to mix with the known hazards of the battle – the clanking of chained ghosts, and the slaughtered Lamb of God which slid down nightly from its gruesome picture in the bedroom and into my nightmares, and the bleeding monstrosities from the first production of *Macbeth* which I saw as too young a child, and the First War Germans grunting under the bed in a dug-out after I had heard some of my father's suppertime stories. All those half-remembered fantasies mix with the memories more recent, their stench still degrading the nostrils, of the German motor-cyclist lying like a waxwork in a St-Aignan ditch, and a British motor-cyclist spread-eagled and forgotten whilst still chilling into *rigor mortis* before Caen, and the officer with an arm shot off, and the loathsome roasted creatures still sitting guard in their shattered tank. All these and the flooding visions of my own wounding, burned in the trap of a sealed tank, or torn by the whirling shards of shrapnel, or ripped apart by the threading series of machine-gun bullets, or blasted to tiny, uncomprehending fragments by a flash of high explosive.

Riding in the tank at less than walking speed, with a blind man's view on a tiny segment of orchard hemmed in by imagined dangers, I have nothing else to think about. Except myself. A whole world at war. Millions mown down by the bullets, the bombs, the mines, the knife thrusts. But I am alone in a fatal, darkened steel niche in an even darker, empty world. And the imbecility of it, the lack of form or reason or intelligence, prevents my thinking of anything. Except myself. And the horrors to come. Sometime in the night I doze into nightmares and awake into worse black reality. The tank roars and trundles on, stopping and starting. By some miracle we keep in sight of the darker hulk in front. And somewhere ahead Bill Fox walks in bow-legged imperturbability through the perilous orchards, guiding the way.

The tank halts. Shudders to rest. Goes silent. The wireless flicks dead. The empty visual world is joined by an empty audio world. Mac taps me on the shoulder. I remove my earphones, and the silence buzzes in my eardrums. 'We're home. We're bloody well home. Old Bill got us here,' he says.

'Where is home?' I ask in my stunned state.

'Anywhere is home for me at 03.00 hours in the morning,' says Mac. 'Dismount, lads. And pray they don't have bloody reveille in an hour's time.'

In the wilderness of night our Sherman is distinguishable
only by touch and by the warmth of its engine after a day
and night of travel. McKenzie, who has been to a brief
commanders conference, comes back and finds me fast
asleep, standing up and leaning against the tank – not the
first time it has happened to me or others on the crew.

'Wakey, wakey. Reveille. Breakfast up,' he crows, once
again the comedian.

'Oh, leave the poor lad alone, Mac,' says another
sergeant in a group of commanders walking past. 'It ain't
really reveille, Ken. It's broad, bright noon-day.'

The Sergeant-Major's voice breaks in, his face only a
paler blotch of night like a faint moon behind thick clouds:
'Get some proper kip, lad. Have to be fit tomorrow to
dodge all those shells Jerry will be throwing at you after
scaring his Tiger away today.'

'Do you think it will be as tough tomorrow, then, Sid?'
asks a sergeant.

'No! Piece of cake tomorrow,' says the Sergeant-Major as
their voices fade like ghosts into the unreality of deeper
blackness. 'Jerry will be on the run now the Black Watch
have captured the hill. Tomorrow it will all be sleeping and
boozing and dreaming of . . .'

Blizzards of sleep drown me and snowdrifts of unconsciousness wrap me around.

17 AUGUST 1944:
After a very late breakfast we have moved up beyond the
hill of last night's adventure. B Squadron is advancing on
St-Julien-le-Faucon, and we sit in reserve in a large field
behind a farm. RHQ (Regimental Headquarters) is in the
next field. A Squadron somewhere nearby. The Black
Watch resting along the road. But on our left and right
flanks we are again exposed. Mac says that Bill Fox says
that Hank says we have got ahead of the rest of the army

and that this road and these few fields are another arrow-head of the advance. So over in those woods to the right and over in that other farm to the left there may be enemy troops. We rest on or by our tanks. I try again to write home.

I sit on the turret and try to write. The pen moves erratically in my fingers but no messages come from the brain. What can I write to my parents? A poem about August sunshine in green fields? My father was in the army in 'the last lot' but not in the front line. Will even he comprehend if I write about the unceasing devilish roar of tank engines and aeroplanes and gun-blasts and shellbursts which drown the echoes of silver trumpets from my boyhood dreams? Will even he comprehend the immensity and ferocity of fire as 88s and 75s and 17-pounders blast away at each other from a hundred yards' range, and where the muzzle flashes from our own guns coalesce with the mortar bomb flashes from the Moaning Minnies and the muzzle flashes from the German Mark IVs until, as at St-Aignan, an entire cornfield can become a storm of fire in which every living being, human, animal and reptile, is grilled to death even before the rolling thunderclouds of poisonous smoke asphyxiate them? So what can I write?

I sit staring at the green fields and the orchards. The silent tanks and the recumbent troopers. The smoke puffs. *The smoke puffs!* Six puffs of smoke as innocent as though from a pipe-smoker's mouth. Men roll over into slit trenches or leap up and run to hide under armour-plated tanks. I vault up and into the shelter of the turret. As I drop, I see another six puffs. The scream of the falling bombs this time penetrates my vacant ears. Six screams, six puffs, six playful bangs like blown-up bags bursting, six cyclones of sods, iron, flame, smoke. Then six and six and six. And one flashing under the very nose of the Squadron

Captain's tank. (The Squadron Captain's tank brewed also at St-Aignan in a green field on a hot afternoon.)

Screams now, not in neat stitches of six, not linked to smoke puffs and blasts. Detached, arrhythmic, agonized screams. Human screams. We are not nearest. Others run before us. Duck, kneel and grovel by the Squadron Captain's tank. Bruce Dickson staggers up from where he was sheltering beneath – battered, bruised, horrified but alive. Men dragging a person from farther under the tank. Poor Len Wright. Back a few days from a head injury in our first battle. Now wounded again in almost the same part of the head. Bleeding but alive. Now they wrestle underneath and drag out more men, swearing, bleeding, living men. And a mashed, minced, murdered tangle of clothing with a crown on its sleeve. Bill Fox running, pointing. 'You, run for the ambulance. You two, stretchers, and you two. Field dressing, you and you. Lay him down here. Get back, and give him air.'

Half-track ambulances ploughing the green grass. The MO running through the hedge from RHQ. A wounded man weeping. Correction: a non-wounded man weeping. 'Shut that bloody noise,' snaps a sergeant. And the wounded men, five, six, seven . . . and eight, lying still, smiling weakly, smoking greedily, stifling the pain.

Hank appears through the hedge (he is Second-in-Command at RHQ now) and confers with Bill Fox. Both of them wearing corduroy trousers which are khaki to the knees and good, red Northamptonshire Yeomanry blood from knees to ankles. Hank pulling a medical orderly away from a pile of clothing and saying, 'He's damn' well dead. Get a stretcher to Bolton there.' With the tenderness of worshipping nuns, the rough-clad troopers move George Bolton, Signals Corporal, on to a stretcher. 'Damn' well get him better,' snaps Hank to the medical corporal. 'He's too good an operator to lose.' The savers of lives rev their mechanical chargers and race away down the one liberated road towards the hospitals and beaches and Blighty. And the troopers bring spades and a blanket and a wooden cross and a pencil to render the only service now left for that fast-joking, darkly sardonic, immaculate Squadron Sergeant-Major who will call no more parades on this earth.

Back on the tank at last I begin to write. 'Our SSM has been killed. You met him once. Very strict but comical with it. Cracked outrageous jokes on parade and challenged you to laugh. At your peril. Stand still and bust your innards sniggering silently.'

Don Pateman, the Squadron Leader's co-pilot, pulls my foot as I sit scribbling on the tank top. 'Bill Fox wants you. Immediate. Come as you are.' I have been sitting bare-chested, bare-footed but Bill Fox requires no spit-and-polish response. I jump down and follow Don across the grass which again sleeps peacefully and unremembering of the storm, except for one oblong of turf which is up-mounded above the rest.

Bill Fox and Hank have been chatting beside the tank. Bill turns to me with weariness shading his face and growls, not unkindly, 'You commanded a Stuart, coming over. Think you can command a Sherman?'

'I'd have a good try, sir.'

'Ah, yes. Yes. You know the Sergeant-Major was killed there? Damn' bomb bounced. Wouldn't believe it. But it's true. Damn' bomb bounced right over young Dickson. Turton was the third one in. Sheltering right under that damn' tank. Exploded right over him. Damn' bomb. Damn' good Sergeant-Major.'

'I saw it, sir.'

'Ah, well. Choose to fight bloody wars, people get hurt. Take over the spare tank, lad. The new SSM is ex-infantry.

Never been in a tank. Hank says "Can't let *him* loose across country in a Sherman."'

'You mean . . . the Squadron Captain's tank, sir?'

'Of course I mean the Squadron Captain's tank. Ah, I see! Only a Lance-Corporal and all that? Squadron Captain's only a messenger boy half the time. You command that tank, lad, and you go my messages. Get your kit. They know you on that tank. Get over there straight away.'

I wonder how to salute, bare-chested and bare-foot. Compromise by gripping the seams of my oily denim trousers with my fear-sweated fingers, about turn, shamble off.

I collect my kit (small pack, bedding roll, water-bottle and little else) and advise McKenzie, who slaps me on the back and goes off to find another 17-pounder gunner. I walk to the tank that was the Squadron Captain's and then the Sergeant-Major's and now a Lance-Corporal's. We are in truth running short of commanders. At various times in England on schemes I crewed with the men on this tank. We shared a barrack-room before D-Day. The gunner was burned and evacuated from St-Aignan. Otherwise they are the same people.

Lance-Corporal Harold Hoult, the driver, who is much older and senior, greets me with a cheerful groan: 'What have we here? This is a tank, boy, not a pram. We'll have to strap you into the turret to make sure you don't fall out. Welcome home to the old Troop.'

'Old Troop!' I growl in a faint imitation of Bill Fox's voice. 'Bill Fox said that everyone on this tank is so old that they need a commander who's not blind, deaf and bed-wetting, to care for all the other old fogies.'

The co-driver, Robin Hood, also a lance-corporal and almost as senior as Harold, intervenes: 'They shouldn't appoint a person as commander until he's had his first shave.' He grabs my small pack. 'Come on. Let's settle you

into your new luxury cruise ship and I'll make a cup of tea.
I think we all need one. Drink to the memory of poor old
Sidney.'

We sit on the grass, not quite forgetting the mortar
bombs, ashamed to retreat inside the tank in times of
silence and now not only ashamed but afraid to dive
beneath it in times of violence. We drink the chlorinated
tea which tastes as horrid today as it did the first day
ashore.

Harold says, 'Look, Ken. We can run this tank on a
democratic basis as far as cooking the meals and dividing
the fags is concerned. But when we cross that start line
into action, you flipping well give the orders, son, and we'll
flipping well obey. You're the commander and forget the
ages. What you say goes.' He wouldn't say that if a
lieutenant of twenty had been sent to command their tank.
But then he wouldn't have given the lieutenant an extra
slice of corned beef in his mess-tin either.

18 AUGUST 1944:

St-Aignan was a dead, evacuated village. But in this area
the French people are still living in their houses, taking
refuge in cellars or ditches when the battle approaches.
Today the extended family from the farm and nearby
cottages forms into a simple procession, and, arms loaded
with summer flowers, comes to decorate the first grave of
SSM Sidney Turton. Later he will, no doubt, possess an
ornate grave with a heraldic headstone provided by the
War Graves Commission.

The SSM's grave is still under close mortar fire. German
big guns shell us. Infantry Moaning Minnies bombard us.
Anxious to get in on the act, both British and American
fighter-bombers strafe us, in spite of the white stars on our
tank which proclaim our allied loyalties and the yellow

smoke bombs which send up messages of allied desperation.

A group of us in the corner of the field, keeping close to the hedge as though that fragile barricade of leaves could protect us from various kinds of fiery extinction. We study each other's faces, and the messages of distress and weariness and apprehension on each face add to our individual distresses. The conversation advances in fits and starts, like a night march by tanks, and meanders endlessly, like a river full of ox-bow lakes.

'Bloody good Sergeant-Major, old Sid.'

'Sarcastic old sod sometimes.'

'If I was a Froggy, I'd be hiding down my cellar. Not coming out to put flowers on his grave.'

'If *I* was a Froggy, I wouldn't be in this bloody war now, would I?'

'You would if you lived five miles up the road.'

'Ferking fool's game, war. Not so bad shooting Jerries. It's when the buggers shoot back . . .'

'Fool's game sitting 'ere, mate. Waiting to get your goolies shot off.'

'Why don't we just get up and go, instead of sitting here like swallows in the sunset?'

'Swallows don't sit in the sunset. They fly.'

'Course they bleeding sit sometimes. Can't fly all the time.'

'Swallows can't land on the ground. They have to keep on flying. Like seagulls.'

'Don't be a dumb twit. I've seen seagulls sitting on the flooding sea. And where'd swallows lay their eggs if they can't sit?'

'Still say we should all get up and go home. They could only shoot us. And we'll get flaming shot, sitting here.'

'They don't shoot people in this war. Not for deserting.'

'Shot thousands in the last war. For cowardice. Shot

50,000 in one battle. That's what they gave the little lieutenants revolvers for. Not for shooting Fritz. For shooting cowards up the arse.'

'Couldn't have shot 50,000 at once. You're a bleeding idiot, Bill.'

'I'd rather be a bleeding idiot taking the chance of being shot for deserting than a bleeding hero being shot for certain by Jerry over that hedge.'

'You're safe if you go bonkers. If you go pissie-cologically sick. They can't shoot you then.'

'Well, why don't we all go bonkers? All start braying like jackasses? All start tickling our armpits and legpits like gorillas? All sit 'ere and stare and drool with our mouths open and refuse to eat?'

'That's mutiny. That *is* a shootable offence. If you *all* go pissie-cologically sick, it's mutiny. You can only go one by one. Every man to pissie-college by himself.'

The imbecilic conversation meanders on, but so near to the borders of stark truth that I wonder if the slightest push, or just one more bomb, will send us all hurtling down the mental precipice on whose lip we teeter.

20 AUGUST 1944:

We pass through the picture-postcard town of St-Julien-le-Faucon. Black-and-white houses like the Welsh Marches of my childhood. The villagers are out on the pavements, cheering us by. Many of them carry pails of wine, buckets of apples. A boy runs out of the grocer's shop of Monsieur Gazareth, his arms laden with Camembert cheese. He throws a cheese to each tank as it goes by. By the church the column halts. Laughing Frenchmen hoist a girl up to the turret, and she kisses the blushing commander. The column rolls. It passes the church and the girl. And I miss the kiss. The column halts and another commander two tanks back is in luck. People wave and cheer and run – run for no other reason than that the adrenalin pumps fast as the liberating troops go through.

We are moving beyond the village, ready to advance on the morrow. My first day in command in a real battle. I look up at the wooded hills in front, so much like the hill above St-Pierre-sur-Dives in the gloaming. I think of Tiger tanks lining the summit, dug in, invisible and invincible. Imagine orchards alive with snipers and bazooka men. Boggy streams. Haunted country. Then evening closes the curtains on the distant view of tomorrow's land of travail.

This is another moment for which all my life has been geared. My patron saints are warriors, George and Michael and Ursula (who liberated these very lands from robber barons) rather than Francis or gentle Clare. My consecration is in terms of the picture at home of the fully armoured knight lifting his sword in front of the altar and praying before battle. In my bedroom as a child there was a huge painting of soldiers advancing at Waterloo, a row of scarlet-coated guards, life-size to me then, who continually marched day and night, and in my waking dreams called me 'Colonel'.

My parents weekly dressed in the uniform of the Salvation Army, my father resplendent in summer in the red tunic with white stripes. His massive monster bass filled our sunny front room with a silver refulgence as of a sacred altar. Although not a front-line soldier, he told rousing tales of the last war. My English master at school introduced me to Sassoon and Remarque, but without pointing out their anti-war implications. I scented only the adventure and the derring-do and the glorious advance. This is the heritage which sends me tall, if scared, towards Lisieux, the city of miracle-working St Thérèse.

I stand tall because it is an imposing thing to be located here in the turret of a moving Sherman, watched by admiring crowds. Perched tight in the turret, head and shoulders out in the air, it is as though the body has grown a monstrous, bulging, armour-plated belly, like a grossly exaggerated Buddha, but omnipotently warlike where Buddha is pacific. The great, challenging gun protrudes with connotations of virile masculinity and earth-destroying wrath. The legs, the grinding tracks, crunch the very ground into submission and mash houses, hedges, dug-outs into desolation. The two machine-guns, at a word from me, spray scarlet flames of death across the fields. Through the wireless microphone my voice penetrates into unseen distances, and through the earphones I eavesdrop on mystic mutterings and weird whisperings out of eternity. And in this landship, this mobile community, this death machine, my writ runs, my word rules, my command utters fire and steel and smoke.

Shorn of the glamour of lances and pennants and galloping horses and trumpets, this is the new enchantment of modern war. Yet fearful: because, for all the armour and weaponry, the internal husk, myself, is a frail human being, able, in a fraction of a second, to transmute into a screaming maniac or a heap of blood-stained khaki tatters with a stripe on its sleeve. Or an evil-smelling cinder.

21 AUGUST 1944:

We cross our start line in the pre-dawn dark, heading up the main road from St-Julien to Lisieux. There is no mayoral farewell committee to see us on our way at this hour. There may be a reception committee. The Germans know it is the day and the hour for us to advance. Around some leafy corner an iron monster of destruction waits, a dinosaur, its wicked telescope eyes gleaming in anticipation of the prey, its fiery breath ready to spit, its whole body coiled for the strike. The Germans know the date and the hour and the place. We know only the date.

2 Troop is up ahead, Bill Fox following and I as his

messenger boy rolling faithfully behind. The first tanks are
proceeding with the caution due to darkness and thronging
hedges and lurking dinosaurs. Dawn and sunrise encourage
us towards the first rural crossroads. 2 Troop triumphantly
liberates the deserted intersection of leafy lanes. Another
Troop turns right and explores towards Livarot. 3 Troop
turns left into nether Norman jungles, and Bill Fox follows
that way. We move into a narrow lane governed by some
of the highest hedges I have seen, even in Normandy.

3 Troop methodically leapfrogs ahead. One tank slowly
rounds a corner, another trailing it, another in more remote
support behind. We wait in the lane as the last 3 Troop
tank swings round a distant corner and Black Watch
infantry prostrate themselves and peer through the roots of
the hedges. The fields on either side are alien country,
defended by unimagined forces. The Black Watch Colonel
walks up to Bill Fox's tank, and Bill gets down to meet
him. They stand nonchalantly, apparently passing the time
of day but doubtless intent on most serious matters.

Leaves fall around my ears as though in an accelerated
autumn. Lounging infantrymen dive into ditches. The
Black Watch Colonel and Bill Fox hurry around the other
side of the tank. Our engine is still running, its booming
reverberations filling my ears. So the momentary panic has
no meaning to me.

'Driver, switch off a moment. Something happening. I
want to hear.' Harold switches off. Peace! A funny kind of
peace with sounds of mouse scratchings on the turret and
snake hissings high in the trees. Machine-gun bullets!

'Ah . . . hello Queen Baker.' (Bill's voice and our code-
sign.) 'Do your best to see off that pesky Hun. Ah . . .
Baker, over.'

'Queen Baker. Will do. Off.'

I am not sure which way the bullets are flying, north or
south. Bill Fox gets into his tank and retreats back the way

we came, as does the Colonel in his jeep. The Black Watch infantry seem to have a majority inclination towards danger from our left. I climb on to the tank top. Here, when I am fully extended on tiptoe, my eyes probably some fourteen feet or more above ground level, I can just peer over the top of this Beecher's Brook *in excelsis*. Another innocent black-and-white farm in an orchard. Or is it the last citadel of a weary SS detachment, determined to halt here and bear the ignominy of retreat no longer?

It seems that the machine-gun fire may be coming from the black-and-white farm. I tell the gunner to traverse left and fire our Browning through the hedge. It might be dangerous to fire the 75mm high explosive which has a sensitive detonator in the nose of each shell, liable to explode on impact against an unseen tree trunk in the hedge or just beyond in the orchard.

I am aware of somebody tapping my arm. Harold, the driver, has climbed out of his little hatch.

'What the Hell are you doing standing up here?' he shouts over the rattle of the Browning gun.

'Looking over the hedge. What do you think I'm doing? Watching a football match?'

'You'll get yourself bloody killed, you idiot. You can be seen for miles around.'

'Wrong! Hedges too high. Not your business anyway. I can't see over the hedge from down below.'

'Then let old Bill bloody well stick his head above the hedge. We've got to look after you, you silly young sod.'

'I'll take care, Harold. Get back in your cab. We're going to reverse to the gate. Try some 75HE.'

I had been too busy to calculate risks. But Harold's nerves are all shot to pieces. Shot, in reality. Only a few days ago he had to bale out of an exploding tank. His hand trembled on my arm but it seems steady enough on his driving controls as he rolls the huge tank backwards like a quiet limousine. We arrive opposite the gate, looking through the hedge, into the orchard, towards the farm.

'Driver, halt. Gunner, three rounds of 75HE. One into the farm and one to each side. Fire in your own time.'

I see the flash from our muzzle even as the tank itself hurtles back on its haunches, keeling over on the springs and then reasserting itself. In the same instant the ball of tracer emerges from the muzzle flame, darts across the orchard and crashes, an unwelcome visitor, through the front door of the farm. It explodes somewhere inside, belching flame, smoke and dust back out through the doorway. Two more shells hurtle after it and boil over into cascades of torrid flame, showering steel splinters on either side of the house. There is no reply from the house or the orchard. With my earphones over my ears and our engine running, I can hear nothing else. But I notice the Black Watch men in the ditch cautiously lifting their heads, shoulders, bodies into a more comfortable and alert position. One of them, a sergeant, gives me a V sign.

'Hullo, Queen Baker,' I report. 'Infantry think area now clear. Queen Baker, over.'

'Ah, hullo, Baker. Good show. Over.'

In a moment Bill Fox's tank reappears around the bend behind me. He halts at my tail. Beckons me over. I vault down, from turret to engine covers to ground. And up the front of his Sherman.

'Good show. Now I want you to take that left turn. Explore that lane for about 400–500 yards. If it is clear, pull back and the infantry will dig in. We are holding a very narrow front. If anything stirs, get to Hell out and we'll call down an artillery stonk. Take care but don't hang about. Should be all clear. On your way.'

Harold swings the thirty-ton tank round the corner into the left-hand lane delicately and without scraping a leaf in either hedge. A hundred yards of open lane lie ahead, running down the side of the orchard by the black-and-white farm. Infantry squat in the ditches on either side. Bill Fox thinks this lane should be clear. But will Hauptmann Fritz Fuchs, somewhere over there in the distance, have thought the same thing? And will he therefore have posted an anti-tank gun to catch the unwary commander who bowls along thinking the lane to be too unimportant to defend? Or shall we run into the tail end of the SS infantry retreating from our main force but carrying with them a bazooka or two, ready for a snap shot at wandering Shermans? Or will a heroic Panzer grenadier, lingering for a last look over the hedge at the hesitant enemy, lob a bomb neatly into my turret hatch?

'Driver, speed up to the next corner. Then slowly round. Operator, load with AP.' (If there is a tank or anti-tank gun awaiting us, we need the armour-piercing shot in the breech ready to fire instantly. The two machine-guns can deal with men on foot.)

At the corner we leave behind our escort of Black Watch. Harold steers the tank carefully into the bend. Now is not the time to slide into a deep Normandy ditch. The new stretch of lane opens slowly before us. Dark and dappled with heavy shadows, the hedges encroaching from both sides. The far hedge, fifty yards ahead, where the road bends again, is almost indistinguishable. A lovely place to site an anti-tank gun.

'Halt a mo'. Ready for advance or reverse.' Only just peeping around the corner, I lean forward as far as I can and focus my field-glasses (good German Zeiss glasses appropriated from a Jerry who will never need them again) on the dark patch of farthest hedge. Our tracks and our sloping front and our gun muzzle preceded me around the corner by two or three feet. The German could have got in a shot. But he may be waiting to get a good clear shot at our turret rather than risk a small target or take a chance on hitting our front slope which is most heavily armoured.

There is a moment in which I can still reverse. Retreat and leave the infantry to explore the darkened jungle track. Tell Bill Fox it was too risky for an unescorted tank. Or go forward and take a chance on the confused topography. Fifty yards – total destruction distance for an anti-tank gun, if the dinosaur is such. Fifty yards – irresistible target for the hand-held bazooka, if the dinosaur is such. Trees overhanging, for the Panzer grenadier bandits to swing down onto our turrets and lob their bombs or fire their carbines in my face. I can feel the bullets tearing, the shards of armour-piercing shot smashing bone, the bombs burning and gouging my flesh, the Vesuvius of white fire opening behind me as the engine erupts. The sweat of fear obscures my eyes as I try to decipher the shapes in that dim, sneering hedgerow. What dinosaur . . . ? I am primitive man again, my uniform, weapons, armour-plated fortress stripped away and my body exposed to the roaring beast. To go or to come? This is the worst place. I am killing myself by degrees.

'Driver, inch forward. Slowly . . . now go! Go! *GO!*' And we charge along the brief lane. If the dinosaur springs, a chance in a thousand he may miss. He did at Noyers. And our charging monster, our own heavier dinosaur will crush him in its paws, its own breath of fire blasting the enemy intruder . . .

'Ah, hello, ah . . . Queen Baker. Report progress. Over.'

'Queen Baker. Two bends behind us. No dinosaurs. Over.'

'Ah, Baker. What the Hell are dinosaurs? Clear one more bend and then let the infantry come up and dig in. Report back then, over.'

'Baker, OK, off.'

Harold tickles his way round the next corner. A longer

stretch of road. A more distant bend. Less overhang. Clearer view. One way to make sure.

'Operator, reload with HE. Gunner, put two rounds of HE just into the neck of that bend. Just in case. In your own time. Driver, halt.'

Surprises still in store! The first shot blasts a large hole in the distant hedge. Three Germans leap from the ditch beneath the explosion and sprint like Jesse Owens for Berlin. Our second shell follows them and sets up a vision of Sodom and Gomorrah and the wrath of God in the centre of the bend.

'Gordon Bennett!' ejaculates Harold. 'We hit something there.'

We sit in our mobile castle and make the entire surroundings of the lane uninhabitable for foes. With the suspicious mind bred by these enclosed surroundings, I glance behind me from time to time. One such glance registers Black Watch men moving carefully into the bend behind me. A lieutenant climbs up the back of the tank. Shouts in my ear.

'That should scare any poachers. Did you see anybody?'

'Only three sprinters, heading out for their lives. And a huge flash. No response otherwise.'

'This corner suits us. Good field of fire. We'll send a patrol up to that next bend when you've pulled out. Watch your heads in these orchards!'

'Apples?'

'Damned stick bombs!'

Back on the main lane of advance we move slowly along in the wake of a tank from 3 Troop, leapfrogging from corner to corner. I glance at my watch and am astonished to see that it is afternoon. Then the afternoon is ripped apart by a vicious, high-powered double crash which says 88mm. Anti-tank. High-velocity. Tiger? I instinctively cower somewhat into my turret in the empty lane. Nothing to see. Nobody to see me. Another double crash. Lighter bangs of a 75mm replying.

'Hullo, Queen 3. Queen 3 Able brewed. Anti-tank gun was firing down side lane. Gun appears to have retreated. No further firing. Queen 3 over.'

'Queen 3. Ah, thank you. Move up and hold the crossroads if you can. Over.'

'Queen 3, OK, off to you. Hullo, Queen 3 Baker and Charlie, cover my flanks and keep closed up . . .'

Walking along the lane towards me are four, yes four men in black berets. One missing. I scan the faces as they pass me, waving despondently, their eyes still full of instant terror unwinding its ghoulish film across dilated pupils and scorched retinas. Sergeant Wilkins' crew again. Spearhead crew again. Brewed again. Wilkie is there. And Michael Pryde, his driver. Co-driver is missing.

'Hello, ah, Queen Baker. 3 Able's co-driver not accounted for. Be a good lad. Go check co-driver alive or dead. Baker, over.'

'Baker, OK, off,' I answer Bill Fox's order.

So that is what messenger boys do? Surely Wilkie, a soft-hearted bloke, wouldn't leave a wounded co-driver behind in a brewed tank? Or maybe as Wilkie himself has been brewed up two or three times in as many weeks, old Bill thinks an additional check is needed?

'Driver, advance.'

3 Troop's Firefly ahead has swung into a lane leading diagonally back in the direction from which we have come. There is room for us to squeeze past his rump. Another 75mm Sherman stands a few yards beyond the corner, on our lane, in our way, its gun cocked at an unnatural angle. The Sherman points to the right, facing down a long, narrow, dark bridle-path between high hedges.

Our lane itself swings slightly left. There is no hedge on the left of the lane, only a white railing fence. Ahead, along our lane and about forty yards from us, another Sherman, presumably Bobby McColl's, snuggles into the main crossroads. Crossroads? Our objective! The third 75mm Sherman, carrying Ken Snowdon and my old mates, has smashed through the white railings, crawled into the left-hand field and now dominates the main highway which forms the crossroads with our lane. On my right the bridle-path looks and smells sinister. Wisps of smoke hover above the ruined tank. Explosion stench soils the air. Just minutes ago an 88mm shot, or maybe two or three, howled and hurtled along this narrow, leafy channel, homing on the target of the exposed Sherman called 3 Able. Bill Fox and Bobby McColl believe that the enemy gun has now retreated towards Lisieux, a mile or two away. But it is Hauptmann Fritz Fuchs and Leutnant von Ruf who worry me. They may guess that they are assumed to have retreated to Lisieux. And they may well send that 88 back into the bridle-path to take another pot shot at any fool-hardy Shermans gathered at our end of the path in support of our brewed comrade.

'Driver, we will not halt just here. Squeeze past the brewed Sherman and halt beyond the bridle-path. Gunner, keep your 75 pointed up that path. Loader, check loaded with AP.' Carefully, unostentatiously as ever, Harold eases past the broken tank. There is not much room. The rear of the thirty-ton Sherman protrudes on our right. A typical deep Norman ditch lies on our left. No hedge, but a vast ditch.

'The ditch! *The ditch!*'

We are sliding. Harold bangs on the revs, brakes the right-hand track. But we are sliding and tipping, the left front dipping, the right flank jolting upwards, the tracks scrabbling at the bank, the ditch collapsing, taking us down, skewed, tilted.

'Hold it! Halt! Get out and have a look before you try

again, driver.' While Harold climbs down and tests the ditch, Robin crawls into his seat and I check that we are out of sight of whatever is along that fatal bridle-path. If a German tank or SP appears now we are helpless. And Bobby McColl up ahead would be trapped. Corporal Ginns in the Firefly behind makes signs that he will reverse and pull us out. Harold looks up at me and shakes his head wearily.

'Ah, hello, Queen Baker. What news? Queen Baker, over.'

I grab the microphone. 'Hello, Queen Baker. We are temporarily ditched. Will report as soon as mobile. Baker, over.'

'Baker, yes, but get over and check that co-driver. Off.'

'What's old Bill yakking about?' says Harold, who has climbed onto the tank behind me.

'Wants me to check on the co-driver in that brewed tank. Alive or dead. And hurry!'

'You can't. What if there's a Jerry up that blinking lane? Stay here. I'll look. On the way to get the tow-rope for Ginns to pull us out.' He vaults off the tank and walks the few feet to the brewed Sherman. Climbs up and looks into the co-driver's hatch. Grimaces and gives me a very negative wave.

I grasp the microphone angrily. A good lad, that co-driver. A shy, quiet boy. Finished! 'Hello, Queen Baker. Co-driver still in tank, but dead. Queen Baker, over.'

'Queen Baker, ah, yes. Have you seen for yourself? Over.'

'Queen Baker. No. We're ditched. I cannot leave my tank. My driver has reported on the casualty. No possible doubt. Over.'

'Queen Baker, ah, my orders were clear. Go yourself. Go means "go"! I don't want damned secondhand reports. Over.'

Ginns tows us back into the horizontal. I dismount. Meet Harold. 'Where you going, mate? Off for an afternoon stroll?'

'Bill Fox wants me to see for myself. That the co-driver is really dead.'

'Of course the poor man's dead. Half his head missing. Take my word. Go, tell Bill you've seen him. Don't go and look in there. It's not nice.'

'It's a direct order from Bill. I've got no choice.'

'Shit!' says Harold, not normally the most expletive of troopers.

I approach the tank from the driver's side. When I was too tiny to know my own age, they took me to pay my last respects to my grandfather. I was terrified by the shrivelled husk that had replaced the kind, laughing, playful old gentleman. Since that moment I have nursed a pathological fear of corpses. It is different to shovel the decomposing remains of an unknown enemy into a hastily dug pit. This is one of my pals.

The driver's hatch is open. So is the co-driver's eye as I look in from the left. Open eye. Staring. He might be alive. Petrified with fear or paralysed with pain. In spite of what Harold says. And a direct order from old Bill. I lift the co-driver's hatch. And age many years. Become world-weary. Too tired to be terrorized any more. As Harold says, 'It's not nice.' There is no face at all this side. No man can live like that. I touch the shoulder and the already cold body falls forward.

I jump off the tank. Wipe my hands on my denim trousers. Stamp across the road, crunching underfoot the silver trumpets and silken banners of my boyhood dreams.

'Hullo, Queen Baker. I've seen with my own eyes and he is without doubt dead, cold, blasted in half. Baker, off.'

I do not wait for Bill's procedural reply. Tow the brewed tank back out of the bridle-path, across the road, through the shattered paling fence. Leave it there. Abandoned. Drive back across the road. Jam our tank into the bridle-path. Dare Hauptmann Fuchs to do his damnedest. Curse war.

Nothing happens. I stare at the bridle-path, and it stares back at me, like two boxers daring each other and making visible their hatred before they start the bout. Gradually the place loses some of its sinister power and becomes just another remote and insignificant bridle-path in the early evening's mellowing light.

Tomorrow our recovery vehicle will tow away the burned-out tank. A burial detail will dispose of the body of the co-driver. And the cows will once again exercise gentle rights of occupation of the lush fields and the quiet orchards. What was it all about? My first day of command. A co-driver's last day of living.

The Black Watch pass us by and dig in for the night around the crossroads and along the bridle-path. Harold backs the tank carefully out into the main lane. We head back towards harbour. Just before the black-and-white farm of this morning's encounter, we swing left into a field where the Squadron has gathered to replenish and rest. Two echelon lorries are driving into the field as we arrive. They halt and give us right of way.

Jack Aris, the Squadron Cook Corporal, leans out of one truck and waves delightedly. Another cook, Harry Claridge, waves from the second truck. Jack stops his truck, jumps out and comes running over to the tank.

'Hey, mate, when did they let you loose in a commander's seat?' he shouts. 'But you got back safe! Great! Glad you got back safe.'

The cheerful greetings of Jack and Harry join with the voices of a host of fitters and echelon drivers and clerks, Jack Copping, Bruce Fulford, the lot, there to welcome the Squadron tanks with all the heady enthusiasm of echelon personnel whose pals in the tank crews have survived yet another day. For a moment excitement and adventure are in the air again. It's like having scored a half-century on the cricket field or a good try on the rugby pitch, and then being cheered into the pavilion.

Jack Aris says, 'They tell us young Tyler's had it. Pity. A nice lad. That's the bloody trouble with war. All these young lads getting killed or wounded. If it wasn't for that, we'd all be having a good old tea party. Look after yourself now, remember, young Ken!'

And they begin to ply us with petrol, ammo, water, food, letters from home and the latest rumours from RHQ: 'Rommel's been shot and Monty says the war will be ended by November. The Jerries are all caught in the Falaise pocket and there aren't any Jerry reserves left between us and Berlin. All we've got to do is drive to Berlin and hoist the Union Jack before Joe Stalin or that bugger Patton gets there first.'

Ken Squires, who has taken over from wounded George Bolton as Wireless Corporal, comes with the call-signs for tomorrow. 'Tomorrow we are Baker,' he says. 'That makes you Baker Baker. Sounds like a baker with a stutter. Or the beginning of a nursery rhyme. Daft, ain't it?'

'Yeah,' says Robin, 'but how much dafter can you get than fighting a war anyway?'

7

Tank in a Hurry

23 AUGUST 1944:

It does seem as though the Germans are now pulling out more rapidly, although still leaving behind them well-organized suicide squads to delay our enthusiastic advance.

We head to the left of Lisieux to capture the river crossings while B Squadron under Major Rathbone, formerly our Squadron Captain, liberates the sacred city of Lisieux with strict instructions to avoid damaging the cathedral. Our river crossings are captured with very little opposition. Our tank fires only machine-guns but not the 75mm cannon. In Lisieux, according to wireless reports, the going is much stickier.

24 AUGUST 1944:

We drive through Lisieux, the streets thronged with jubilant people. We see how difficult it must have been for B Squadron to ascend the narrow streets by the cathedral. That vast building appears to be undamaged and now St Thérèse can continue to perform her healing miracles without hindrance from the warlords.

Beyond Lisieux we camp behind a hedge and wait for tomorrow's orders for advance. After supper we sit on the grass and idly converse. Harold and Robin are there, and Don Pateman and Pete Pedder and Bruce Dickson, now apparently recovered from the shock of the bomb that bounced over him to kill the SSM. Somebody mentions the echelon talk about Jerry high-tailing it for Berlin.

'Ah, bloody gossip,' growls an aristocratic voice behind us – old Bill Fox himself. 'Don't you – ah – damn' well believe it. Better face facts. Some bloody fighting to come yet.'

'Jerry doesn't give up that easily,' comments Dick Bates, the Troop Sergeant.

'The Hun isn't finished yet, whatever Monty may say,' confirms Bill. 'We have to capture those damn' Channel ports – Le Havre, St-Valéry, Calais – street fighting, much worse than the Bocage! And when we get to Holland there will be the dikes – damn' big banks along the canals, every 500 yards, and damn all else to stop the 88s in between.'

I stand looking across the hedge towards the orchards of tomorrow's exploits and hope that tough old Bill is mistaken. Something tells me that his pessimistic assessments may be nearer the truth than some of Montgomery's press releases.

25 AUGUST 1944:

We are lined up on an anonymous French road in our onward advance. Something up ahead has delayed the lead tank. There is no evidence of warlike activity. But war there is, for in a ditch alongside us lies a young German, his face waxing white and fragile as a magnolia blossom, the blood drained away by an invisible wound, and the sunburn diluted in the catharsis of death.

I get out to look at him. Harold emerges from his driver's hatch clutching a water-bottle. In this bitter human strife sometimes the rite of death intervenes and the winner offers a solemn ceremony of sympathy and aid celebrated in chlorinated water rather than communion wine.

'The Hitler Youth!' says Harold, reading the man's badges and scanning his young but ancient face. Harold crouches by the ditch and offers the water-bottle uncorked. Enemy mortar bombs express their wrath in smoky bursts across the adjoining field.

The young Nazi snarls. His lips and nostrils impeded by

the weakness of ebbing life but impelled by the rictus of death. His weak right arm lifts upwards and in the hand is a revolver. The yellowing fingers squeeze about the butt and the trigger, aiming at Harold, who is protected only by the water-bottle. I grab the revolver from a baby's grip and hurl it towards the bomb-bursts in the field.

'Well, strike me dead!' Harold begins.

'He nearly did,' I smile sourly. 'Let's mount up. Nothing we can do for him.'

Harold remains a moment, looking down at this alien creature from a recidivous culture. His eyes seek the blearing eyes of the boy but find no human empathy with the mind raped at birth by the Nazis.

'Well, strike me . . .' Harold begins again. He looks me in the eye as he climbs back into his hatch. 'Damn that bloody Hitler!' he shouts at me, as though the Nazi boy, young enough, were his son.

Our column moves on, leaving the Hitler Youth casualty in his ditch with fading hopes of entry to some remote Wagnerian paradise. C Squadron is given an objective through and beyond yet more orchards loaded with the bitter cider apples.

'Hullo, Item 3 Baker,' (one of the other Squadrons) '88mm gun firing from beside farm. May be SP. May be Tiger. I am bogged down. Item 3 Baker, over.'

We push through the uncharted orchards with the ominous report still echoing within our padded earphones. 'May be SP. May be Tiger.' The same gun in either case, able to blast us to pieces at 2,000 yards. And the range here is more likely to be twenty yards. For the orchards add a new dimension to tank warfare. Worse than the Bocage. At least in the Bocage with luck it was possible to see fifty or more yards at once.

Now we are in a thickly planted orchard of heavily pregnant trees. The trees are so close that it is an intricate job driving a tank between them. The boughs of the trees, totally armoured in layer upon layer of thick green leaves, join together in one dense, jungled mass commencing at about six feet above ground level. And my eyes are trying to pierce this same opaque foliage at about ten feet above ground level. My vision is restricted to millions of chubby red and green apples like pixies hanging in the branches. Mischievous, hindering, fatal pixies playing amid the leaves as our bruising turrets set the trees dancing.

The commander's hatch set in the top of the turret, through which gunner and operator also must pass, is protected by twin hatch covers. These are semi-circular pieces of heavy steel which can clash closed to provide a kind of manhole cover over my head when I duck. A touch on the springs which normally hold these covers aloft will bring them crashing down, their edges like guillotines for the unwary skull or fingers. Now open, these two hatches form a protective barrier beside my exposed cheeks as I peep out of my turret. My feet tingle at the thought that somewhere ahead, invisible through the apple branches, lies an 88mm anti-tank gun, able to see our tracks and lower compartment clearly as our turret rushes blindly through the tree tops. That gun will blast a shot through the co-driver's seat and through the lower turret and through my shins and through the rear of the turret on its way, at such short range and high velocity, into the engine space primed with fuel fumes.

I hardly notice the menace of the loaded apple branches for the steel turret flaps beside my cheeks bend back the insolent apple branches like heralds clearing the lesser mob from the path of a powerful ruler. The apple branches crack and fall, or bend and sweep back slowly behind the turret like courtiers doffing plumed hats and cloaks as the royal chariot passes. Like a riot of peasants in revolt, the massed apples on a tough, resilient branch suddenly plunge over the restraining flaps. They leap, slashing at my face, crashing home with the brain-stunning, explosive force of a hand-grenade!

Blackness . . . Echoes of distant chariots . . . blood . . . on my face, nose, hands, chest. Warm, thick, gentle, flowing blood mingled like red syrup with a mash of apples. The white, worried face of Johnny Martin, our gunner, bending over me.

'Thought you'd got your bloody head blown off,' he gulps. 'Thought a Jerry 88 had hit you fair and square in the mug! Blood and gore all mixed with apples all over our nice clean turret floor. Hope this new bloody SSM doesn't arrange a turret inspection parade tonight!'

He drifts from concern into humour, from the concern of the tank crewman who lives with the constant fear of seeing his decapitated commander collapse into the turret. But, having survived a wasp wound in the St-Aignan holocaust, I also survive an apple bombardment in this even more remote orchard. I pick the splinters out of my face, spit the apple pulp out of my mouth and wipe the blood from my collar with my khaki handkerchief. I realize that the tank has halted and that Robin is looking anxiously into the turret too.

'What a bloomin' indignity,' he complains, 'if we had to report on the wireless, our Sunray killed in action by ten pounds of apples. We'd never live it down. And you'll have to tell your kids, when you have 'em, when you're picking the splinters out of your face in ten years' time, tell 'em it's shrapnel. It *is*, sort of, ain't it?' He too laughs his own fears away.

I sit up in the bottom of the turret where I had landed. Now I am attacked by what seems to be piles. Another indignity. Piles indeed! In the rear end. But piles of apples, for in its blundering career through the trees the tank's turret flaps have plundered what appear to be tons of apples, now knee deep in the turret.

'Can't traverse the flaming turret for apples,' says Johnny. 'We'll have to bail them out.'

'Hey, Johnny,' says Harold, 'if you could get the old turret traversing and mash all that lot we'd have a few pints of scrumpy slopping around there by evening.'

Other tanks in the Regiment have dealt with the menace of that lurking 88mm in the orchards. We pass through a tiny village where the inhabitants are emerging from their shelters. Bill Fox visits me and orders me to stay put in the village and generally 'watch our tails'. The rest of the Squadron fans out and advances again. From my turret top I exercise the very temporary and insignificant sinecure of military commander of a dozen houses, barns and pigpens. At least the local inhabitants recognize our presence with the usual tributes of wine, fruit, cheese and flowers.

For us this is a mere halt along an unending road towards an uncertain objective beset with unimagined dangers. For them this is the Day of Peace and Liberation and consummation of the hopes of years. So they laugh and dance and tilt the wine bottle while we sit watchful in our tank, chewing an apple but storing the wine against future celebrations.

The jollity does not last long. Someone brings a kitchen chair out onto a green apron of land in front of a farm building. Two men come from the building dragging a thickset farm girl with pale face and red eyes. They sit her roughly on the chair. The sparse population of the minuscule village gathers round. One of the men grabs the girl's hair and the other wields a pair of sheepshears, chopping through the long locks and ripping the strands from the scalp. The tiny crowd jeers and laughs and shouts 'Collaborator!'

'That's ruddy cruel,' says Harold from below. 'Can't we stop them, skipper?'

'Not as long as they are not interfering with us or blocking the road. Or causing real bodily harm.'

'Serves the filthy bitch right if she's been sleeping around with Jerries,' observes Johnny. 'You must expect the locals to take it out of her hide. Me, I'd be shoving a red-hot poker right up where she wouldn't misbehave any more.'

Leaving Robin perched on the turret top, exercising supreme civil and military authority for the time being, I move in the opposite direction from the shearing party to speak to a Frenchman who is standing apart from the scanty mob. He is leaning over a wide gate leading into another inevitable orchard.

'*Bonjour, mon ami. Comment ça va?*' I begin in my best fifth-form French.

'Very well, thanks. And you?' he replies in surprisingly fluent English, for we have found few Normans who speak more than a word or two of our barbarian tongue. I ask if there is any word locally about the Germans' intentions. Are they running or will they stand and fight again? He has no information. He refers to my shattered face, not deeply scarred but scratched and pitted in every direction as though I had been attacked by a wildcat. I blame the cider apples. We talk about orchards and apples and cider and Calvados.

'Are you English or Canadian?' he enquires.

'I'm English. Why?'

'They told us the Canadian Army would be liberating us. What part of England do you come from? London?'

'No. From a small city in the west. You would probably not have heard of it: Hereford. An old cathedral city. Farming country. Bulls. Orchards like these. Cider works. Mud on your boots.'

'Do you know Bulmers' cider works?'

'I ought to. I was born and bred within the smell of their

cider presses. Old man Bulmer was a governor of my school.'

'Then we are almost neighbours. Before the war I exported my entire picking of cider apples to Bulmers in Hereford. Perhaps now I can send my apples to Hereford again instead of Berlin.'

He invites me and my crew to supper and champagne – saved since 1940 for the liberation. He was a soldier himself, badly wounded, captured and repatriated. But only Bill Fox knows where my crew and I will be taking supper. And I fear it will not be at my friend's table.

26 AUGUST 1944:

It wasn't. Our supper table last night was not at the home of my friend, the cider-apple grower. We bedded down under the shade of yet another anonymous orchard. The Medical Corporal looked at my scratches and 'ooh'd' and 'aa'd', whilst I responded with less gracious noises as he dabbed raw iodine on the red network of devastation that was my face.

'Doesn't quite qualify as a Blighty wound,' he said cheerfully.

Our objective today is a place called St-Léger, and on this road the orchards are thinning out into cattle and horse country. I sit on the turret top in bright sunshine and let Harold roll the tank gently in Bill Fox's wake. There is nothing to do except enjoy the verdant countryside, totally unspoiled by war, and wave to the occasional liberated Norman homesteader. We collect a bottle of Calvados, a bottle of wine, several assorted cheeses which vie in strength of smell. And we exchange a couple of cigarettes for a pack of rich butter and a grey loaf (our staple ration is still the hard biscuit).

'Hullo, Xray 4 Baker. Hullo, Xray 4 Baker. Sunray

injured. We are halted awaiting medical. Xray 4 Baker, over.'

'That's Corporal Brown bought it,' says Robin. 'He was up in the lead. Haven't heard any great sounds of battle though.'

'You don't hear great sounds of battle if it's only a sniper's bullet,' answers Harold. 'And if you're lucky you don't even hear that.'

'Aha . . . Hallo, Xray Baker . . .' (Bill Fox calling me.) 'Ah, Baker, get up there in the jeep and take over 4 Baker, that's a good lad. Off.' Not exactly purist wireless procedure, I think, as I thumb the microphone, answer Bill and then switch to I/C.

'Robin, come up and command. I have to go up and take over 4 Baker.'

'Hope you don't find old Brown spattered all over the landscape,' says Johnny somewhat crudely. I share the sentiment, however it is phrased.

I climb down into the Squadron Leader's jeep and we go buzzing along a fine, white road. The countryside here reminds me of Newmarket Heath, rolling, green and open, with woods in the distance and a village away to the left. Holiday country and holiday weather. Holiday speed as we race along the road in our open vehicle. Holiday time. Except for grumbles of war coming from somewhere ahead on the left. Xray 4 Baker stands all on its own behind a low tree which offers it no cover at all. But although the tank rests at the extreme point of advance, there seems to be no enemy reaction. In fact, the driver, Cliff Cuthbertson, is standing outside the tank, looking disconsolate but unafraid.

'The lad chopped 's fingers off, then, didn'a,' explains Geordie Cliff. 'The blinking flap fell on 's fingers and chopped 'em right off, see. The lad's awa' wi' the ambulance already.'

'Aren't there any Jerries over there in those woods, Cliff?'

'Aye, there's Jerries over there but they're taking no notice of us, like.'

'Well, it will be safer inside the tank, I think. Let's get in.'

The jeep crashes gears, spins in a circle and roars off, raising clouds of dust to signal the Jerry gunners' aim. Cliff and I retreat to our separate steel sanctuaries, he below and I above. We wait for the distant woods to react. Another Troop advances through the village and takes up the lead.

Now people begin emerging from holes and folds in the ground. Suddenly we are surrounded by French people. But instead of the usual Calvados or cheese or apples, their arms are full of flowers. It is as though all the florists were arriving for an expensive funeral. They strew flowers across the front plates of the tank, and stick flowers under the ugly steel projections of the hull, and lob bunches of flowers on to the turret. One comedian even sticks a bunch of roses, stalks first, up the muzzle of our 75mm gun. I pick up a handful of roses and lay them over the roseate mess where a steel trap clashed down on a human hand only minutes ago.

The French people dance a maypole jig around the tank while we watch and wait. Inevitably a batch of Moaning Minnies splashes dirt across the fields not far away, where the infantry are digging in. The continuing explosions cause the civilians to retreat in a leisurely, friendly way – liberated, not cowed, but taking sensible precautions, waving as they go.

I descend and find that our grim Sherman has been transformed. The sloping front of the tank reminds me of one of those floral clocks at a seaside resort – radiant, multi-coloured, reflecting and magnifying the sunlight.

Cliff climbs out of his hatch, looks at the display, takes off his beret, scratches his head and then looks down towards the woods where the enemy still reign.

'The buggers'll see's a mile off,' he says. 'Bloody dangerous, that lot.'

'Have you no poetry in your soul, man?' I ask. 'Are you so ungrateful towards our welcoming hosts? The Chelsea Flower Show just isn't anywhere in it! Come on, let's dump this lot in the ditch and get back to war before Jerry wakes up from his afternoon siesta.'

Reluctantly but hurriedly we undo the artistic handiwork of the locals, consign the outrageous flowery signals to the ditch and then resume our posts to look out upon this present non-event of war. Once again we have pushed ahead of the rest of the army and must wait for the strategists to sort things out.

As evening draws on, we are moved back from the open racing country into another orchard for the business of replenishment. On this hot day we have used more petrol and water than ammo and food. Shouting attracts our attention towards the nearby house. I have returned to Harold, Robin & Co, leaving Cliff to his pals to await a reinforcement commander tomorrow. Johnny Howell comes running past us, brandishing a spade.

'This old French goat buried his wine store before the Jerries invaded. He wants us to dig it up for him. Free booze for all afterwards. Grab your spades, lads.'

Kempy and Bruce and others follow Johnny towards the house. Harold and the rest reach lazily for tools and amble off in the same direction. 'I don't drink, so I'll do the washing up,' I offer. I dump the greasy mess-tins in a cut-down petrol tin and boil water over the primus stove to do my chores. Kitchen duties done, I follow to the scene of gaiety. The lads have dug down knee-deep, dislodged a course of brickwork and found a veritable wine-cellar

cached away there. We form a human chain and pass up
bottles with much more appreciation and enthusiasm than
in the similar duty of passing HE shells.

Johnny Howell's 'old French goat' is indeed an elderly
man with a luxuriant grey goat-beard. He fusses like a
hissing goose, fearing that we who handle fulminating
explosives may fail to catch his precious bottles of wine,
dark with ageing Burgundy and dim with dust and soil.
The last bottle excavated and safely lodged within the
house cellar, the thirsty Squadron circles round his door
and waits to be rewarded. The 'old French goat' brings one
bottle to the door, one miserly, meagre bottle as bearded
with cobwebs as the old man's chin is with hair. He mutters
something to the nearest troopers.

'What? For all of us?' shouts somebody who sounds like
Kemp. 'Bloody Hell, that's not a sip each. After all that
donkey work. No ferking likely. Come on, lads. Help
yourselves.'

A mass of baying, shouting troopers pushes past the old
man and begins the process of extracting bottles which
have only just come to rest in their racks. Hands pass the
bottles to other hands. Legs scamper in the darkening
night. Troopers at ground level gently elevate bottles, with
the delicacy of priests elevating the Host, and troopers on
turrets just as carefully store bottles away in racks intended
for more militant purposes.

'It's not robbery,' Harold explains to me. 'We are only
taking two bottles for each tank. And the old miser has
hundreds and hundreds of bottles down there in his cellar
now. He won't even miss the few we took. Serve the silly
old blighter right.'

But the wine-owner rages around the orchard in the
gloom, shouting dimly understood imprecations in French.
Eventually someone points him in the direction of Bill Fox,
who is sitting on a camp stool, eating a chunk of

Camembert cheese. Bill soothes the man in a complicated conversation, for neither speaks the other's language.

'*Scandaleux . . . brigandage . . . abominable . . . pénitentiaire . . .*' we hear the owner cry in high-pitched cackles.

The voice of Bill Fox rumbles on in specious prevarications. 'Damn' dark, you know. Difficult to play detective at this time of night. Have to have a full investigation tomorrow. That's right. Full damned investigation tomorrow. Come back tomorrow afternoon, old chap, when we've had time to investigate. That's it, *mon ami*, run along home and get some bloody kip.'

When the owner has eventually retreated, still muttering seditious uncordial sentiments, Dick Bates whispers to Bill, 'Will you also be investigating that bottle that's hiding under your camp stool, sir?'

28 AUGUST 1944:

Our pre-dawn start yesterday eliminated the possibility of Bill Fox's investigation into the wine riot. Perfidious Albion once again!

Our lead tanks hurried ahead with little opposition and soon liberated the sizeable town of Bourg Achard. In the square in front of the town hall stood an apparently undamaged German Panther tank. Each Sherman commander rounding the bend let out a gasp of instant apprehension. Not since La Taille had we bumped into Panthers at ten yards' range.

This Panther was, in fact, 'dead'. The story I was told by jolly drinkers from the local underground movement was that it had gone to ground in the square during the night, the crew apparently exhausted by the retreat. The local blacksmith had then crept up to the tank and deftly knocked out one of the track retaining-pins, so that the entire track sprang loose. With Resistance fighters invisible in the darkness sniping every time the Germans opened the turret, the crew eventually took the sensible decision of waving a white cloth and surrendering their vehicle inviolate.

Today we advance to the north of Bourg Achard. In a long, narrow wood the enemy have established another nuisance line, with an anti-tank gun and several Spandau machine-guns. We sit at the opposite sides of an immense field and blast off expensive ammunition which will make tax-payers at home poorer but munitions workers richer. This suffices for our military aspirations because we know we can go on firing longer than the Germans. It also satisfies them for when they have fired off all their bullets there will be no more supplies. They can retreat with honour across the fields to the safety of the River Seine.

The stationary battle rages on, more than anything else like a children's firework display on bonfire night. Until a lonely figure appears in the middle of the battlefield. An elderly bowed civilian. At a typical ploughman's pace he plods out into the field, undeterred by the pyrotechnics. The blazing patterns of tracer in front of him fall away, as the young soldiers on either side stare and wonder. The old man trudges on, looking towards neither ally nor enemy. He approaches a ramshackle, partly destroyed hut in the middle of the field. One clean 75mm hit would have blown that hut into invisibility. The old man reaches the hut and goes in.

'Must want to pee bloody bad,' says gunner Johnny, 'if he goes all *that* way in all *this* lot just to relieve his bladder.'

'More likely got his girl friend there,' suggests Harold. 'Calls on her every day at this time. While his wife's washing up the dinner pots.'

'It wasn't a girl, Harold. It was a cow,' I observe from my higher point of vision.

'Same difference,' says Harold.

The old farmer leads from the hut a single cow at the end of a rope. Begins his slow walk back the way he came. I imagine I can hear a tidal wave of laughter rolling through our serried tanks and sounding above the noise of tank engines. Perhaps I can. I am laughing myself. Maybe Jerry over there is laughing too? The pathetic yet intrepid procession of man and cow winds its way slowly o'er the lee, as that poet might have said. And the guns remain silent.

'That bugger deserves the Victoria Cross,' says Johnny.

'They do have a sort of Victoria Cross for animal-savers at home,' comments Harold. 'We ought to recommend him for one when we get back.'

The man with his beast turns into a lane beyond the enemy wood. From the opposite end of the line a machine-gun stutters. Another and another. German Spandaus and Yeomanry Brownings and Highland Brens. Spitting fire and noise and lacking the true heroism of the old Norman farmer. Eventually the enemy fire falters and dies away. Out of ammunition. He has justified himself and will now be withdrawing in order to annoy and frustrate us another day. If his supply columns are still mobile!

Presently a furtive Sherman edges along the lane in the steps of the farmer and the cow. The Sherman moves at an even slower pace and with much stopping and starting. At an average speed of about one mile in the hour, its commander urges it forward to the act of liberating that strip of wood which the enemy, foreseeably, has now evacuated.

Now bold, we all charge over our hedgerow, like huntsmen chasing the fox, trundle across the intervening field, past the broken-down hut and into the opposite wood. Nothing moves in front of us. But one, two, three field-grey bodies, lying sprawled on the foremost edge of the trees, witness that for some of the enemy it was not just a show of fireworks this afternoon.

29 AUGUST 1944:
Bill Fox thinks this might be the last advance before the River Seine. With its bridges destroyed, the river presents an impassable barrier across our line of advance. A great expanse of forest, the Forêt de Brontonne, fills a huge U-bend in the river. And it is into this forest that we advance in one last mopping-up operation before we rest from the battles.

Again I meekly follow Bill's tank as we speed through a tiny village at the outskirts of the forest. The inhabitants throng their doorways and wave jubilantly as we roar past. Beyond the village the trees close in. Not nice country if there are guns hidden among the trees, deep in the thick, leafy undergrowth which rises half-way up the sides of the tanks. A bad place for mines, too, if the Germans have planted any under the bracken.

As we bounce and sway over an open space, a grassy mound like a bald pate rising out of the surrounding woods, Bill Fox's voice calls to me.

'Ah – hallo, Roger Baker. Lead tanks are taking prisoners. Stay put and round up the prisoners as they come. Talk nicely to them. Check if any useful information. Roger Baker, over.' Old Bill orders his tank away on the trail of the lead Troops which have disappeared along various rides in the woods. He leaves me once again occupying a patch of France.

Three Germans come walking hopefully down one of the rides. For them the war is over. They raise their arms again as they see us. Another two figures in field-grey appear through the trees along another ride.

'Better dismount, lads, and round up the fugitives. Use your fluent German. Learn all Hitler's top-secret strategy.'

Glad of the break from the hot, fetid interior and cheered by the thought that this really is the end of the Normandy campaign, the crew dismount, carefully holding their Sten guns or revolvers so that the approaching Germans can see them.

Of the first three Germans one, a major, is a medical officer. The other two are medical orderlies. The Major speaks English and has studied medicine in Edinburgh. We sit on the grass for a pow-wow. The first piece of information is irrelevant to the battle. They are hungry. Starving. Ravenous. Three days since they have seen supplies. Only a remnant of the army remains in the wood, and the supply columns can no longer cross the Seine. Robin climbs into the tank and lobs out tins of corned beef, cheese, packets of biscuits. Johnny fetches the makings of a large brew of tea. We loan our mess-tins to the passive Fritzes. More recruits for the prisoner-of-war cages arrive. We hand them biscuits and ask for news of Tigers and Panthers lurking in the woods. There are none. They are all destroyed. The last one in Bourg Achard.

A single prisoner emerges from the woods to our right rear. Claims his biscuit and slice of corned beef. Wolfs them down. 'Are there any more troops in those woods?' I ask. He does not understand. The doctor translates. Words are spoken. Earnest conversation. The doctor smiles wanly.

'He says his two friends are still there. In a gun-pit. With a gun. Arguing among themselves. Whether to shoot you or to come in and be taken prisoner.'

My crew and I instinctively duck behind the tank in the direction opposite the invisible gun-pit. Stalemate!

We have left nobody inside the tank. If we try to climb up into the turret or into one of the driving hatches, the enemy gunner will have us in his sights. And our movement may induce him to fire. At the same time he cannot see us and can do us little harm whilst we hide behind two

thick walls of armour plate. And eventually the rest of the
Squadron will return from its wanderings. But maybe not
for several hours yet. We hold a quick conference but come
to no clear conclusion. We interrogate the latest arrival
again. His story remains clear: 'Arguing as to whether to
shoot you or come and surrender.'

'Let me try a quick scoot up the front of the tank,' says
Harold. 'Catch him unawares.'

'No hope!' I counter. 'He has nothing else in the whole
wide world to watch, except us. A quick, suspicious move
and he'll be catching you where it hurts.'

'Line some of these other buggers up in front of us, and
nip up the tank behind them?' Harold tries again.

'Against the Geneva Convention,' I say.

'Do we have any weapons in the outside storage boxes?'
asks Robin. 'A Sten or a pistol is no good at that range.
What about Mills bombs? Make a nasty mess of his gun-
pit.'

'Too far! Even if we had a bomb handy,' I reply.

'Might just as well try chucking a corned beef tin,' grunts
Johnny. 'That's all we've got available. Might bounce on
his ruddy nut and knock him out.'

I slap Johnny on the back as we crouch behind the tracks
of the Sherman. 'That's the beginning of an idea.' I turn to
the man from the gun-pit and the Major. 'Ask him to go
back to his trench. Take them a biscuit each. Tell them if
they surrender there is a whole tin of corned beef between
the two of them. They haven't eaten for days, right? Tell
him!'

The Major, as anxious as ourselves to preserve the new
but fragile peace, speaks emphatically to the soldier. The
soldier, a boy of eighteen or nineteen, looks reluctant.
Then shrugs his shoulders, nods, stands up. We give him
three biscuits, one as a bonus for his services. We lie flat,
squinting through the tracks of the tank, and watch him

head back the way he came. He enters the trees and ploughs through deep bracken. After twenty yards or so he drops out of sight. We wait. I look at the German Major. His shoulders rise to about level with his ears, in a universal sign of doubt and wonderment. We wait.

'Pity we didn't have any sauerkraut on the tank,' growls Johnny. 'That would have brought the bugger running.'

'I know one thing,' I comment. 'If I'd not eaten for days and was surrounded by a regiment of tanks, I wouldn't be sitting there discussing my loyalty to Hitler.'

Movement in the wood. Our emissary rises out of the invisible trench in the bracken. Waves. Another man climbs up beside him. Waves a white rag. They move towards us. Two men only.

'Keep down, lads. This may be a trick. Keep your Stens on them when they are in range.'

Behind the two men who are now at the edge of the wood, another heap appears surmounted by a long object. It wobbles and tips. Rises higher. Becomes a man holding a Spandau high above his head. Advances towards us. Suddenly brave, we rush out with our Stens and pistols raised. A line of us. All except Johnny, who vaults up into the turret and begins to hand traverse the 75mm in the general direction of the newcomers.

'*Kamerad!* Corned beef!' says the German with the gun, in fair English. Some of the most welcome words I have ever heard. 'Three days no eat. Three days bloody Hitler army no eat. Now join Tommy army and eat. Corned beef.'

Learning by experience, we leave one of our crew sitting in the gunner's seat and one in the commander's perch, surveying the circle of woods and rides around us. The other three of us sit and talk to the Germans. The chorus is always the same. All the bridges over the Seine are down. The Germans on this side have been abandoned to their fate. We exchange family photographs, German and British. The Wehrmacht machine-gunner talks proudly of his four kids. The war might indeed be over. Almost!

Into our tiny, green sanctuary of peace and goodwill scream the familiar insults of descending shells. Flashes leap up on all sides. Pounding concussions knock us off our haunches where we squat. The usual vicious ghosts of smoke, dirt, clods, dance around the glade. Devilish tom-toms thrash out their persistent beat. Shards of shrapnel wail and snarl and shriek in all directions. Again and again and again salvoes of shells blast upon us like inverted volcanoes. German and Britisher, Jerry and Tommy alike, we fling ourselves under the tank or into a nearby fold in the ground. Shell after shell dives into the earth with muffled thud spawning an instant roar. One and then another shell clangs horribly on the steel of the tank. Disintegrating steel venting its rage on the unmovable, solid plate of alien armour. A clangour as of a thousand knights-at-arms in one combined collision.

We bite the dust as though trying to gouge with our teeth a shelter in the heaving soil. 'Ours or theirs?' Harold yells at me. 'Ferking whoever's,' yelps Johnny. 'That was red-hot shrapnel on my bloody hand.' I hazard a glance to see if, improbably, the shells are accompanied by advancing infantry or unexpected tanks.

'Must be an observer somewhere out in those woods,' I gasp in Harold's ear. 'Seen us from a distance. Thought it was a staff conference. Loosing off a few last rounds.'

'Few?' gripes Harold. 'I've counted five blinking million already. Cripes! If I want my arse scratched, I'll do it myself. I reckon that one drew blood.' He rubs his nether regions cautiously, suspiciously. One last ferocious clash of steel upon steel at the back of the tank. Then silence . . .

The erstwhile Spandau gunner is beckoning frantically from a ditch. The German doctor lies in the ditch. His face is as field-grey as his uniform. Eyes half-closed. Breathing rapidly and stertorously. His body strangely stretched and rigid. I look for blood. None evident. The Spandau gunner clasps his heart, says 'Ughhhh!' and pretends to collapse.

'Heart attack!' snaps Robin, dropping on his knees and wrenching at the Major's collar, slapping his face, banging his chest.

'Do you know what you're doing?' I ask.

'No, but this bloke'll die if we don't do something quick. Where are his medical orderlies?' One of the orderlies is bandaging the leg of the other. The only blooded casualty, it seems.

The elderly Major fights his way back to consciousness. I shout at him, 'You must tell us what to do to get you better. We will do you permanent harm if you do not!' The humour of the situation seeps through into the striving brain. The doctor's mouth curves into a wan smile. Harold mutters in my ear: 'We've been trying to kill the beggar for two months. Now we're trying to save his blinking life.'

It is early evening before the Squadron rolls back into our clearing. The commanders grin unsympathetically as their tanks bounce and rattle over the bomb-ploughed field which now surrounds our tank. We respond to their rude gestures in kind. With our prisoners, now fourteen of them, loaded on the back of the tank we fall in behind the homeward procession.

In the little French village on the outskirts of the forest we are astonished to find that, whilst the villagers wave ecstatically to the tanks in front, they greet *us* with clenched fists and jeers and sneers. Looking behind me, I find that my German prisoners are treating the villagers to Churchill-style V signs. Not difficult to guess why!

For these Germans the war is over. They are safe!

Our laager is in just one more orchard, where we examine the damage to the tank. The air-filters at the back are shot through and through like sieves. I unroll my bedding. The blankets fall in tatters and patches between my fingers. Harold wraps a rag of blanket round his waist like a kilt. It is the largest piece of material in his bedding roll. We gather up the remnants and make our way to where the Quartermaster's truck has just arrived. SQMS Pete Mapley looks at the damage with tears of laughter in his eyes.

'Was you so hungry, you lot? Got to chew your blimming blankets? Real negligence, I calls it. Negligence in the face of the enemy. No respect for WD property. What's wrong with this blanket, Corporal Hoult? Can't you wrap bits of it round your fingers and bits of it round your toes and bits of it round your . . .'

'Bollocks!' says Harold irreverently to the SQMS.

'Yes, them too,' says Pete, busily sorting through his piles of stores for replacement blankets and groundsheets.

'Now, don't go near no bombs with them new 'ns, look!'

30 AUGUST 1944:

We have now advanced from the outskirts of Caen to the Seine, covering ninety miles in fifteen days. We could have done this journey in our tanks in four hours if unimpeded, but an advance of about six miles a day has to be considered almost precipitous in comparison with the 500-yards-a-day average for the better days in the Bocage. And, of course, compared with Great War advances averaging a mile a month, it is hares compared with tortoises. It even betters the Germans' own progress through Belgium to Dunkirk during the 1940 Blitzkrieg.

Now we relax and hope for a few days of break from travelling in our noisy, bone-shaking mobile homes. There are many loose horses roaming the forest, and there is fun to be had in riding them. Some Yeomen have been huntsmen or stablemen to one or other of the officers.

These men, George Smith and mates, now relapse into their civilian pursuits – which word is doubly relevant, for the horses have to be chased before they can be ridden.

Bill Fox comes trotting through the Squadron harbour on a frisky chestnut horse, its temper not improved by the cheers and antics of the troopers. 'Safer in a tank, sir!' yells Tommy Tucker. 'Damn' sight more comfortable to ride,' Bill retorts, holding tight as he digs his heels into the horse's ribs and gallops bareback through the trees.

'O Great God Montgomery!' cries one of our humorists, clasping his hands in mock prayer and turning his eyes to the skies. 'Leave us here in Heaven for a few ferkin' days at least.'

8
In and Out of Tanks

2 SEPTEMBER 1944:

The Great God Montgomery did not heed our prayer. He or his minions scheduled us to cross the Seine today. The Royal Engineers have worked their usual miracles with Bailey sections and pontoons to provide a crossing. Thirty-ton tanks can safely pass over a river much wider than the Thames at London Bridge.

The main road towards Belgium is already being cleared by the Guards Armoured Division but we are able to claim liberation of several V1 launch sites. These are ramps in open fields from which for months flying bombs have been released to torment Londoners and others underneath the route of these mechanized pests. It has been exciting to liberate French villages to the visible delight of the residents. It is equally satisfying to know that our advance today spells greater safety for our own kin in devastated home towns.

We hurtle along open roads in our fastest advance to date. We admire the long avenues of poplar trees – reminiscent of framed landscapes at school. But the roads are dusty, and the holiday atmosphere is spoiled by the mash of dust, stones, smoke and fumes churned up by our long column of vehicles.

Evening finds us harbouring in a narrow wood above the town of Doudeville. In my progress from tank to tank I have failed to carry goggles. My eyelids feel as though they are packed out with grit and dust and splinters.

'Better go to the quack and get it seen to,' Robin advises,

'otherwise you won't be able to open those eyes in the
morning. They're as bloodshot as a red cabbage already.'

My worry is *closing* my eyes. It is agony to blink. There
is no way I can close them to sleep. I hobble off, stiff from
the day of frenzied rocking and bucking in the turret, to
find the Quack Corporal. As usual he exudes total lack of
sympathy.

'Looking for your third wound stripe?' he laughs as he
delicately directs drops into my eyes. 'Wasp sting at St-
Aignan. Apple scars from Lisieux. Now granulated eyeballs
at Doudeville. What's next: haemorrhoids at Le Havre?
Bus-driver's balls at Boulogne?'

3 SEPTEMBER 1944:

The rest of the crew are either on guard this evening or
taking to their beds for an early night. I set off to walk the
two miles into Doudeville with Harry Brown, who shares
my taste for Shakespeare's plays. We used to sit in the
woods near Bury St Edmunds and read *Henry V* or
Macbeth aloud, aided by one or two other troopers of the
same mind.

I am teetotal and Harry rarely drinks but the only place
to sit in Doudeville is an *estaminet*. We enter and I bend
my feeble French to ordering a non-alcoholic drink. This,
to the *estaminet* keeper, appears to be a contradiction in
terms. He searches the shelves in his dilemma. Seizes a
bottle of yellow liquid. '*Eh, bien,*' he smiles. '*L'apéritif. Le
bon apéritif, n'est-ce-pas?*' He looks askance when we ask
for bigger glasses. We taste, savour, swallow the delicate
liquid.

Harry and I work our way down the bottle. The heady
vapours of military success begin to turn our boredom into
exuberance. We finish the bottle. Order another. Tell each
other tall stories. Quote yards of speeches by Henry V.
Revive memories of Tommy Handley's *ITMA* radio shows.

Order another bottle. There is no closing time in the *estaminet* but the Squadron observes a routine curfew at nightfall, so sunset prompts us to swig the dregs of the latest bottle and say goodnight to the host.

'Bon sieur, monsoir!' says Harry.

'You mean bon soir, monsoon!' I correct him.

We laugh outrageously at nothing and step out into the cool evening air. Comradeship suddenly seems something infinitely desirable. We wind arms around each other's shoulders. God is in His Heaven. God is on our side. Harry shouts, 'By the quick, left march!' We step along the road. I start singing 'Onward, Christian Soldiers'. Harry joins in, a half-tone higher. After a verse or two it seems as though somebody in Heaven, annoyed by our caterwauling, has opened a window and is dousing us with Niagaras of water. The rain flushes down in a veritable cloudburst. We are standing in the middle of an empty road. There is no shelter in sight.

Harry opens his mouth wide, and sticks his tongue out. 'It's raining flooding lemonade,' he grins. 'Taste it! That's where the Froggies keep their lemonade.'

We return to harbour just on nightfall, soaked through to the skin. And stone sober.

5 SEPTEMBER 1944:

We move a few miles to the smaller village of Gonneville. Rumour has it that we are to attack Le Havre. Street fighting. The ultimate terror of the tank man. The Germans have retreated from central France. But here in the Channel ports they are standing fast. Defying us to storm their coastal fortresses. By comparison Caen seems a picnic.

We are lodged in another of Normandy's million orchards. The farm labourer's family at the nearest cottage regales us with presents. They cannot adequately express their joy at being liberated. They do not wish to barter goods with us. They give us eggs, potatoes, bread, butter, cheese, wine. We in return, but in the spirit of gifting rather than bartering, take them chocolate and cigarettes and soap and tinned peaches and corned beef.

In the tiny cottage a bottle of Calvados is passed round so that we all may celebrate. As we drink a toast there is a knock at the door. Two artillerymen offering to barter corned beef for eggs or butter. The artillerymen see us sitting there.

'Bloody tank crews,' says one of the RAs, partly in jest, 'always arriving first. Ferking locusts, getting all the good things.'

We donate a couple of our eggs to the artillery, who move on to the next door swearing happily.

7 SEPTEMBER 1944:
The old Colonel is back. Doug Forster, who was wounded at St-Aignan, has returned from hospital and is taking command of the Regiment again. He is to hold a conference for all commanders.

We sit on a grassy slope, and the Colonel makes his glad-to-be-back speech. He gives the appearance of being nervous and hesitant. In fact, he is very determined and, almost single-handed, fought to keep the Regiment from being broken up before D-Day, when a number of Yeomanry regiments were disbanded or diverted to other duties.

'The last time I spoke to you was immediately before our famous Night March to St-Aignan. Now I have returned in time for another challenge. We are to liberate Le Havre. We are to line up, the entire Regiment of fifty tanks, and carry out a long-range, indirect shoot, fifty rounds per tank. Before the shoot David Bevan and I will go up to an observation point. Each tank will fire off a couple of shots to our dictation, checking range and direction. We will all then, at my word, fire in unison, bombarding the enemy front line through which we shall later pass. I am proud to return to you for this very special occasion.'

I look around the officers, sergeants and corporals, all lounging at ease on the grass but all attentive to every word from a revered commander. There is no formal military 'bull' about this meeting. Rather it is like a convocation of relaxed, committed friends, trusting each other as they plan a communal adventure.

The Colonel continues his chat. Our 'Second Line', the 2nd Northamptonshire Yeomanry, has been broken up, and a number of their officers and men have joined us as reinforcements. One of them, Major the Lord George Scott, will now become second-in-command of the Regiment. David 'Hank' Bevan comes back to command our Squadron. Bill Fox steps back into the Squadron 2-in-C's tank and Captain Todd moves back into the Squadron Captain's tank. *My tank!* There is no mention of the fate of one Lance-Corporal (acting, unpaid, temporary, unwanted, as they say) 147 Tout.

Bill Fox imparts the news to me personally after the conference. 'You go back and sit with the echelon for a few days until we need you again. You've had some damned nasty moments, taking over from the dead and wounded. Enjoy a week's holiday. Forget about the war, that's a good lad.'

I console myself that Le Havre is going to be a brutal battle through those narrow streets and under the naval guns from the great fortresses. I once again collect my belongings and depart in the Squadron Leader's jeep. Back to our orchard and to a quiet barn piled with deep and cosy hay. Paradise for weary soldiers!

10 SEPTEMBER 1944:

The 51st Highland Division has decided that our efforts
during the Normandy campaign merit the honour of our
wearing their divisional sign on one arm. As an indepen-
dent armoured brigade we would not normally wear an
infantry sign. Some of us will like to swank with an HD
sign on the arm when we go home on leave, but the hard
core of old soldiers simply say, 'Another bit of bloody bull.'
Surely they never dreamed of silver trumpets and waving
banners in their childhood?

Apart from the stitching of the red and blue HD sign on
my sleeve I've nothing to do but sit in the barn, read one
of the books in my pack (*Memoirs of an Infantry Officer* by
Sassoon, a couple of poetry books and a Bible) and catch
up on long-delayed letters home.

The tanks do their big shoot tonight. Tomorrow morning
they will be crawling into the hazardous streets while I sit
here menaced by nothing more fierce than a couple of
apparently pro-Nazi geese which resent my occupancy.
Perhaps geese pass on genes which make them alert to
invaders. According to legend, they once saved Rome by
their cackling when disturbed by unseen invaders. No
doubt generations of geese have also had reason to fear
omnivorous liberators?

11 SEPTEMBER 1944:

Someone shakes my shoulder as I lie on my imperial couch
of downy hay. I stir reluctantly and grumble at the
intruder.

'Get up, Ken. Get up. You're wanted. Hank wants you.
Tout de suite, Mr Tout. Bring your clothes and kit with
you. It's that urgent.'

The Squadron Leader's jeep-driver, Lowe, whom I now
recognize in the pre-dawn darkness, has his jeep engine
still running where the vehicle stands parked close up to

the barn door. I scrabble in the hay for socks, boots, mess-tins, while Lowe picks up my American tommy-gun, equipment belt with pistol in holster, and small pack. I stumble after him, still lacking my trousers and boots, arguing, 'What's all the hurry? What's it all about?'

'Sorry, pal. Don't know. Got a message over the wireless. Just "Come and bring spare Sunray most urgent." You'll know about it sooner than me.'

'But where are we headed?'

'Up to where the Squadron was doing its indirect shoot last night. By heck! You should have seen and heard that. All the tanks, more than fifty of the beggars, lined up in a long line. Then at zero hour old Doug called over the wireless "All stations Yoke . . . Fire!" And they all fired at once. It was like somebody hitting a bloody drum as big as the earth with a drumstick as big as the moon. We'll all be stone deaf at thirty after that lot.'

As we swerve and skid along the narrow lanes, I manage to insert myself into my trousers and pull on boots (although I normally wear shoes inside the tank). Thousands of troops and hundreds of vehicles are on the move in this area, yet the roads seem totally deserted. Lowe drives like a racing driver on the Brooklands circuit. I hang on tight, in between fastening buttons.

A glimmer of light is in the sky as we almost crash into the first of our tanks, halted by the roadside. Tail to tail, the huge Shermans bulk like castle battlements against the grey-black sky. The paler blobs which are the faces of commanders are unrecognizable as individuals. Wisps of smoke rise from the engine outlets of the tanks as the drivers keep the engines idling. At the head of the column a small group of figures obstructs our progress. Bill Fox's face emerges out of the gloom, and his rasping voice calls, 'This way, lad. At the double.'

Behind Bill are Hank, tall, slim, and cool; the tiny, pert

figure of my old Troop Leader, Lieutenant Bobby McColl;
the well-remembered face of my old commander, Corporal
Ken Snowdon. I am back in 3 Troop.

'Ah, right. There we are,' continues Bill. 'We want you
to take over the Troop Sergeant's tank. Damn' bad accident. Poor man smashed his arm falling behind the 75 as it
recoiled. Nasty thing to do. Damn' nasty. Ah yes. Lead
tank too. Damn' inconvenient. So you take over Sar'nt
Wilkins' hot seat.'

In the increasing light I see that the Troop Sergeant's
tank is indeed at the head of the column and pointing
directly towards those horrific streets of Le Havre. I look
up at the turret of my new tank and see it as a condemned
cell, a prime target, an unwanted seat of honour.

'We move off in five minutes,' says Hank calmly.

'I'd better brief you quickly,' says Bobby. 'Here's a map
already marked up. We are at this point, here . . .'

'And I am to go in as lead tank without time to study the
route, sir?'

'No, that's not sensible,' says Hank. 'Corporal Snowdon
will have to lead. He has had opportunity to get to know
the general plan.'

I look at Ken Snowdon, and his face seems to be
portraying what I believe my face was revealing only a
moment ago. He swallows hard and says very gallantly,
'That's quite correct. I do know the plan and the route. It
would be impossible for young Ken to take the lead. I'll
do it.'

'Then keep your own call-sign, Sugar 3 Baker,' says
Bobby, 'and Corporal Tout will take the Troop Sergeant's
call-sign, Sugar 3 Able.'

'Now, what I want you to watch particularly,' Hank
intervenes, 'is this major crossroads where the main traffic
route goes off to the left, down into the centre of Le Havre,
while we go straight across the junction towards the naval

barracks at the Cape. There is certain to be anti-tank defence, either situated on the crossroads or firing up this long straight road out of the town centre. Take care there. Take all the time you need.'

We study the innocuous lines on the perspex covers of the map but, whilst our own faces reflect on the shining perspex, I imagine Tiger tanks and SP guns and infantry with bazookas, massing in those side streets and setting their sights on those too long, too straight, too open main roads along which we must enter the city.

'Thanks, pal, for taking the lead,' I say to Ken, as the officers move away to mount their own tanks.

'Nothing to it,' says Ken. 'It would have been more dangerous to have you up front and not knowing which way we're supposed to be headed. It doesn't do any good to calculate the odds, let alone complain about the way the dice roll. Come on, let's mount up. Get your driver to move over into the field so that I can get by. And, for God's sake, keep closed up behind me, mate.'

I swing up to the turret and pick up the microphone. The engine is already running. I switch to I/C and tell the crew to be ready to go. I do not know this crew. The tank has been knocked out so many times that the crew now consists mainly of reinforcements.

The light is still insufficient to see more than a hundred yards down the road although behind the western hills (which are actually the landward slopes of Channel cliffs) the sky is the steel grey of a wintry sea. Around us the sound of artillery swells stupendously into storm violence. All I can see is the dark shape of the tank ahead and the similar shape of the Troop Leader's tank behind. I stare intently at the barely visible map lines and try to memorize our route. If Sugar 3 Baker ahead is suddenly knocked out, I shall have to overtake and find my own way.

We come to a very sharp right bend in the road. Corporal

Snowdon halts until our tank has nosed right up to the tail
of his. Then he moves slowly round the bend. The hedges
fall away and we are in an urban area. There are no houses
intact. There is only the familiar desolation. The houses
look as though they have been crushed by giant feet and
mashed down into dusty footprints.

These ruins are not delved deep as in Caen. They are
flung wildly about the face of the earth. There are no huge
craters to explore, only mounds of ugly rubble. This is the
devastation caused by lighter shells in infinite numbers.
Our shells. Fired in unison at the Colonel's call.

Sugar 3 Baker chooses a way through the rubble, a
scrabbling climb over featureless rubbish. Sugar 3 Baker
looks like an immense grey lobster crawling over a rocky
sea-bed, whilst above us the sky lightens and the mists
begin to disperse. The rubble mounds up into individual
ruins that are discernibly demolished houses. Here and
there a house stands aloft, only its roof and doors and
windows shattered beyond repair. Between the ruins the
channel of a street appears. Hickey, in Sugar 3 Baker,
drives carefully into the resurrected street. Men walk past
me. Infantry. Black Watch, I think. The lead section
spreads out beside and behind Sugar 3 Baker. The rear
men crouch.

'Hullo, Sugar 3 Baker. Have crossed an area of total
ruins but the road is now open and negotiable. Sugar 3
Baker, over.'

'Sugar 3 Baker,' (Bobby McColl answering) 'take good
care. Off.'

The new stretch of road widens into a kind of small
circus some hundred yards or so ahead. That must be the
crossroads. Sugar 3 Baker moves a few yards. Stops. Waits.
Inviting the unseen enemy to shoot. Moves. Stops. Waits.
We watch for the flash which will signal an enemy shot
aimed to brew up Sugar 3 Baker.

No flash . . . but puff! puff! puff! A familiar batch of Moaning Minnie explosions right on the crossroads! Another batch falls at the entrance to our street. A third batch just in front of Sugar 3 Baker. The fourth batch, scorching flame and screaming steel splinters between us and Sugar 3 Baker. I yank at the hatch catches, remembering somebody else's mashed fingers, carefully pull the flaps down over my head. Wait for the next batch of Minnies, on top of us!

No more fall. I open up again. Peer out. The Black Watch are snuggling into the bases of walls or cuddling up behind our tank. More explosions at the crossroads. I press the mike again and say to my crew, whom I have not yet *seen*, 'Strange. If they were defending that crossroads, they'd hardly be shelling it with their own artillery.'

The same thought obviously occurs to the commander up there ahead.

'Hullo, Sugar 3 Baker to Able. Cover me. I'm going across. 3 Baker to Able, over.'

'3 Able to Baker,' I reply. 'I'm with you. Off.'

3 Baker seems to squat back on its haunches as Hickey in its driving seat revs up and then launches the Sherman forward under full power. Even through my headphones and over the constant grumbling of our own engine, I hear the thunderous boom of 3 Baker taking off.

'Driver, close up to the corner.'

3 Baker hurtles across the intersection and into the continuation of our street. Halts. A split-second afterwards a massive rose of flame blooms off the wall of a building at the corner, flames like a huge climbing plant, sprouting leaves of soot-black smoke.

'Gunner, traverse left. There's something shooting up that left-hand road. Be ready to shoot back if it's still there and visible. Driver, slowly forward until we get a view down that side road.'

We roll forward into the vacant crossroads. Wait for the obliterating flame to erupt from our front plates or left-hand track. As the view into the side road, a wider road than ours, unwinds there is . . . nothing . . . and nothing . . . and still nothing . . .

'Gunner, right a bit. That alley. On! Fire!'

I can see nothing moving, nothing outlined in that distant alley, but it is the obvious hide for an anti-tank gun. Our 75mm flashes, growls, spews smoke. Through the smoke I glimpse the tracer swoop down into the alley, impact, flash.

'Operator, reload with HE. Gunner, that far corner. Give it a couple of rounds of HE, just to scare nasties away. Fire in your own time.'

Red fires, like visible lion's roars, rage back at us from the house at the focus of the far street corner as our gunner (whose name I do not yet know) stamps twice on his 75 firing button. But there is no responding flame of enemy guns. It looks as though 3 Baker's opponent fired one unsuccessful shot and then beat a retreat. But we cannot be sure.

The world has again become a dead place. 3 Baker sits motionless fifty yards ahead in our continued street. Behind us a group of Black Watch lies or crouches in gutters and doorways. At the street bend behind us Bobby McColl's tank stands waiting. Down the wide, long road to our left, the road which leads down to the centre of Le Havre, there is nothing to waken my fears. The bright sun darkens the doorways and alleyways. Its blazing light mists the walls with veils of incandescent dust. Only the *pavé* of the road lies clear, open, bleached and desolate.

Nothing to see. In this kind of tank advance there is nothing of the stimulus and mass movement of waves of infantry climbing out of their trenches and marching forward, bayonets gleaming, across the open land. I sit above the immediate world and watch for movement, for fire, for smoke, for outlines which do not belong. But nothing moves. Except in my mind.

My mind supplies visions of Tiger tanks moving just beyond that street corner, their omnipotent 88mm guns already loaded with the immense, lethal missiles which will destroy us. Or the resolute Panzer grenadiers crouching behind windows and loading their bazookas ready to blast us, who present such a vast target sitting here unmoving at a few yards' range. Or the invisible, tank-shattering mines dug into the road and neatly covered over so that, when our track crunches a few yards further forward, fire and steel splinters will burst up through the thin bottom of the Sherman and riddle our bodies with bloody agonies. And I remember the men in tanks who travelled at the arrow-point of advance. The four Germans cooked to a cinder in the tank above Creully. The headless co-driver still watching along the bridle-path before Lisieux. The Sherman alongside us, boiling up into a fifty-foot column of fire at St-Aignan. The officer with an arm hanging by a single muscle. The waxwork motor-cyclist in the ditch. The sacks of flesh with no names attached.

Whilst I try to close my mind to all else, so as to analyse the sinister signals sent out by the ominously silent street, these spectres crawl up out of the cellar of the subconscious. Hammer at the mind's door. Demand admission, consideration, relief from their mortal agonies. For I am not yet convinced about death. Will it indeed be simple oblivion? Or flowery fields of green peace with music ever wafting on fresh breezes? Or will the soul for ever wander in dark passages, screaming from the final agony impressed in the flesh by the bullet or the steel splinter or the cauldron of fire which killed?

I sense, rather than hear or see, movement behind me. Black Watch infantrymen, crouched and shuffling rather like Red Indians, trot up beside our tank and run quickly across the intersection.

'Hullo, Sugar 3 Able.' (Bobby McColl to me.) 'What news? Sugar 3 Able, over.'

'Sugar 3 Able. No movement. Road apparently clear. Over.'

'Sugar 3 Able, wait . . .' (Bobby reports back to Hank.)

'Sugar 3.' (Hank to Bobby.) 'Stand fast whilst our little friends consolidate and Sugar 4 takes up counter-attack positions . . .'

More and more Black Watch file along our street. Shermans of 4 Troop squeeze past Sugar 3 and past us. They turn into the crossroads. The tanks and infantry slowly move down my empty main road, populate it, occupy it, secure it, fortify it.

I duck inside the tank to introduce myself to the crew, two of them totally unknown to me. Now we are suddenly bound together in a mortal peril which may end in us sharing one common headstone for ever more.

'Hullo, Sugar 3 Baker. Continue advance. Sugar 3 Baker, over.'

'Sugar 3 Baker, OK. Off.'

'Hullo, Sugar 3 Able. Close up and support 3 Baker. Sugar 3 Able, over.'

I press the microphone switch. 'Sugar 3 Able, OK. Off.'

As I order the driver to follow 3 Baker, a door in a house on my right opens and a teen-aged girl looks out cautiously. Reassured, she runs into the street, waves a box camera at me, motions me to smile. From my lofty perch I assume a smile which is only lip deep. The girl snaps for posterity her photo of the liberating tank, blows a kiss, retreats to the safety of the house. Our tank rolls forward and I peel off my thin smile, replacing it with the sour scowl more appropriate to those silent streets ahead.

Occasionally an enemy machine-gun chatters abruptly

and we swing our guns in that general direction, dousing the houses with high explosive and Browning tracer. Frequently the ruins of a bombed building obstruct the street and we have to make a detour through a back yard or send our Sherman clambering over the rubble. Never do we see the devastating flash of an anti-tank gun ahead. But always, behind the eyelids and around the next corner, lurk the spectres of Tigers and bazookas and suicide bombers.

After a while Ken Snowdon ahead halts and waves me on. As the street rises towards the naval barracks, I begin to believe that our fears about street battles in Le Havre were as insubstantial as this morning's thin sea mist. We are trundling along in low gear, a gaggle of Black Watch walking serenely behind us, Sugar 3 Baker following on, Ken Snowdon head and shoulders out of his turret, leaning on his elbows on the turret, as am I, not a care in the . . .

The whole spinning world jolts, halts, shudders. The hillside leaps at us. Gravity thrusts upwards. Centrifugal force lashes outwards. The Gates of Hell open and all the infernos of earth's primeval belly gush towards us. Choirs, millions of lost souls, scream damnation over our heads. A force like an invisible aeroplane smashes into the turret. Leopard's claws dig and drag at the folds of my cheeks and the joins of my eyelids. A solid giant fist of air crashes into my face. The Sherman shrieks in an agony of oppressed springs as it wrenches back against its sprockets and fights against its striving pistons.

I am inside a resounding black drum the size of the universe, and Thor's eternal hammer is beating upon the reverberant drum-head. The noise comes from inside my skull and tries to explode my eardrums outwards. My eyeballs and nostrils bulge with the expanding ferocity of solid darkness. The world shudders once more and then begins to spin again. The darkness in front of my eyes thins into shapes of houses and streets. The battering monsters of noise power away into the distance.

Bobby McColl, away to our rear, recovers first. 'Hullo, Sugar 3. Naval gun firing point blank from fort. Sugar 3, over.'

Comes the deliberate voice of Hank, reassuring as ever, 'Sugar 3, I believe I may possibly have heard it. Stand where you are . . .'

'Driver, swing into that right-hand street. Gunner, traverse left,' I say between parched lips. For the Germans have turned their naval guns inland. The fortress guns at the Cape, intended to sink 30,000-ton battleships at twenty miles' range, are now shooting at our thirty-ton tanks at 400 *yards*' range! Fourteen-inch guns against my 75mm (barely three-inch) pea-shooter. Guns firing a projectile almost as massive as the turret in which I stand.

We tuck ourselves away into a side street. That first shell soared over our heads. Maybe we shall be safe. Maybe the huge naval gun will not be able to depress sufficiently to do us harm. Maybe this is only a demonstration of futile resistance. Maybe!

Hank will not wish to take the risk. He will be planning a flank attack. Or perhaps the infantry will infiltrate through the surrounding houses. Now we move into an incredible style of battle. The area is almost silent except for idling tank engines. Once in a long while a brief burst of machine-gun fire breaks out in the distance. Then into the silence, at long-spaced, agonizing intervals, there erupts the sense-dulling thunder of a naval gun just up the hill. The huge shell churns through the injured air above our heads, creating for itself a howling wind-tunnel through which it whirls away towards some far, random point of fiery disintegration.

Then silence again. Idling tank engines. Wireless atmospherics. In such a silent moment someone hammers on our side armour. Callers at this time of day? I lean out over the turret. A Black Watch lieutenant, young and baby-faced, shouts words that are inaudible through the grumble of our engine. I climb out on to the engine covers behind the turret.

'Sorry! Can't hear!'

'Engage it! Damn' well engage it! Why don't you damn' well engage that bloody gun?' shouts the wild-eyed Lieutenant.

'What? Engage a naval gun with a 75mm?'

'You've got a big enough bloody gun on this tank. Use it! Get up that hill and engage that Hun instead of shirking behind these bloody houses!'

'Sorry, sir. Nothing doing. You carry on with your war and I'll carry on with mine.'

'I'll have you bloody court-martialled for insubordination.'

'Complain to your colonel, sir. He knows what our orders are.' (Infantry and tanks work in collaboration but this infantry lieutenant has no authority to countermand the orders of a tank commander who is in direct wireless contact through Troop and Squadron to colonels and brigadiers.)

The lieutenant hammers the hollow engine exhausts with his pistol in fury and stamps away up the side street. A wiry, wrinkled Black Watch sergeant comes over to the tank and leans negligently against it, pulling a cigarette packet from his pocket. He is wearing the Africa Star. As he lights the cigarette, he looks up through the flame of the match at me and chortles.

'Dinna' fret, laddie. Yon boy's new out. He's raring for his MC the noo. Anither week in action, he'll be for the deepest slit trench wi' a' the rest of us. Keep y'r wee head doon, Mac, whilst yon battleship's perched at the top of the brae, till Jerry gaes off duty.'

Eventually the colonels and brigadiers decide to send the infantry crawling in under the vast but clumsy barrels of the naval guns at the top of the brae, rather than sending tanks – ponderous and obvious targets – up the hill. And soon afterwards God himself decides to send in an army of black, glowering clouds from the sea, to curtail the tanker's day and impose night a little early. We withdraw to rendezvous with the rest of the Squadron on a local football field surrounded by buildings. Each Troop forms into a square laager of four tanks, nose to tail, steel armour presented to the outside world and the crews nestling safely within. Two sides of the football field are occupied by the Black Watch. The other two sides are still possessed by German defenders, fortunately quiescent. We sit in the middle.

Within the easy, confined intimacy of the laager Bobby McColl calls us together in the darkness for a quick tactical talk, forecasting tomorrow's movements and dealing with code-signs. Some of us sit on the grass, others lean on a tank. I and one or two others sit on the side of my tank, and Bobby leans his map on the 'mudguard' which covers the front of the track.

A wild wisp whirrs out of the darkness, pings against the turret next to my ear and transforms itself into an ugly lead slug which bounces back on to Tommy Tucker's leg. Tommy picks it up curiously, looks at me and says, 'I saw that. It went right in one of your bloody earholes and out through the other. Nothing in between.'

Everyone laughs heartily, but those of us sitting on the tank slip down to the ground and others who were standing idly now drop into a crouch.

'Aye,' says Bobby. 'Ye'll need to keep your heads down tonight. I said the Boche was within spitting distance.'

Undaunted by the spectator enemy ranged somewhere along the touchline of the football pitch, we light our primus stoves, make tea, boil our usual mess of mixed tinned meat and vegetables. Jerry over there, undoubtedly hungrier than us even if no more frightened, observes in silence and soldierly sympathy. We all take turns at guard duties. My gunner and driver may need to be as alert as I shall be tomorrow, may need to stamp on firing button or tug at track braking level whilst I am still mouthing the words of an order. These September nights are more convenient for us than June's midsummer nights. Then we had time only to replenish supplies, maintain guns and engine, eat and, if lucky, sleep for perhaps two whole hours. Tonight there is time for each member of our five-man crew to take one hour of guard patrol. Five hours! For sleeping!

At 03.00 hours I am prowling around the outside of our tiny laager, savouring all the disquieting thrills of this ultimate frontier. The night is black under dense cloud that seems to mute whatever sound of distant battle there might have been. Four or five of us prowl silently in and out of the Squadron tanks whilst the other ninety crew members sleep the deep exhaustion of battle. Now and again some-one emits a snore, a grumble or a curse.

Then: '*Wilhelm, warum konnen Sie nicht schlaffen?*'

'*Wilhelm! Konnen Sie . . .*'

'Oh, shut your pissing face, you great Teutonic square-head! Go home to Heidi.'

'*Ach, so!* Very sorry, Tommy.'

In the silent night the words of Wilhelm's anonymous companion come with startling clarity. It is one of our prowler guards who responds with less than common courtesy. And the tired German voice obviously has no wish for middle-of-the-night conflict or controversy.

12 SEPTEMBER 1944:

Again we head up the hill. I find myself in a street of quiet, respectable houses. I might be a tradesman plying my peacetime van along a street like this. The two or three Black Watch privates standing beside the tank might be simply waiting to buy my wares.

The first hour or so of the morning has passed by with few warlike noises in our neighbourhood. Now it is surprising suddenly to hear the ripping sound of a Spandau machine-gun, unmistakable in the velocity with which it pours out bullets. The sound comes from behind this nice row of decent houses. A group of Black Watch assembles beside our Sherman. I climb down to enquire what is happening. I have met this Black Watch Sergeant before – a very placid, self-controlled man, older than most of his company. Now he appears to be unusually agitated.

'What is it, Sergeant? Can I help?'

'Nothing you can do, Corporal. Bloody Huns. Bloody SS. Up the back of these houses in a machine-gun post. Waved a white flag. Going to surrender. Our lads got up off their bellies and walked openly up the hill to accept the surrender. When they were a few yards away, the Spandau opened up. Mowed them down. Good lads. Tricked by a white flag. Bloody SS. Must be. Ordinary Jerry soldiers don't do that.'

'Can I get the tank in behind the houses and brass them up?'

'No room. Not unless you knock the bloody houses over first. Don't worry. Our lads are going in now. Bloody mad they are. Taking their tin hats off and putting their bonnets on. They're going in for revenge. And there will be no bloody survivors from that machine-gun pit.'

The infantrymen, wearing their conspicuous Scottish bonnets, run up the road and burst through the front doors of a number of houses. The morning pleasance is disrupted by a gale of battle echoes from behind the houses, bomb blasts, volleys of Sten-gun bullets, rifle shots, shouts, screams. Silence.

Four or five houses up the hill, the Sergeant emerges from a front door, waves me past him, nods his head savagely. As we ascend the steep street, the Sergeant is taking off his khaki bonnet with the red hackle, stuffing it in his pack and putting on his tin hat again. Bloody mad they were.

At the hill-top there is a sudden view to the Cape and a row of fortress buildings, the last defence of the German garrison. Our Troop lines up facing the southern end of the buildings. Over to the right 2 Troop is already in line. In the turret of the nearest tank, clearly profiled, is the face of little Sergeant Warren, fierce moustache visibly bristling in the morning sun. His tank fires. The tracer of the shell seems to slide lazily in a slight arc from the gun to the main door of the buildings. As the tracer hits the door, fire and smoke shoot upwards. The door swings open. A large white sheet pokes through the doorway and waves vigorously.

'Gunner, try that door straight in front of us. See if you can get the same effect,' I say. 'One round 75 HE. Fire!'

The crash of our gun firing merges with the muzzle blasts from our Troop Leader and Baker tanks and the three tracers race each other towards the buildings. Three corresponding flashes from the door and walls in front of us. Opposite Sergeant Warren's tank, at the main doorway where the white flag waves, a tall, elegant German naval officer emerges. He marches resolutely out into the road, about 200 yards away from our lines. Behind him come two other officers. A rank of seamen. A second rank. A third, fourth, fifth. In full uniform. No weapons. All in step. Arms swinging. Lines correctly formed and dressed. Marching out of the massive main gate where the white flag still waves. More ranks. A dozen. A score. Maybe a hundred.

'There's hundreds and hundreds of the buggers,' says Sergeant Warren, his voice coming unexpectedly over the external radio waves. (Presumably, in his astonishment, he

has forgotten that his set is on 'A'. He quickly realizes this.)
'Hullo, Nan 2. Hullo, Nan 2. Have put one shot into main
barracks. Doors opened. White flag up. Prisoners marching
out to surrender. Hundreds of them. Please send little
friends. There are too many for us to look after. Nan 2,
over.'

'Hullo, Nan 2. Bloody good show. Sending for little
friends. Off.'

The great procession continues from the main gate. Still
in good order. Heads high. Marching to peace. Sergeant
Warren is standing on his turret top, a tiny man to
command so many hundreds of great striding prisoners.
Opposite us another door opens. Soldiers emerge from this
door. Hands high in the air. Each one holding a white flag.
Great numbers of them. Hosts of them. Not marching. Not
in files. Simply trudging across the open space between
their barracks and our tanks. I begin to count the prisoners,
but there are so many I soon give up.

The Black Watch are coming up behind us, lining the
road, holding their rifles and Sten guns at the ready in case
of trouble. Bobby McColl leaps off the front of his tank and
trots towards the leading prisoners. Selects one with a
considerable array of braid and badges. Engages him in
conversation. No doubt checking out on any recalcitrant
troops remaining in the barracks. It occurs to me that our
Troop has not reported. The other two commanders are
down there with Bobby. And Sergeant Warren's Troop is
getting all the glory.

I report: 'Hullo, Nan 3 Able. Barracks opposite us also
apparently surrendering. Considerable numbers of prisoners emerging. Sunray forward interrogating prisoners.
Nan 3 Able, over.'

'Nan 3 Able. Keep a good watch in case of last-minute
tricks. Off.'

But there are no more nasty tricks this time. The battle

degenerates into farce. The reports of prisoners surrendering sounds like a Bingo game as tank after tank comes on the air to quote numbers now evacuating their barracks and defences on the Cape.

In a little while I am left alone with four tanks. As I am the junior commander, I remain sitting on my turret, headsets by my side, ready to respond to any urgent message. Meanwhile the entire Troop, from Bobby McColl down, takes a quick tourist trip into the vast barracks complex, which is now empty. They return laden with bottles of wine, cheeses, Nazi flags, naval caps, field-glasses and all the booty of war.

One of the lads shouts to me, 'Pity you weren't with us, Ken. There was a band room down there and a whole set of brass instruments. Trumpets and tubas and saxophones and trombones. You could have taken your pick to take home for the Sally Ann Band. Anyway, we didn't forget you. We didn't know which instrument you play best. So we brought you this one.' And he hands me half a clarinet. The bottom half! As an enthusiastic amateur musician, I drool at the thought of a band room full of shining new brass instruments, going free. I contemplate asking Bobby's permission to hurry over there and help myself. But at this precise moment the headphones chatter busily.

'Hullo, Nan 2 and 3.' Hank's voice. 'Hullo, Nan 2 and 3. Prepare to move at a moment's notice. Nan 2 and 3, over.'

13 SEPTEMBER 1944:
For reasons of the kind evident only to higher strategists, we pulled back to our football field – now abandoned by Wilhelm and his comrades – and waited in reserve for any eventuality. What eventually might be expected when the garrison had completely surrendered was beyond our comprehension.

I saw the Squadron Leader's driver and presented him

with my useless bottom half of a clarinet. He is a clarinet-player and carries a clarinet with him. He seemed more pleased with the thing than I was.

14 SEPTEMBER 1944:
Back to our little orchard in Gonneville-le-Malet. Whilst a number of tank commanders jostle for parking space near the big, central farm buildings, I direct our driver to a far corner of the orchards where I remember there is a row of modest cottages. In one of the cottages lives a very friendly farm labourer, a repatriated prisoner of war from 1940. His wife, daughter and a small son form a delightful family. We knock on their door and announce our return. They dash for the coffee cups and Calvados bottle. They overwhelm us with the unabashed hospitality of simple folk. We are only too happy to sit on a civilized chair with a roof over our heads.

15 SEPTEMBER 1944:
All our wheeled transport has been called away. The advance of the British Army through France and Belgium has been so precipitate that the supply columns cannot keep up with the forward tanks. There is no enemy opposition, and the only limiting factor on the advance is the availability of petrol and other basic supplies. So a number of regiments like ours have been left sitting in the orchards whilst our lorries join the almost continuous convoy from the Normandy beaches to the Belgian border and back.

Meanwhile our old friends the Black Watch startle and then amuse the inhabitants of Gonneville by marching into the village square with bagpipes groaning and shrilling and drums beating. For an exhilarating hour they march back and forward across the square 'beating the retreat', which seems an inappropriate function for soldiers who have just completed an unprecedented advance. Our Yeomen stand watching, reluctant to make the normal raucous comments of Sassenachs on hearing the Highland skirl, because we now proudly wear the HD sign on one arm.

'Sounds like the end of the war,' says my driver, Fred.

'Wish it was the end of the bloody war,' answers Eddie Bollens, the gunner. 'Now we've won the Normandy campaign, perhaps they'll let us go home.'

16 SEPTEMBER 1944:

A tiny procession, much more subdued than the Black Watch bombast and brilliance of yesterday. Reminiscent in its way of the small group of farm people who brought flowers to cover Sid Turton's newly dug grave. The farm labourer, his wife, his thirteen-year-old daughter and eight-year-old son. They process through the orchard towards our tank, bearing gifts: an oven-roast chicken, roast potatoes, a kind of apple cake and a flagon of white wine. Our lunch! True, we have given the farm labourer a packet of excellent English cigarettes. We have given his wife some pure, pleasant-smelling soap. We have given the daughter a slab of Duncan's blended chocolate from Edinburgh, and for the son a box of Army-issue boiled sweets. But this is a liberal and free exchange of gifts for gifts, rather than the normal barter system which takes place at cottage doors.

So the tiny procession comes in homage to their liberators. For again we recognize the difference in concept between how *we* regard ourselves – a gaggle of lads conscripted into huge war machines but scared for our very lives at each new turn of the road – and how *they* regard us – the tough, heroic campaigners for peace and liberty.

'*Le Boche a pris tout*' is the watchword of our friend. 'The Boche has taken everything.' He took this man's elderly horse. He took all the horses from the farm. In his

haste and anxiety to retreat, the German soldier was
pressured into grabbing any and every primitive means to
escape the oncoming Allied hordes. '*Le Boche a pris tout.*'
And so we inherit the gratitude of these people whose
orchards we are desecrating and whose towns we have
razed to the ground. For a moment everything seems
worthwhile. This Frenchman tells us haltingly that he was
afraid for his girl, rightly or wrongly. Afraid she would
come to a certain age before the liberators arrived. Now he
feels that she is safe.

'He doesn't realize,' says Fred, 'that his girl might be
safer with disciplined German troops, anxious to get a good
name with the Frogs, than with some of the drunken
buggers on our side.'

17 SEPTEMBER 1944:

The French family's little boy comes to watch us as we
virtually take the guns and engine to pieces in order to
carry out intensive maintenance. He plays in the turret
and fancies himself quite a soldier. Today he picked up my
belt, which was lying on the front of the tank, pulled the
loaded revolver out of the holster, pointed it at me and
said something which I took to mean 'Stick 'em up!' He
then tried to pull the trigger. His aim was good but his
finger was not strong enough. So I live on. And we have
hidden our personal weapons.

22 SEPTEMBER 1944:

Today we assemble in the big hay barn for a concert given
by the lads of the Squadron. Harry Brown, Harry Graham
and other leading wits have been concocting a version of
the popular radio series *ITMA*, which features many
strange personalities who revolve around comedian Tommy
Handley. Harry Graham is a great impersonator. He will
supply a number of voices. Ralph Hill, an amateur actor in

civil life, will provide others. Several of us help to swell the handwritten script.

We sit on the straw and hay in the barn. Captain Bill Fox and RSM George Jelley are in the front row. George jumps with surprise to hear his own voice bark from the rear of the barn: 'Stand to your feet there. What-do-you-think-you're-bloody-well-doing, then?' as Harry Graham launches the hilarious hour of rough and tumble, bawdy jokes, sentimental songs and tunes on the clarinet from Lowe. Norman Plant and friends sing a useful imitation of an Inkspots' song, including that deep bass voice which narrates the second verse.

'The RAF have dropped me a bullock!' complains the high, imitation voice of Quartermaster Sergeant Pete Mapley. The audience roars with laughter for, whilst the phrase has connotations of a sexual character, the RAF have indeed been dropping meat to advanced units and . . . 'They dropped a bad egg on me at Magny,' answers the voice of the RSM, who was on the receiving end of both British and American bombs around St-Aignan way.

'Why does the Colonel go to see the Brigadier?' asks one. 'Because he's *Fors-ter!*' says another.

Showers of straw descend from the audience upon the jokers and script-writers who perpetrated that pun. But the quality of the jest matters little compared with the idiotic behaviour which releases the turbulent and persistent tensions of war.

I laugh as loudly as the rest, but when we return to sleep in our little orchard nook, I lie looking up through the thick leaves of the apple trees at the glittering stars and am not reassured. The future holds only the promise of more isolated arrow-head advances, surrounded on all sides by legions of invincible fears. More sinister, deserted roads ridden by the ghosts of fire-blackened comrades or decapitated opponents. More night hours whilst the hairs at the

nape of the neck rise in atavistic response to the wild
creatures, human and mechanical, which prowl the wilderness, waiting to leap.

Now I understand why the trench soldiers of 1914–18
yearned for the 'Blighty One'. Why they calculated that
maybe the loss of a hand or an eye or even a leg would
be an acceptable price for release from the fear of death
or permanent wounding even more appalling. Why, if
what they say is true, lieutenants in that war carried
revolvers not to shoot the enemy but to coerce the friend.
In this war lieutenants in tanks have little need of
revolvers to restrain or compel the crews. A tank man is
immured within a sealed steel cell – a travelling tomb.
When needle-sharp iron slivers and molten fire lash the
outside of the vehicle, he has little option but to remain
seated, enclosed, trapped, able to express himself only by
the curse which goes unheard under the roar of the
engines, or by emitting the ultimate statement of horror
via the seat of his pants.

24 SEPTEMBER 1944:
A free day in Bolbec, not the most interesting town in the
world. I stand and watch processions of tiny 'Brides of
Christ', all in white gowns, going to their First Communion. Literally hundreds of little girls hardly old enough to
remember the traumas of France over the last five years.

Free tickets for the theatre where the Highland Division
Concert Party is performing. Usual kind of male presenta-
tion. Hefty Highlanders, heavily made up and dressed in
frilly skirts and knickers, doing the can-can. Not, I think,
as good as Harry Graham and Ralph Hill and Harry Brown
in our humble barn. Clumsy sexual innuendoes. Flashing
brawny thighs. On reflection most of us preferred the
innocence of the little 'Brides of Christ'.

26 SEPTEMBER 1944:

Some under-employed staff wallah has had the bright idea of removing us from our sheltered orchards at Gonneville, where we lolled in luxury like Lotus-Eaters, and setting us down on the edge of dank, ploughed fields somewhere near Criquetot.

Nothing to do. No friendly farm labourers. (I have bequeathed my German field-glasses to an enthralled farm labourer's son.) Football is not easy to play across ploughed fields or on a grassy patch parked thick with great tanks. Sergeant Bert King has obtained some boxing gloves from somewhere, and we expend a certain amount of energy in trying to punch the elusive and skilled boxer Bert on his chubby chin. With very little success.

28 SEPTEMBER 1944:

We battle-worn warriors had thought we were now immune to shocks. We had under-estimated our new Squadron Sergeant-Major, who was promoted on Sid Turton's death. The new SSM has ordered us out for First Parade on the ploughed field with boots clean, brasses shining, and carrying personal arms.

'My God,' says Tommy, 'these days I only shave when a piece of shrapnel passes me close enough. What does the bugger think he's playing at?'

One of the older, long-serving sergeants goes to complain to Hank or Bill Fox. Discovers that all the officers are away on some sort of Brigade exercise. So, like sullen convicts commencing a twenty-year sentence, we slouch out on to the ploughed field, our boots apologetically wiped clean with handfuls of grass, our brasses given the benefit of a rub with a shirtsleeve, our webbing rescued from under piles of Calvados bottles, half-empty Camembert cheese packets, dirty socks and spent cartridge cases.

'Right! Less-ave-a marker from each Troop! Brighten

yoursel's up. Itsaluvlymornin', can chew see?' cries the SSM, as perky as an early blackbird and the only grinning face in the whole wide, ploughed world.

'Go on, Ken, you're tallest,' says Tommy to me, exercising his democratic right as a British Yeoman.

'It's beneath the dignity of a Lance-Corporal,' I reply. 'Our duty is to oppress the proletariat and make you do the work. You're tall enough. And ugly enough.'

'C'mon, c'mon, c'mon, 3 Troop. Dyuhwanna do some extra drill after?' shouts the SSM, still grinning happily.

'Pass me a red-hot poker,' growls a voice. Some joker pushes me in the back and I stagger forward from the top of a ploughed rut into the bottom of a ploughed furrow.

'Ah, at last, the h'aristocrats of 3 Troop have decided to send us a volunteer,' crows the SSM. 'C'mon, lad, at the double. Quickly. It's nearly sunset. Juggle your balls a bit.'

I hop and totter over the furrows of damp, clinging clay where even an elephant would be hard pressed to raise a canter.

The SSM in his wisdom lines up diagonally to the furrows so that forming a straight line across the undulating field becomes a physical impossibility. I hear some of the sergeants enter into the party spirit. 'Up a bit on your left. Kemp, you're out of kilter. Try balancing on that cow turd . . . Graham, pull your belly in. It's out of line with your skull . . . Somebody rescue Bollen from that hole he's fallen into . . . Rushton, are you standing back to front?' The SSM's smile begins to falter. But he is willing to leave us to it. There is nothing else to do anyway. Once we are placed in approximate lines, he then strolls around to inspect us, moving at the pace of a large khaki slug and carrying out what is virtually a personal interview with each individual on parade.

'Haircut, lad! What? "Where d'you get your hair cut?" Don't the Froggies have bloody barbers in the villages?

Who do you think's been shaving the hair off the Jerry whores? Angetchur brasses bloody well polished. Parade before breakfast tomorrow for me to see. Where's your creases? Eh, what's that? What bloody battles? You don't stop creasing your trousers till you gets your bloody legs shot off!'

So it goes on, man after man. I escape lightly. Perhaps he remembers that I took over the tank he would have had to command, had he been a tank man.

29 SEPTEMBER 1944:

Don Pateman whispers that when Hank came back from Brigade and heard about our parade he called the SSM to task. 'We don't want any of your damn' infantry ideas here. This is a Yeomanry Regiment and these are tank crews. I don't care if their brasses are not polished as long as the breeches of their guns are clean and oiled. Some of those lads are going to bloody well die in the next shoot-out, and they won't die any more willingly and efficiently for parading on some damn' sodden patch of French ploughland.'

Hank's decision is popular and irrevocable. But I can't help wondering whether some glimmer of ancestral military wisdom has not been transmitted to us by the over-eager SSM. Idle troops are discontented troops are poor troops are soon defeated troops.

Today for the first time since Aldershot we are served with real bread as part of the rations. Soft white bread after months of 'dog biscuits' or the grey sawdust bread of occupied France. We dance a jig and wave our slices of bread to a benevolent God in the skies and His servant on earth, the gentle Pete Mapley, SQMS. And Fred has been to a brothel. Well, not exactly a brothel:

'You see, I heard that this Frenchwoman was, like, inviting people in. The old mother was at the door in a filthy black dress collecting the subscriptions. Almost turned me off at the start . . . There were all these blokes, see, on the stairs – infantry, artillery, ordnance, even bloody pioneers. Anyway I went up just to see what was happening. There was just this farm wife on her own, with a bloke, if you know what I mean. But muck! The place stank like a midden in the middle of a sewage farm. And this farm wife, well I've seen better talent out in my old cow byre. So I apologized to the other blokes for pushing up front . . . and slung my hook pretty quick. Never know what you might pick up just walking up the stairs in a place like that. Only went out of curiosity, like. But old Tommy's there, of course. Waiting patiently . . .'

Later there are shouts and jeers and laughs from across the field. Tommy has returned from the house of subscriptions. He has been unwise enough to boast of his doings. So some of the lads have decided that he needs an FFI.

In normal barrack circumstances the FFI (Freedom From Infection Parade) is a regular proceeding when an entire squadron or even a regiment lines up, usually in a draughty gymnasium, each man wearing only his unbuttoned trousers. A medical officer, accompanied by one or two lackeys, passes along the patient, shivering rows. As the MO approaches, the individual drops his trousers. As the MO reaches him, he extends hands and fingers for inspection (scabies, impetigo and so on), then raises his arms and does a slow ballerina twirl, during which time the MO peers and pokes for lice, 'crabs' and more virulent infections.

But the Yeomen have decided today that the MO is not needed. Tommy is mobbed and debagged. He leaps up like a startled stag on the Highland moors and gallops away across the field, stark naked. A howling, baying pack of two-legged staghounds chases him hither and thither over plough and thistle and grassland. One by one the hounds sink exhausted whereas the indefatigable Tommy bolts for refuge into a convenient and discreet patch of woodland beyond the ploughed field.

Bill Fox has been watching the performance. He catches my eye. 'That'll damn' well larn him,' he says.

These frivolities sustain me until I am snuggled into my rough blankets, head on my small pack, watching the stars and squirming on the hard ground to find a more accommodating hollow. I chew on a piece of white bread, raw, soft, untarnished by butter or cheese or lesser staples. Gourmet stuff. But as the stars go blind with approaching sleep, my subconscious mind prepares to stage another of its midnight improvements on Shakespeare's ghost scene from *Macbeth*.

9

Piggy-Back Tank

4 OCTOBER 1944:

We are to move at last. Possibly to Belgium. Possibly to the Netherlands, where the Allied armies have, as yet, little more than a toehold.

The distance which we must cover is vast for tanks with their limited track life. So we shall be lifted by huge Diamond T and Scammel tank-transporters. We shall be moving out of this haven of peace, never fought-over and now of no interest to the combatants. And we shall be coming once again within the sound of the guns.

6 OCTOBER 1944:

The transporters arrive. Each tank is driven up on to the back of its transporter and then locked and chained into place. We shall travel at will within the cab of the slow, grinding transporter or perched in the turret and driving hatches of our tank.

7 OCTOBER 1944:

At dawn we set off, the transporters wriggling with great difficulty through the narrow lanes between Criquetot and Goderville. Out on the main road we pick up speed a little but not so much speed as would cause serious injury to any one of us who happened to fall off our cumbersome steeds.

We stop for a break at a tiny place called St-Saëns, outside an *estaminet*. Orders prohibit our entering but the Frenchwoman owner comes out and pours us each a mug full of *vin blanc*. I happen to remember that my father was stationed here during the First War.

'I probably served him,' says our hostess. 'I was only a little girl but I loved to serve the English soldiers. I married one eventually. He died before this war. Have another drink for your father's sake.'

This morning I received a letter from home. The Post Corporal came driving up the column handing out mail. For the first time since Aldershot my folks have a fair idea of where I am. In Bolbec I met an old friend. So I wrote home and said I had met Bram Millest from Sheffield. My father knows that Bram is in the 49th (Polar Bear) Division, and the BBC have announced that Le Havre was liberated by the 49th and 51st Highland. So my father will have deduced that I am somewhere near Le Havre and not battling up the fatal Arnhem road.

It is strictly forbidden to write home with news of our movements. Officers read our mail and 'blue-pencil' out any leading references. My parents must not know that I was in St-Aignan or Bourg Achard or Le Havre. Otherwise they might accidentally gossip in their shoe shop or at the Salvation Army meeting and some lurking German spy would hear, rush to report to the Nazi High Command, frustrate the best-laid plans of Montgomery. Yet any German commander, perched on a hill using his excellent field-glasses and watching us advance, could see and identify the cap badges in our berets and the Brigade signs which army orders require us to paint boldly and clearly on our tanks.

Random thoughts usurp my mind until *we* reach the Somme battlefield where, during the 'first lot', my father and uncles and schoolmasters endured sufferings far beyond anything we shall ever know in this more mobile war. My crew sit on the engine covers, dangling their legs, cutting the cards and playing Pontoon. I spread the map on the turret top and look right and left to identify the sacred places, near which we are rumbling: Mametz and Thiepval, Montalmaison and Beaumont Hamel, the innocent and tiny River Aisne, High Wood and Delville Wood. Places made sacred by Father's tales at the supper table. And by the serried regiments of white gravestones dimly visible to us today across this corn-gilded landscape.

We halt again at Bapaume Station, another name which conjures up Great War photos of British infantry standing in the rain outside this same station building, upon those same cobbled stones, whilst surely this same grey, grizzling rain seeps down from a grim heaven.

At evening we come to one of the most evocative names of all: Mons. Every military man has heard of the Angel of Mons and wonders why no such angel presided over the road down into Caen, or the trackless *via dolorosa* up the Bourguébus Ridge or the gully at St-Aignan.

We are delighted when we are told to park along the boulevards of Mons. Delighted because the juddering journey of the day is done. Delighted because this is one city of which all of us have heard and which all of us wanted to see. Delighted because, as long as we leave one crew member on guard, we can go off to the *estaminets* and the streets where the red lights glow. Delighted because, although there are no celestial angels in Mons tonight, there are plenty of terrestrial beings crowding out to welcome us and offer friendship tokens in the usual forms: wine, coffee (even though ground from acorns), flowers, kisses.

The rest of the crew have gone off to an *estaminet* where they will probably do nothing more outrageous than drink a Belgian beer and ogle the serving girl. I hang around the tank doing odd jobs. (We have been unloaded by our transport friends who have now departed in their transporter vehicles.) I unlash the bedding rolls of the crew and push the individual rolls underneath the tank where we shall be able to sleep, fairly well protected from the thin, greasy rain which continues to fall intermittently.

A small crowd of Belgians stands watching the tanks. A little nine-year-old girl and her father approach me. He speaks in excellent English.

'My daughter wants to know if you sleep underneath the tanks.'

'Yes, we do. That is what we have done ever since we landed on the Normandy beaches.'

'You were in Normandy?' (Some of the troops now arriving are new reinforcements who did not fight in Normandy. This particularly applies to some American divisions.)

'Yes, we have come all the way.'

'Monique thinks this is a very uncomfortable way to sleep.'

'When one is tired, one does not think too much about the softness of the bed. By the way, would you and your daughter like to see inside the tank?'

They both clamber over the tank and poke about in the turret with avid interest. Then, it being Monique's bed-time, they thank me and depart. It is around ten o'clock when the crew returns, slightly intoxicated, gently cheerful and droopingly weary. At the same time Monique and her father return from the opposite direction.

'Corporal, Monique insists that you cannot sleep out here when we have a bed to spare. And her mother agrees. So we have come to invite you to spend the night with us. Just two minutes away. And other soldiers from your tank if they will sleep on our sofa or share the bed.'

We hold a crew discussion. We do not move off until 10.00 hours tomorrow. Plenty of time. One man must stay with the tanks. One man per crew. Fred is on guard anyway, so will stay. Four of us can go. Two have been invited back to the *estaminet* by the Madame ('Nice people.

Just like English publicans. Not really a brothel at all.')
That leaves two of us to go with Monique.

Another Belgian approaches us. '*Messieurs, s'il vous plaît. Est-ce que quelqu'un voudra dormir chez nous?*'

So, quickly collecting my small pack with my shaving kit and some chocolate and smokes and pushing a tin of peaches into my pocket, I accompany Monique and her father.

Their hospitality consists of a huge supper, scraped together from ration oddments, a bottle of champagne – which, even though normally teetotal, I valiantly assault – and a roaring fire which must be consuming their entire winter's fuel supply. The father is, or was until the Germans came, a commercial traveller for a British firm, Port Sunlight soap, so they squeal with delight when I produce and hand to them a gaily wrapped cake of genuine, softly scented Erasmic soap, real British soap, which my mother included in my latest parcel from home. The local soap substitute, after years of enemy occupation, is loathsome and inefficient.

My first night in a house since my forty-seven-hour leave back in May! Paradise! A huge flock bed, the sheets and blankets old but scrupulously clean and inviting. I approach the bed with some sensitivity, considering my grimy feet and unbathed body. The only ablution facility is a china jug with a couple of pints of cold water.

My Belgian friends will be deeply disappointed if I do not use their bed. I overcome my repugnance at my own body and climb into the vast, warm desert of yielding flock. Roll about in ecstasy. After a minute or two I begin searching for the familiar hard lumps of earth and stone. On the soft mattress my body contorts into unaccustomed shapes. Pains develop in sagging back and twisted shoulders. I toss and turn. Groan and argue with myself. Ungrateful sod. Uncomfortable idiot. I get out of bed, remove the quilt and pillows. Doss down on the carpet. I sleep the sleep of the Elysian Fields where, no doubt, the souls of departed soldiers lie down with lion and lamb on the verdant green sward rather than tolerate the heavenly mattresses of cast-off angel-wing feathers.

8 OCTOBER 1944:

As daylight filters through the unfamiliar curtain shapes, I hear the rattle of a cup and a footstep on a stair tread. With the urgency of a tank man bailing out of a burning Sherman, I gather my pillows and quilt, fling myself back into the great bed and pretend to sleep.

The door opens gently and a female voice says, '*Bonjour, monsieur! Bonjour! Sept heures! Du café? Avez-vous bien dormi?*'

'*Oui, madame. J'ai dormi . . . toute la nuit dans le paradis.*' (Liar!)

As I eat a leisurely breakfast, I experience a strange lesson in the frustrations of Babel. Monique has just started studying Latin in school. Last night, because of the English soldiers, she did not finish her homework, her '*devoir*'. She sits at the table and asks her father what is the Latin for 'table'. He does not know. '*Mensa,*' say I. I ask her, faltering for the French words, whether she wants the '*nominatif, accusatif ou génitif.*' She appears to understand. '*Les tables sont noires.*' Ah, then it's '*mensae*', little lady. We 'Babel' on in three languages. She finishes her homework, gazes at me in my strange uniform, with the little silver horses of Hanover on my lapels and beret – gazes at me with a kind of idolatry which children reserve for visitors from distant planets. I think that it will be a very bold schoolmaster who will dare correct any of the Latin translations, however stumbling, enunciated by the Liberator who stayed the night in Monique's house.

On the way back to the tank I meet Norman Plant and Howard Reid, who have also been sleeping in a civilian house. 'What was it like?' I ask.

'Bleeding awful. Kept rolling out of the bed. Or both sunk in the middle and all coiled up like a pair of bleeding snakes. Had to get out and sleep on the floor in the end. Be glad to get back to sleeping on a good old slab of granite again.'

The good folk of Mons come out and wave us on our way as, at 10.00 hours, we start up our engines and proceed under our own tremendous horse-power. The Madame from the *estaminet* is there, and the girls from a more colourful establishment, and a cohort of neighbours who vacated their beds last night (and maybe for several nights before that). And little Monique, in school uniform and clutching a satchel, has special permission to watch us go before taking her Latin exercises off to the more mundane happenings at school.

Our route takes us through wonderful Brussels. Even though we are just another tank in an endless conveyor-belt kind of operation going on day after day after day, the citizens halt and turn and wave and cheer, along the streets and through the squares and under the shadow of towering spires and frowning façades and away again into the widening suburbs, wave and cheer and halt and look and smile and run and wave and fetch their neighbours and dance and . . . .

Malines – grey buildings in the seeping rain but golden sunshine smiles on barely glimpsed war-worn faces. Small villages, and farmers stretched up from the pigpen or furrow and waving. Bowed, thick-limbed, multi-skirted women still bending over the potato rows but nodding and laughing as we thunder past.

In the thickening rain, cloud, darkness, we come to our objective, Gierle, a village with a school. We are to sleep

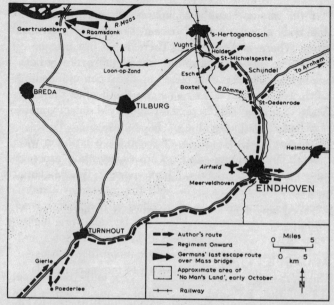

1NY in North Brabant, Netherlands, October 1944

in the school tonight. Suddenly, after months of flinging our blankets down on the island of turf, mud or stone on which we have halted, we are given billets.

The disadvantage of lodging in built billets is that one does not have the choice of the entire countryside in which to exercise certain natural functions. After a long day's drive, the objective of every man in the Squadron is the school latrine. War conditions have created havoc with waterworks and water supplies, even in the humid north of Belgium. The latrine is mounded high with paper. A Trooper strikes a match in order to see better. In a flash, literally in a flash, the match slips from numb fingers, falls into the mounded paper and the entire latrine flares up into an inferno which burns with a peculiar acrid smell.

'Fire!' shouts somebody unnecessarily. 'Water!' yells somebody else, with more reason than hope. There is no water. There are no hoses. There is no fire brigade on hand. The fire-extinguishers in our tanks are remote, beyond the school perimeter.

'There's only one way to get water,' cries a third Trooper. 'Make your own, lads.'

A circle of long-travelling Troopers surrounds the blaze and assaults it with accurate if insignificant jets of innovative fire-fighting equipment. The fire gradually wavers and, probably as much from astonishment as saturation, dies away.

'Saved ourselves a bloody court-martial there,' says Alf Rushton.

9 OCTOBER 1944:

The Squadron moves back a mile or two, to the tiny hamlet of Poederlee, a church, a stretch of common land, a farm and a few rows of houses. Our first surprise is to see the Flemish wives scrubbing their doorsteps at reveille time, scrubbing their windowsills and then scrubbing the entire area of pavement and road outside their house frontage.

'God, my wife would drop dead at the thought,' says Fred.

11 OCTOBER 1944:

As always the local folk are most friendly. Too friendly at times. The children swarm all over the tanks whilst we are trying to do routine maintenance and cause us to mislay split pins and springs and 'four-by-two' pull-through rags. Little Eddie Bollens, my gunner and the only D-Day 1NY man on the crew, leaves his personal kit on the mudguard of the tank whilst stripping down the guns inside the turret, an oily, heavy task which takes every inch of available space. When he comes to retrieve his kit, the revolver is missing.

'One of those blessed kids must have taken it,' gripes Eddie miserably. 'But Hank will still have to make it a court-martial offence if we don't find it.'

We grab our remaining personal weapons and, hunched together like a gang of Chicago heavies, present ourselves at the door of the leader of the local Resistance. He is a friend of ours but we try to adopt Hallowe'en countenances and Corps of Military Police voices. A curious group of locals gathers and gabbles away in the unknown language. I try a piece of transparent bluff, cobbling together a few words that sound to me like Flemish and which, I hope, will make them think we have understood their talk.

'What was that "tweezer" bit about, Ken?' asks Eddie.

'Giving them two hours. Two hours to find that revolver. I hope they got the message.'

Tommy, who has joined the group, asks, 'What do we do after two hours? Traverse left and five rounds of 75HE? Or call in the flame-throwers? Or shoot a few hostages and rape a few women??

We go and report to Bobby McColl, who looks serious and dubious. 'I'll give you until sunset. After that I'll have to report it,' he says. We go back to our maintenance. Brew some tea. Sit behind the tank disconsolately sipping the bitter brew. It is Eddie's voice which eventually rouses us as he prowls around the tank. 'Ken, come and look.'

On the mudguard lies the pistol. And a bottle of sinister-looking gin. Harsh spirits from the still behind somebody's cottage.

As I crawl into my blankets at sleep time, I wonder why, when some horrific death or maiming awaits us just up the road, the words 'court martial' have such a dread impact. At the worst a court martial for losing a revolver would only mean a spell in a military prison, possibly until the war was over and we could all go home. Yet the fear of military discipline impelled us to urgent action as though we were being threatened with the rack, the thumbscrew, the boot and the axe. For a moment I have clear insight into what makes a man climb out of a trench and rush at a waiting machine-gun churning out hundreds of bullets a minute. Or what makes me lift my head out of the protection of the turret as a target for every gun within thousands of yards.

My moment of clarity is disturbed by the subtle, insistent crump of shockwaves racing through the earth from battles raging away along this road, in unfamiliar names like Eindhoven, Nijmegen, Arnhem.

12 OCTOBER 1944:

We go to Turnhout for our first bath since leaving Aldershot. Throughout the Normandy campaign we relied on pouring water over each other as time and temper permitted. Now we go to an old factory which has been rigged up with lines of showers. The water is almost unbearably hot. After our showers we are released into the forecourt. Our towels and underclothes are taken away for laundering and will be reissued to later bathers. Meanwhile we shall be issued with rehabilitated towels, pants and vests bequeathed by earlier bathers.

Unfortunately the baths Staff Sergeant is away at NAAFI break and nobody has a key to the stores. So we wait in the early winter frost, our bodies dripping water and exuding steamy sweat. The great God Pneumonia stalks up and down our ranks. We double up and down at a speed which the SSM could not exact from us. We curse the Staff Sergeant and shout mutinous slogans. The Staff Sergeant returns and with the sanctimonious disdain of the headquarters functionary for the fighting troops calls us strictly to attention in the nude. We respond by giving the Hitler salute and shouting '*Sieg Heil!*' He gains revenge by having trouble with the lock of the stores door.

The front-line trooper may win the moral battle but not the war. As we depart from the ill-fated baths, I discover that my 'new' towel and underclothes appear to be First War relics which have recently been dragged through the Ypres mud.

In the evening we console ourselves with a drink at the fireside in the Flemish farmhouse. We play our usual five-a-side game. The family lines up in chairs on one side of the blazing wood fire. Our Resistance friend stations himself at one end of their team, and the old, partially deaf grandfather is at the other end. I take the end of our row, and Fred sits farthest from me. Our Flemish host makes a remark in Flemish. Jan of the Resistance translates into French, his only other language. (He had to escape to France when hunted by the Gestapo.) I listen to Jan's rustic French and then pass on an English version. Eddie or Roy answers back. I translate. Jan ponders over my schoolboy French. Translates into Flemish. We all nod happily and wisely. The bottle or the coffee pot passes round again.

Meanwhile, nearest the fire, the old Grandpa chats away in broad Flemish about farming to Fred. Fred, an East Anglian who comes from a region to which Flemish weavers have emigrated over the centuries, somehow understands. The broad country dialects of the Flemish and the East Anglian flow slowly back and forward, with no haste to understand and with comprehension of mutual farming terminology glowing at every fifth or tenth sentence end.

15 OCTOBER 1944 – SUNDAY:

A football match has been arranged between the village and the Squadron. We have some good lads playing for us. Jimmy Sables is on Newcastle's books. Little Ripley and even smaller Yo Preston, together with Alf 'Coon' Rushton, form a vigorous and skilful forward line. Sadly our goalkeeper was one of our battle casualties. The press gang appoints me goalkeeper. 'You're a rugby player, Ken. You can catch a bloody ball. We haven't got another 'keeper. You've got to get out there and stop 'em scoring. For the honour of England, and chop yer balls off if you don't.' I goalkeep.

With the score at eleven to nil in our favour, a discussion develops between our full-backs 'Jesse' Pye, Pete Pedder and myself. 'You've got to let one in, Ken,' says Pete. 'Eleven–nil looks bad. We can't do that to them, not after taking their wine and their gin and their meat and their eggs. Let one in, mate. Restore their pride.'

At last the local lads boot the ball in our general direction. Pete Pedder makes an impressively dramatic attempt to stop it but does not quite get a boot in the way. The Flemish wing pounces on the ball and lashes in a drive of First Division ferocity. It almost amputates my hand. It crashes through the goal like an 88mm anti-tank solid shot.

'Goal! Goal!' shout spectators and players in the international Esperanto of football. The Flemish players leap about as though they have won the World Cup. Allied solidarity is saved. The ref blows 'Time!'

'That was really good acting, Ken,' whispers Pete to me.

'That blessed shot came nearer killing me than any Jerry shell,' I shudder.

10

St Michael's Tank

17 OCTOBER 1944:
Suddenly we move. We are required in the line. We say
goodbye to Grandpa and Jan of the Resistance and the local
football team and the scrambling, interfering children and
the pavement-scrubbing housewives.

Evening finds us in a suburb of Eindhoven. We park on
the main street in Meerveldhoven. A slim, under-
nourished youth invites us into his house, up an alley and
into a yard behind some shops. He is employed by Phillips
of Eindhoven as a radio technician.

From a bookshelf he takes a thick book. Opens it to
reveal a square shape cut out of the middle pages. There
nestles a cigarette tin. Inside the cigarette tin is a mass of
intertwining coloured wires and terminals. Another hidden
tin contains miniature headphones. He connects up. Fid-
dles with coils. Listens. Clearly over the war-tormented
ether comes the music of the BBC. Our friend built the set
himself, listening in to the BBC for the Resistance, in spite
of the Gestapo searches. These were the real heroes,
unsupported by big guns and tank armour and marching
battalions of infantry.

I wonder, 'How would I have reacted had *my* parents
raised me under the Nazi occupation of Meerveldhoven?'

18 OCTOBER 1944:
We drive solemnly through the avenues of Eindhoven,
past the bombed railway station. We see our first Dutch
canal. We laager in a farm beyond St-Oedenrode, the tall
church at our backs, a narrow river curling through the flat

fields to send up perpetual mists around our parked tanks, and the single road towards Arnhem riding away straight in front of us.

We are told that in those woods over on the left, there, and in those other woods, away on the horizon there, the German infantry are still entrenched. Allied troops spaced along the road and defending the fields on either side. We are in a military vice, a trap narrower than that near St-Julien-le-Faucon where SSM Turton was killed.

19–20 OCTOBER 1944:

All ranks share in night patrols and static guards. Tonight I am paired with Sergeant Prentice. Ted Prentice sports fierce moustaches like a Uhlan of the Great War or an RAF Squadron Leader of this war. He seems immeasurably older and more mature than me though our birth certificates show only five years age gap. So significant is seniority to recent schoolboys.

Last night, we are told, enemy infiltrators from those woods, there, crept across the fields, through our pickets, and cut the throats of several Scottish Highlanders lying asleep in their blankets. We are ordered to patrol in pairs. And back to back!

This is an inclement, hostile world of bewitched darkness. Upon a dense backcloth of moonless black skies, river mists move like Hell-tormented ghosts seeking a resting-place but never able to alight upon the moisture-brimming sod. We squelch to the start-point of the patrol route which we have observed in daylight. We place ourselves back to back. Ted steps forward, Sten gun at the ready. I step backward, close against him, my US Navy tommy-gun loaded and pointed at the mists. My fingers frozen. My heart palpitating. The Celtic depths of my subconscious conjure up invisible, blood-sucking vampires and hideous ghosts to inhabit this haunted wilderness. Normally terror is projected from the imagination. Here it is plainly visible. The only shapes our eyes can discern are the mobile mists which multiply the horror, depicting it in ever-changing shapes.

We cross a tiny footbridge. As we plough into the mists beyond the steaming rivulet, the footbridge creaks with stealthy footsteps. Both Ted and I halt, arrested by our mutual terror. We listen to the dripping silence. We prowl again into the midnight mists. Our hearts almost stand still when a sinister, mausoleum-shaped Sherman dome appears out of the overhanging fog. We retrace our circuit. Again, the footbridge. Again, we pass into the mists. Again, the footsteps. Again, the sodden, inhuman silence.

It seems unlikely that a Squadron of our mates lies sleeping around us. They could not be so silent. They are all dead. It cannot be true that a battalion of the Black Watch lies snoring along the road. They too are pale corpses with throats slit and eyes staring. It is too silent for life, for war. It is not the Germans who prowl – warm-blooded, comfortable enemies. There are the Things of the unholy night, whose horses we see galloping in the mists, whose wings beat suddenly out of the darkness, whose low moans sough on the chill wind and whose cloven feet snuffle through the muddy grasses.

I shrink back into Ted's rough khaki and, as we approach the footbridge again, whisper, 'You go on. I'll duck behind that bush and find out who's following us.' We tread softly over the bridge. Under our feet the malevolent rivulet boils and hisses though its water is near freezing. I step to the left and crouch behind a thick bush as Ted shuffles off into a lost eternity. I wait.

The footbridge crackles. Eases. Moves. Footsteps tread over the bridge and nothing is there. Nothing is visible. Nothing materializes. Only the white-sheeted ghouls of moisture wavering around the bridge. But no human body

superimposed upon the unseen feet which tread the empty
bridge. The footbridge creaks and eases and adjusts itself
and sighs through the length of its old, sodden, elastic
timbers. Easing itself back into shape. Untrodden. I shudder at the maniacal laughter which floats through the mists.
Then realize I am listening to myself. I hurry after Ted.
Hurry to the warmth of his human body and movement.

21 OCTOBER 1944:
There is a football field beyond our laager. We challenge
the artillery to a match. Someone from Northampton has
sent us a new set of football kit. I save a penalty. The
artillery forward snarls, 'You didn't ferking save that. I hit
it straight at you.' Harry Graham shouts from behind the
goal, 'Take no notice of the bugger. Jolly good save, mate!'

Another penalty is awarded against us by the impartial
referee, our own RSM, big George Jelley, who is a
professional referee. Being a rugby man, I am not aware of
the rule which requires the goalkeeper to stand still until
the penalty is kicked. I decide to baffle the odious artillery
forward by dancing up and down, back and forward, wave
my arms, shout insults. The artilleryman watches me in
amazement. George Jelley opens his mouth wide and in
his well-known paradeground voice yells: 'STAND
STILL!!!' Automatically, I shoot to attention. Heels
together. Arms rigid at side. Head back. Chin up. Eyes
straight to the front. The artilleryman slaps the ball past
me. Laughs and waves his arms. We lose, 5–4.

22 OCTOBER 1944:
Another football match amongst ourselves. One Troop
against another. A knock-out tournament among the five
Troops. Dear old Ralph Hill, wit, amateur actor and
chocolate salesman, goes careering down the wing with
little accurate idea of where he is placing his feet, lashes

the ball with one foot, puts the other foot in a pothole. The ball spins through the goal, winning the match. Ralph crashes to the ground in mortal agonies. A dislocated cartilage, the most painful of injuries. The half-track with the Red Cross on the canopy tears across the field. They load Ralph into the ambulance and rattle him away down the enemy-infested road.

'I bet that was a Blighty One,' says Pete, torn between sympathy and envy.

Tomorrow we go into action again. Reveille an hour before dawn.

23 OCTOBER 1944:

The fateful roulette wheel of war fortune continues to spin in its own haphazard manner. In the dim hours of the night Bill Fox appears beside my tank, accompanied by Bobby McColl, to announce that Sergeant Thompson has returned from hospital and will take over my tank in its true role as Troop Sergeant's tank. Failing other available seats for my redundant body I am to 'ride shotgun', as Bill puts it, in the Squadron Leader's jeep, *pro tem* and until needed and all that, which may be damn' soon.'

I am loading my bedding roll and small kit into the confined space of Hank's jeep when Captain Bill again taps my shoulder. 'Come along, my lad. You're needed. We have two cases of flu. It's a wonder it isn't double-bloody-pneumonia in these God-blasted fields. Come and gun in 4 Troop. There's a reinforcement corporal commanding the tank. But it's only for today. Attacking one of these outlandish Dutch villages. Unpronounceable name. St Miggles Giggles or some such thing.' And kindly, hoary Bill conducts me to my new home, which is waiting with engine ticking over and the unfamiliar face of the reinforcement Corporal staring down from the turret. 'Panter's the name, kid,' he says. 'Who are you? Climb in quick. It's draughty with the front door open.'

Our objective today, the village name unpronounceable according to Bill Fox, is Sint-Michielsgestel. The four-mile sector as far as Schijndel has been cleared by the 4/7th Dragoon Guards, whose Sherman tanks now line the route and whose crews seem very relieved that they are not required to advance further.

We have now a similar advance of between four and five miles, not far for an energetic walker on a hiking holiday, but a very considerable distance for a tank column advancing through unknown country in face of a determined defence. Indeed, the enemy has barricaded the main road with fallen trees, so we move to the left and outflank the enemy position. Soon the tall tower of Sint-Michiel's church comes into view. At some 800 yards from the village we turn into the fields on the right of the road and survey the houses carefully. Ahead of us Arthur Dwight's Firefly moves down into a dip in the field. A 75mm Sherman moves alongside Arthur. Sergeant Warren is advancing along the road.

Out of the pleasant, peaceful day there bursts the familiar slamming sound of a German 88mm gun, a vicious noise we've not heard at close quarters since Normandy. Tremendous speed and hitting power. Nerve-shattering menace. As we look feverishly for significant smoke or flash or movement or square shapes, the double slam echoes and re-echoes among the buildings and across the fields. A geyser of fire gushes from the front of Sergeant Warren's tank. Another double crash. Another flare of fire, this time rebounding from the Sergeant's track. Men bale out of the tank. Oozing smoke hides it from view.

'Gunner, traverse right,' shouts Panter. 'On! Right of the church tower. Between those two houses. Now! Fire!'

I fire three or four shots in succession into the area

indicated by the Corporal. I can see no shape or movement. Other tanks are firing into the same area. Out of the corner of the periscope I see Arthur Dwight climb from his turret. The field slopes down so sharply to a narrow, hidden stream that the muzzle of the immensely protruding 17-pounder gun has struck into the muddy bank at the other side of the stream. Arthur walks forward to look at the gun muzzle. Huge, flaring, bulging flame springs out of the ground at his feet. As he reels, flung to the ground, a cloud of smoke wraps itself round the scene. Someone else jumps from his tank. Another figure from the next tank. Run to pick him up.

'Bloody SP!' Panter screams with rage. 'Put some more rounds into that same area. Fire! Can't see the bugger but he must be there.'

I pump shot after shot at an invisible target. My flying tracers blossom into blinding flame amid the houses. I glance back sideways in the periscope to Arthur's tank at the edge of my vision. A Black Watch medic is bending down there in front of the stricken Firefly.

'Doubt the poor sod will survive that,' says Panter. 'Who was it anyway?'

Lieutenant Skipper's voice sounds over the wireless, urging us to move out along the road into the village. We follow Harry Graham's tank towards the first houses of the village. Harry will now be thinking of more serious matters than impersonating the RSM. We have heard his gun booming away on our left several times.

'They suspect observers in that church tower,' says Panter. 'Gunner, give us five rounds into the openings in that tower.'

We halt, traverse and desecrate the church tower. There is no response. We start up and roll on. A tiny square at the foot of the desecrated church tower. A small town hall opposite us. Moving a few yards forward, we can see along the main village street, right and left. To the left, along a hundred yards of cobbled street, Harry Graham's tank is roaring triumphantly on to capture our target, the bridge over the Dommel river. As the tank reaches the bridge, the wooden timbers and cobblestones all disintegrate and are transmuted into a rising, writhing column of fire, smoke, dust, detritus and shattered rubble. A hundred feet high the erupting column rises. Hovers. Begins to descend. Then the flailing, paralysing physical noise lashes our tank.

'Bloody Jerry's blown the bridge,' groans Panter. 'Now we're stuck for the night. Old Bill said it's a deep river. Too wide for us to wade over.'

We turn right, and through my telescope I examine and memorize every tiny detail of that inoffensive street, along which an enemy 88mm gun, self-propelled or tank, has recently rolled. Is he there somewhere in a gap between the houses, watching us advance?

Throughout the afternoon we edge forward through the village, pausing at each corner and bend and surveying the land. Small groups of Black Watch follow us along. Every corner and bend is yet another dying time. Every lurch forward into another stretch of open street is to savour all the imagined agonies of wounding, the mind screaming within the skull from the wounds which the body has not yet sensed. The ripping of flesh, the mangling of bone, the shredding of muscles, the agonizing laceration of nerves . . .

The village is a hundred miles long, and the day lasts a hundred years. At last we come to an open space on the left. A gateway and lane leading to a large house. A street junction diagonally to the right. The end of the village. Our final objective. The day's work done. The 88mm gun chased away. Sint-Michielsgestel liberated.

'That's it, then,' exclaims Panter. And, as though he has given some weird order, the Sherman begins to slide and tip. To the left. Stationary but tilting. I glimpse through the periscope a huge ditch to our left. We are toppling into it. Falling. Spinning. I crash out of my seat against the solid, unyielding gun breech. Other solid iron objects rain on me. Something heavy and brutal smashes across my left leg above the knee. Then the final crash: a spine-battering halt, tilted over at a wild angle in the vast ditch.

In the silence, as the engine stalls, somebody begins to laugh. 'Shit!' shouts somebody else. I kick my left leg with my right foot to make sure it is still there. I have somehow become jammed under the gun. We readjust ourselves gingerly in our places, careful lest the tank should entirely turn turtle and seal us off in a tomb flooding with the petrol which could so easily ignite.

Panter puts out a distress signal. It seems only moments before Sergeant Shadlow and the ARV (tracked recovery vehicle) arrive and unleash a massive towing-rope. The ARV tugs us back into the horizontal with a series of bangs as bruising as our descent. We sit upright again and I massage my aching leg. No real damage done. No 88mm shots into our skin-thin bottom plates.

Darkness approaches. Our tank is withdrawn to the miniature town hall with its double ascending staircase. Over the doorway a coat of arms features St Michael himself bearing a flaming sword. Two tanks are to remain alone in the village when the remainder withdraw for the night: our tank pointing towards the east along the main street, Harry Graham and his pals looking west across the wreckage of the bridge. The engineers will work all night to put a Bailey bridge into position.

'Bugger me!' grumbles Panter down my neck. 'Why couldn't they leave one of the other Troops in the village overnight? We've been up front all day. No chance to get out and stretch our legs either. There's a sodding Jerry

Spandau firing from across the river where the infantry can't get at him yet.'

We settle down under the watchful eye of St Michael, running our engine occasionally to top up the batteries, then sitting in a silence broken by odd stutters of machine-gun fire. But our night is not to be undisturbed. Either the Germans are aware that the engineers are moving up with a Bailey bridge, or else their artillery commander is suffering from dyspepsia and is determined that, if he cannot sleep, nobody else shall rest. Crashing shells vomit fire at us. The clashing of shattered roof slates mixes with the tinkling of broken glass and the crunch of fractured brickwork.

Smoke from exploding shells and dust from shattered bricks permeate the tank, mixing with the animal odours which we ourselves produce after a day in our mobile iron cistern. Our driver has 'Gypo tummy' and at our advanced battle station he cannot open his hatch to empty the tin ammunition box which he uses frequently as a chamber pot.

'Bugger this for an all-night picture show,' grumbles the driver as another series of explosions fills our dark world with blinding flashes that leave the night even darker, purple-black, in their wake.

'And how do we see if Jerry does come up the road?' I ask.

In the middle hours of this interminable night of torture for all the senses – blinded eyes, battered ears, offended nostrils, aching, cramped limbs – there is a scratching and tapping on the back of the tank. Panter pulls out his revolver and thrusts it over the edge of the cupola, to be confronted by . . .

A Dutch civilian carrying a tray of coffee. 'Gut evening, my friends,' he says, smiling at our surprise, 'or may it be not a gut evening. You will like some coffee, please? This is not the very gut coffee. There is a war. May it be you know there is a war. So it is the very bad coffee. But you are welcome in Sint-Michielsgestel.' The coffee may be very bad coffee but it is preferable to any of our ration drinks. And it is served in tiny blue-and-white china cups which contrast oddly with the grim brutality of our cell. And it bespeaks the warmth of welcome of the Dutch doctor, for such he is, who walks bravely through the shell-blasted night whilst we skulk low within our steel armour.

When we have finished our coffee and the imperturbable doctor has gone away, a tiny speck of human sense amid the erratic and imbecilic flashes of mortar bombs and shells, Panter says, 'I'm going to call up Squadron Headquarters. See if we can pull back or forward out of this square. It's obvious that Jerry has got this crossroads pinpointed on his maps.'

He calls headquarters. There is no reply. For almost half an hour we take it in turns trying to raise our control station. The only response is a message from Harry Graham's tank to the effect that, 'We've been trying to raise them too, but the buggers have obviously gone to sleep and left us in the ferkin' manure.' So we lapse into silence again. The troubled silence of unceasing radio atmospherics, and our engine grumbling into idling speed from time to time, and the immense cacophony of the barrage.

'Hullo, Xray 4 Able to Xray 4 Charlie. Has the waiter called on you? Over.'

'Charlie to Able, yes, he served us coffee. Did you get served? Over.'

'Able, we got coffee. But what else did you buggers get? Over.'

'Charlie, nothing more. Only coffee. Over.'

'Able, you ought to be with the élite crew. We got cigars as well . . . .'

Normally   some   superior   commander   would   call

instructing us to observe wireless discipline and not waste radio time. Tonight everybody seems to have gone home except two Shermans, a Dutch doctor and an insomniac German artillery commander.

I sit and stare through the periscope at the fitful world which flickers between total black obscurity and rending red lightning not of God's creating. In the red glare the Dutch street stands solid under the continual pounding of high explosive. Rain, the colour of blood, streams over the cobbles and grins back at us amid the lunatic fire flashes. Mirroring the dead waxen grins of so many we have seen along the way.

Tonight my usual nightmare transmutes into living faces. Today at a corner a mile back along the road, Arthur Dwight's tank squeezed past us. I saw his face clearly, in telescopic close-up. The pale, drawn face of a lad my own age. Sending his driver forward into the unknown deserts of fear that used to be pleasant fields outside a quiet Dutch village. Where is he now? Has he survived that fearful explosion in front of his tank? I cannot hope . . . And other living faces. Scared faces. Masks upon scarred minds. The living who turn the dead over, examine them, look in their faces and then pass on along the road – carry the scars of death struck and struck again, like white-hot iron, into the soul. The faces of the living. Their soiled minds and tormented memories are vehicles for real ghosts.

25 OCTOBER 1944:

Dawn breaks sullen, damp and smoke-blackened. Above our heads St Michael still grasps his flaming sword upon the coat of arms of the burgomaster's house. After the filth and destruction of the battle St Michael looks somewhat bedraggled and weary. But no more so than the young Michaels squatting in this reeking tank.

The engineers have erected a Bailey bridge over the

river during the night. B Squadron tanks file past us, their commanders looking curiously up and down the village street, making obscene gestures at us, then bracing themselves to keep watch over the fields and woods beyond, still unconquered territory. Behind the tanks walk platoons of relaxed Highlanders, easily keeping pace with the rear tanks. The front tanks will be venturing slowly and agonizingly towards the first, blank savage corners. Their caution filters back along the column, dictating a snail's pace, a pace of monster snails with armour-plated shells on their backs.

Behind B Squadron come even more familiar faces above the turrets – Ken Snowdon, Bobby McColl, Ossie Porter, Bert King, Squadron Leader David Bevan himself. C Squadron again on the move, for each Squadron has a new objective today. We trail along behind in a reserve role.

If given any other role today, we would be of little use. We are battle-weary, noise-crazed, body-sullied. It is more than twenty-four hours since we trod on firm, steady ground and since we washed or cleaned out our mouths; and any natural functions performed have been negotiated from a cramped position into an empty brass shell or an ammunition box; and we have not stretched our limbs beyond the strait-jacket requirements of our noisome den; and whilst a normal strait-jacket is manufactured from yielding cloth, our strait-jackets are of totally rigid armoured steel; and we have been forced to endure unceasing noise levels which would constitute a safety hazard in a civilian factory; and during the night we have walked the deepest darkness of soul, trying to find a mental slit trench or dug-out in which to cower from both reality and phantasms.

'Esch, Hal and Halder are the three Squadron objectives,' announces Corporal Panter, after Lieutenant Skipper has lined up his tank alongside ours and 'come aboard' to brief the sleepless Panter. 'Esch, Hal and Halder: sounds like a Dutch music-hall act. Tight-rope walkers or comedians.'

'Sounds more like a new school of Dutch painters to me,' I reply, but our attempts at humour fall as flat as an unexploded shell.

'That twerp Kemp,' explains Panter, 'was on wireless watch when we were trying to get through in the night. Fell fast asleep. Bloody lucky it wasn't a squadron of Jerry Tiger tanks breaking through!'

'Any news of Arthur Dwight? And Sergeant Warren?'

'Old Bunny Warren is all right. Just battered about a bit and cussin' even more than usual. They say that Dwight lad lost a leg and was blinded. Don't hold out much hope.'

The morning drags slowly by, the sluggish progress of the clock accentuated by our jolting, ten-yards-at-a-time advance as we wriggle and jerk about in our tight coops, like battery hens, vainly trying to restore circulation in legs, buttocks and shoulders.

In the afternoon wireless messages buzz busily from neighbouring battles. We progress along a straight, tree-lined lane that ends in a railway crossing. Our tank bumps on to the railway tracks and halts there. Fortunately there are no trains running today. The ruler-straight track runs away into misty invisibility both northwards and south-wards. At some point down and up the line our empire ceases. At some point the enemy still holds the banks on either side of the line.

A solitary German stands up, about 300 yards away. Surveys the scene. Races across the tracks. Dives into the bushes at the other side of the rails. Snakes of tracer slither from our immediate right and send sparks off the rails where the German crossed. I sit in amazement and fail to tread on my trigger button.

'Where there's one bloody Jerry there's bound to be

fifty,' growls Panter. 'Keep your eyes and bowels moving, mate, and get your ferkin' foot ready on that button. Operator, check you're loaded with HE. Give 'em a few extra creases in the arses of their trousers.'

Two Germans sprint from the right of the tracks. 'Range 300!' I stamp, swing the gun, stamp again. The field-grey figures arrive at their leafy destination without my shot impacting. Somehow I'm not too sad about that.

Far to the right, through the trees, I see movement. Traverse the turret. 'Not that way,' commands Panter. 'Those are Jocks advancing.' Yes, the Highland gamekeepers and poachers and deer-stalkers, disguised in khaki, are moving across that field, beating the bushes as though driving grouse. Flushing out two-legged prey whose only escape route is across the rail tracks under our guns.

A batch of field-grey figures detaches from the right-hand bushes. My foot stamps without command from my brain. Fire and smoke lash out from two unseen tanks to our right. Distant running figures shudder, freeze, stagger, are flung upwards, catch fire, disintegrate, collapse, roll writhing on the railway lines, lie still. Others race, jump, duck, crawl prostrate towards the security of the far undergrowth.

'Bloody murder,' grunts Panter. 'Stay alert. Keep it going. We're winning.'

I sit in my tiny judgement seat. In a funk. Think of Arthur Dwight, blinded and disabled. Search for anger to speed the downward beat of my feet, sentencing petrified Huns to Hell at 300 yards' range. They take their pick in the lottery of battle fate. Surrender and risk a stray bullet or an avenging Highlander. Fight back against the overwhelming numbers of the Jocks. Lie still as though dead and take a probing bayonet through the liver. Or run across the railway lines where the stupendous volcanoes of searing flame and flailing shrapnel constantly erupt as I and the

Harry Grahams and Bruce Dicksons tread gently on tiny buttons unleashing cremation power.

As the grisly game of man-hunting fizzles out, I gaze along the rail tracks, empty of movement except where a contorted body still twitches as its spirit takes a darker and more distant journey.

The infantry, our Scottish infantry, dig in. We are released. Back to a field at the crossroads. Our Sherman bucks over a green bank and sways gently across a grassy level. 'Driver, halt. Unload all guns. Driver and operator, switch off.' A painful, unbearable silence hammers on our eardrums and tears at our brains. This is the climax of our Chinese torture. Incessant clangorous noise for thirty-six hours without respite. Then silence. Mute, harsh, virulent silence.

'All right, lads!' Panter shouts down inside the soundless tank. 'Get out! That is, if you're not that solid to your seats. And I wouldn't be ruddy surprised if you was, 'n all.'

We haul ourselves up by reluctant arms. Roll off the turret on to the engine covers. Slide down to the ground. My left leg folds and I fall flat on my face. Strong arms pick me up. Cooks and drivers. Waiting as ever to welcome us in and provision our tanks. Known and friendly faces. Jack Aris and Harry Claridge and Scotty and the rest.

'Had yer legs shot off, then?' asks Scotty.

'No, can't you see he's been out all night boozing in that Dutch village? Jong Genever, they calls that drink,' suggests Harry Claridge.

'Aw, come on. Can't you see the poor lad's tired out?' argues Jack Aris. 'Wakey, wakey, boy. There's double rations for you all today.'

They stand me up and I grope my way around the tank. 'What's a matter, mate?' asks Panter.

'My leg's crocked. Got a bash from something falling on it yesterday when we went into that ditch. I'll be OK.'

'Just you sit there and take it easy for a few minutes. We'll brew up a nice old cuppa. That'll solve all your problems. D'you know it was thirty-six hours you lads were packed inside that old corned beef tin? No wonder your legs comes out feeling like bloody corned beef.'

Fortune's wheel gives another jerk. Panter's gunner is waiting to resume his place on the tank. So I gather my few belongings and limp in the general direction of Squadron Headquarters. At least Panter has the kindness of heart to order his gunner, fresh from a couple of days' rest, to clean the guns I've been firing. I slump on my blankets and share rations with some of my old mates from HQ(F) – Pete Pedder, Don Pateman, Sergeant 'Basher' Bates (the least 'bashing' of men except for his driving methods), Ken Squires and all.

A new sound – as of ten military bands marching through a tunnel – funnels across the field. Memories of the invisible tanks at midnight in Audrieu. Now invisible military bands. A large loudspeaker van, perhaps our old friend from Audrieu, bounces into the field, the music of 'Stars and Stripes' also bouncing as the needle of the gramophone takes the jolts from the van's wheels, so that the 'Stars' stumble in their courses and the 'Stripes' become distinctly wavy. A hoarse cheer greets the van. 'Play some Glenn Miller! What about Salome? Up with Vera Lynn. Feed us the hot stuff, man.'

The invisible NCO I/C gramophone records within the van remains impervious to our suggestions, artistic or philistine, and serves up what appears to be a job lot. 'Stars and Stripes' are followed by 'White Cliffs of Dover', then by an amputated section of Beethoven's 'V for Victory' Symphony, and eventually by a banal song which nobody, classicist or jazzman, has ever heard of. The tinny but over-amplified music must be audible also to the Germans on the other side of the railway tracks. We almost expect to hear Wilhelm's distant voice requesting a Wagner extract.

As the van eventually retreats, to a round of jeering and banging of mess-tins, Dick Bates passes round supplies of field postcards. We sit and strike out the inapplicable sentences. I indicate that 'I am well' for there is no printed sentence to say, 'My left leg is aching like blazes.' And additional written comments are not permitted.

'Hey, you guys,' says Bruce. 'Why is there no message on here which says, "Dear Mother, I'm dead"?'

'Because,' says somebody else, 'for you it would have to add, "from the neck upwards".'

That remark triggers off an all-in wrestling match, as though we have not seen enough combat today, in which more and more people become involved. I keep my left leg gingerly out of the way and join the cheerleaders. The fun is much more entertaining than the Army's official music-delivery van.

As I divest myself of footwear and trousers and slide into my blankets on the hard, friendly earth, I remember my mother's old mangle. An immense machine with huge wooden rollers to batter recalcitrant sheets into dryness on the wettest day, it took all my mother's energy and will to spin the huge wheel which turned the churning rollers. One day, intent on pulling the wheel to mangle a thick flannelette sheet, she did not notice my thumb holding tight to the sheet as I tried to help her. The thumb was dragged between the awful, pounding rollers and, it seemed to my moment of utter agony, mashed flat like a penny for ever. The thumb survived, and so did the memory of griping, pulsating pain – so very much like the pain that persists in my leg as I twist and double up into the blankets. I attribute the worst of the pain to the familiar cramp that follows a day and a night and another day of imprisonment in a tank. Explosions of smoke-black sleep kill the day and drive me down into instant unconsciousness.

11

Goodbye to Tank

25 OCTOBER 1944:

As I sit on my blankets in the cold, grey morning light and pull on my trousers, the leg of the garment jams around my left knee. I look down with bleary eyes and see something reminiscent of an elephant's leg, huge, distended, shapeless and mottled purple-brown.

Dick Bates is sitting on his blankets a foot or two away. He looks at my leg with disbelief. 'You wants to get that attended to, young Ken. Go and see the Quack Corporal. I'll tell Hank.'

'No. It's all right. Just a bit of bruising from when we went head over heels into that ditch I told you about. I'll be all right when I've jiggled about a bit.'

'Looks bloody painful to me. I'll tell Hank anyway in case you have to go off before the final whistle today. He's still at conference. Says you must go up in his jeep again. Reserve commander as usual.'

By sheer force I drag my uniform into place, taking care to wear my shoes today rather than the heavy regulation boots. Hank, tall, slim, as unruffled as ever, ambles back from his conference and calls for Troop Leaders. He turns to me.

'I want you to go back to Sint-Michiel and bring up Sergeant Warren's tank if it's mobile. Or see that it is recovered. I'm sending Corporal Hunt back to get Corporal Dwight's tank. Take my jeep. Then report back to me. We shall be advancing along this route . . .' He points to arrows on the perspex cover of his map.

'Yes, sir. By the way, is there any news of Corporal Dwight?'

'No news, I'm afraid. The medical evacuation system is so fast, people vanish into it and are never heard of again.'

I join Lowe in the jeep and we head back the couple of miles to Sint-Michielsgestel. The villagers have already begun cleaning up the village although flesh-red scars show on the brick tower of the church where our high explosive concussed. We skid around the narrow corner and speed out into the country road. Arthur Dwight's tank still stands in the marshy dip to the left, its gun hanging brokenly over the tiny brook. Sergeant Warren's tank should be over to the right.

I get out and hobble across the field. There is no tank, but a great patch of scorched ground, spattered with metallic detritus, the grass for yards around fouled by smoke and splintered shrapnel. A civilian approaches me and extends his hand in greeting. 'Do you look for a tank? The tank which was aflamed? It is not here. It is gone away. The flamed tank, the tank with the wheel joins smashed, the soldiers in the black hats like your hat, they came and take it away to your working shops, they say.'

So the fitters have preceded me. My task is accomplished. I shake hands with the Dutchman again. Refuse his hopeful offer of a cigarette. Offer him a couple of real English cigarettes which I always keep handy in a pocket.

We drive back through St Michael's village. See a shop open. A shop actually selling goods. We stop and buy some Dutch cheese to share with our pals. The shopkeeper and his customers insist on drinking our health. We continue back to our overnight laager. The Squadron had disappeared. After wandering along a number of back lanes, we find Hank's tank tucked in under trees on a long, straight avenue. A number of other Squadron tanks are visible, their guns traversed to all points of the compass, even towards *us*. We are obviously at the all-too-familiar arrow-point of advance, and the fields on either side of the road have not yet been flushed clear by the Jocks. I report to Hank on his turret.

'Very well,' he says, after listening in to a wireless message between two 3 Troop tanks out on the flank. 'There is no tank for you to command today. But when the replacement comes up tomorrow you take it over permanently and put up another stripe. Today, just follow me around and be available.'

Lowe and I sit in the jeep and nibble cheese whilst odd bangs sound from the woods on our flanks. Occasionally a puff of smoke and dust, enclosing a red fiery eye, blinks at us from the fields or ahead on the road. The sun shines brightly to dispel the rains of the last few days. The Netherlands are smiling at us. An hour or so passes before Hank waves me back up to his turret. I climb on to his tank, wincing at the sharp-clawed pains in my knee and thigh.

'I have a job for you. Or rather two. That young lad over there – I don't know him. He's a reinforcement – has been arrested for refusing an order. He was told to go with a stretcher party into a burning house up the road where there were one or two wounded Black Watch fellows. Take him back to RHQ and hand him over to Major Fraser, HQ Squadron Leader. You don't need an escort. He won't give you any trouble.' A pale-faced boy in a black Yeomanry beret is standing wearily at the side of the road, guarded by two burly swarthy Black Watch privates.

'And call at Bill Fox's tank up front on the road there somewhere. They have captured a wounded German colonel. Walking wounded. We don't have any officers to spare to escort him. Take him back to the Adjutant who knows about it. That's all.'

'Excuse me, sir . . .' The Squadron Leader listens in on

a message, orders 4 Troop to swing wide to the left, looks back at me with cool gaze. 'Yes?'

'Whilst I am at RHQ, may I drop in and see the MO? I gave my leg a bang in Sint-Michielsgestel. Perhaps the doc can give me some lotion or an elastic bandage. It's nothing much. Just badly swollen.'

'So I heard. Yes, do that. No hurry. We shall need you tomorrow. Good luck.'

I herd the young English prisoner into the jeep. He is totally subdued and does not appear to know what is happening.

'Bloody shell-shocked, poor blighter,' says Lowe. 'It's a sight worse going around picking up bits of bleeding bodies than sitting inside a tank pressing a trigger.'

Down the road beside Bill Fox's tank is a small group of people, an infantry captain, a tall, imperious German officer, an assortment of British lieutenants and sergeants. I motion the arrested trooper into the front seat and climb into the back seat with the German. Lowe spins the jeep around almost in its own length and, accelerating hard, sends snorts of defiance through its exhaust pipe towards the group of watching officers. We again roar through the streets of Sint-Michielsgestel.

The German Colonel speaks for the first time, in precise English and with a pleasant, cultured voice: 'St Michael. Chainmail armour and flaming sword. More leisurely wars. A man could distance himself from death by leaping back a pace or two. St Michael was one of the more militant of saints. I wonder, would he have been made a saint, had he been on the losing side?'

'Was he on the winning side, sir? I don't know that much about him.'

'Neither do I. But he was a Christian warrior, and the Christians conquered the "powers of darkness". Until Hitler, that is.'

'Strange thing for you to say, sir.'

'Not strange at all. The only strange thing is that we didn't say it sooner and more often. We are losing the war now. You are winning it. So all the saints will be on your side, all the sinners on ours . . .'

We ride past Arthur Dwight's scene of martyrdom. (Dead? Or suffering pains worse than death if he has survived.) But I find it difficult to rouse myself to animosity towards this man in the German braid and badges.

'Of course,' he continues, 'knowing the British ability for self-criticism, it is quite likely that your future generations will cast *you* as the villains, as they did with Haig and Rawlinson. And turn even to our SS for their heroes!'

He smiles a thin, sceptical smile, similar to Hank's smile, then winces as the jeep bounces over a ditch into a field, jarring the shoulder through which he has been shot. This is RHQ. A couple of wireless vehicles. An ambulance. A sentry at a barn door. One or two signs painted on tin plaques and hung on gateposts or stuck in the ground.

The adjutant, Captain Llewellyn, is a small, friendly man with a fierce moustache which disguises his hymn-singing tendencies. He is walking between the two wireless vans. He stops, turns, waits for us to bump to a halt.

'Hullo, Corporal. C Squadron, is it not? Thank you. I will look after the Colonel here. Would you come this way, please, sir?' The German Colonel nods at me, taps my knee and climbs clumsily out of the jeep. Then straightens up to his full imperious height, winces again and marches off, apparently the prototype Nazi, behind mild, music-loving Llew.

Lowe drives up to HQ Squadron headquarters in the barn. A corporal emerges at my call. 'Sorry, mate. You'll have to wait a mo', if you don't mind,' he says, 'because the major is having his back powdered. He's just been taking a bath and isn't in fit state to come on parade.'

We hang around for half an hour while the world war progresses in all its horror on various fronts. At last the Major emerges, bathed, powdered, dressed and twirling his riding crop. 'Ah, yes, Corporal, I believe I know about this. Damn cowardice in the face of the enemy, eh? Leave this man with my Sergeant here. We'll see he pays for the crime.'

Throughout the journey the young reinforcement, whose name I've not asked and not been told, has sat rigidly, the horrified victim of rape. Rape of the mind, not the body. Eyes unblinking. Fingers permanently seized up in one traumatic convulsion. Unspeaking. No vibration of human affinity. The only apparent evidence that he is not totally paralysed or mummified is a thin trickle of spittle frothing from one side of the mouth.

'Poor sod,' says Lowe. 'If he'd been shot through the lobe of one ear a moment before he funked, he would have been a hero for ever.'

'Or if he'd been blasted to blazes and buried in a hole,' I add.

The MO is in the tent alongside the ambulance. 'Let's have a look at the leg,' he demands. He and the 'Quack Corporal' watch with undisguised interest as I struggle to wrench the tightened trouser leg from the ever more swollen elephantine limb. 'Oh, my word,' he whistles.

Later: 'I'm not going to touch that. Have you still got the use of the jeep? Get him to run you back to the Brigade MO. I'll give you a note. The Brigade MO is an orthopaedic specialist. Bone man. He will sort you out in five minutes. Now if you'd come to me with lungs . . .'

Lowe drives me back another couple of miles to Brigade HQ, a marginally more auspicious gathering of vehicles than our own Regimental HQ. The Brigade MO is doctor first and soldier second. He agrees to look at me straight away. 'Nothing better to do,' he grins disparagingly. He and his sergeant wait for the unveiling performance with professional curiosity. His examination is long, detailed and painful.

'When did you say this was? That's almost two days ago. Bursitis obviously. But what's underneath . . . ? Well, it's hospital for you, my lad. Dismiss your driver and I'll send you straight there in an ambulance. Lucky you came to see me. There's bone damage. Could have been bad if you had landed with some unqualified quack, a pill-and-ointment man. Don't bother putting those damn trousers on. Nobody's going to see inside the ambulance. And your own driver's seen a pair of male legs before, surely?'

I walk out with trousers over my arm. Legs bare. Am talking to Lowe, when the extremely tall, imposing Brigadier himself walks by. Does one salute when one is bare-legged and carrying one's trousers? The Brigadier does not seem to notice.

'Say cheerio to the lads for me. Tell Hank what's happened. I'm sure to be back in a week or so. Just let the swelling go down. Ask them to look after my kit.'

Lowe drives out past the Brigade Headquarters sentry, leaving me with what I stand up in, including a pistol belt, one revolver and six rounds of ammunition. No small pack, mess-tins, personal belongings, greatcoat, gas mask. I remember the words of Job: 'Naked came I into the world . . .'

I am the only passenger in the ambulance. We trundle along at a gentle pace through Schijndel and St Oedenrode, where Ralph Hill was taken away by another ambulance after that silly football accident. Then through Eindhoven. A long, long way in tank terms, from the Regiment. Out on the Helmond road. To a real hospital. Occupied by the Army.

In a draughty waiting room a nurse in starched, pure white apron offers me a cup of real English tea made from clear, boiled water – not the chlorinated stuff we have drunk since Castillon. And a queen cake, a delicate bun made with sufficiency of eggs and butter and sugar – after all our dog biscuits and sawdust bread. A doctor subjects me to an X-ray examination. The same nurse, middle-aged but handsome and friendly, shows me to a bed in a ward. 'Not so many casualties as we had expected,' she comments as I look around the half-empty wards and wonder how many beds death has emptied.

I didn't say goodbye to the lads. They'll still be sitting in their tanks, tucked in under the trees along that same avenue or its continuation. Their limbs will be cramped whilst I stretch out within the cool luxury of clean sheets. The hospital bed is hard enough to respond to my ground-hardened bones.

Unchlorinated tea, butter-rich cakes, nurses' aprons starched as stiffly as a Guards sergeant-major's moustache, smiling mouths, friendly eyes, soft-soled shoes, clean sheets. I shudder at the thought of my filthy feet as the nurse, unblinking, removes my socks and levers me into bed. They said I can bath later. Rest now!

I smile softly into sleep.

26 OCTOBER 1944:

A nursing sister brings labels which are pinned to each patient's pyjama jacket or shirt. Khaki-coloured cardboard labels. Each label carries our name, number and religion. And a blank space in which the doctors write either BX or UK. BX stands for Brussels, to which most of the cases, trivial or imminently fatal, are evacuated. UK stands for UK, the top prize in this final spin of the roulette wheel of war.

The doctor holds my label and writes: 'UK'.

'Does that mean what I think it means?' I ask hesitantly.

'Yes, of course. We're sending you back to the UK.'

'But I don't want to go yet,' I protest. 'I'm supposed to be taking over a new tank. And I haven't said goodbye to the lads. And there is nothing really wrong with me. I'm not badly wounded or ill.'

'Young man,' he smiles, 'I happen to be a surgeon and I happen to believe we cannot look after you properly here. Your leg is excessively swollen because it has filled with fluid. But there is more significant damage to the bone, as shown by the X-rays. We can't touch that here. And they wouldn't want to be bothered with that in Brussels. So it's back to England and your sweetheart, whether you like it or not.'

'I haven't got a sweetheart,' I mumble.

'Well, you needn't be without one for very long when they see you hobbling around in hospital blue. Take my word for it.'

27 OCTOBER 1944:

In the early morning a young medical lieutenant does the routine rounds of the wards. He looks at my label and reads my documents.

'You don't need to be going back to England,' he exclaims. 'You're a soldier. You stay where the war is. Brussels for you.' And grasping my label he strikes out the UK and writes BX.

Several other squads of doctors and their minions visit various beds. Last of all comes the matron, a fearsome, brawny woman who stamps upon the floor as though treading on cockroaches. She stops at my bed. 'Be ready to move today,' she orders. 'All being well you will be in England before supper, boy.'

'I'm afraid not, matron. My label has been altered.'

She grabs my label as though intent on throttling me. Stares at it with protruding eyes. 'Who altered this label?' she calls. 'Answer me, please. Sister! Nurse! Who had the effrontery to alter this boy's label? Doctor who? That young runt? Fetch him here. This moment. At the double . . .'

Eventually the young Lieutenant appears, not now so arrogant as when he last stood by my bedside.

'And tell me, sir . . . what authority do you consider you have to go around my hospital altering the damn' labels? You may have two bloody fried eggs on your epaulettes but in this hospital you are a pip-squeak, sir. That's what those pips are on your epaulettes. Pip-squeak authority. These boys in this ward have been in a bloody war which you know nothing about. We have top specialists here, sir. When we decide someone is going back to the UK, we shall not consult you, sir. For all your pips and squeaks. Nor will you alter another of my labels unless you want to be out on your ass, sir. Yes, sir, "ass" I said, and "ass" I damn' well mean!'

Red-faced and puffing hard, the burly Matron turns towards me and with surprisingly gentle fingers, detaches the label, deletes BX, writes UK again, signs it and pins the label back. Suddenly she smiles at me, winks and says in a low voice, 'Bloody whippersnappers. Who do they think they are? Enjoy Blighty, boy.'

After an early lunch a number of us who wear the lucky UK label are pushed in wheelchairs or carried on stretchers to where a number of ambulances are waiting for us.

'Eindhoven aerodrome, it is,' says the orderly who is pushing me. 'Lucky bugger. You'll be home for tea.'

'Where do we arrive?' I ask.

'Don't ask me! Luck of the gods. Some convoys go to Scotland. Some straight in to the good old Smoke. Some to the Midlands. Anywhere. But one thing is sure. It's bloody Blighty for you, you lucky young sod.'

I restrain myself from telling him that I want to go back to say goodbye to the lads. I relax, lying on a stretcher in the back of the ambulance, and contemplate my first ever flight in an aeroplane. But contemplation seems to be about as far as we shall get for the time being. The mists which have hampered our advance through the Netherlands now envelop the runway of the simple airfield cut through the pinewoods near Eindhoven.

'Typical bloody British army balls-up,' grumbles a medical orderly to me. 'They've released all the flooding ambulances. Let them go off somewhere else. Now the met. office tells us that we shall have this mist right through the night. And the RAF say they can't take off. And we can't get you poor sods back to hospital. You'll have to camp out here on your stretchers. We'll see if we can get you some more blankets brought out on the fifteen hundredweight. And some char and chow as well. Poor sods!'

The inconvenience of lying here does not worry me. A stretcher is not much more uncomfortable than a decent patch of grass in an orchard. What disturbs me is that I am not eager to leave the war-shattered Netherlands yet. I am in no hurry to go home to Blighty or Tipperary or the white cliffs of Dover. It is as though that other England over there, that green and pleasant civilian land, is no longer my country. I belong to a new nation of wandering gipsies. Nomads who travel and live in tanks rather than caravans. Who are as sun-browned and hilarious as the raggle-taggle gipsies. Who call themselves Northamptonshire Yeomen. When I leave them, I abandon my adopted people. I renounce the blood tie of the pagan tribe which befriended me. Having said that, all the more romantic notions about soldiering have been blown out of my brain by the incessant explosions of shells. Visions of medals and honours have become tarnished by the memory of the greying faces of the dead and the haunted eyes of the wounded.

Only the other morning in that shop local Dutch people told us that in the town of Vught, a mile beyond where I left the Squadron, there is a concentration camp containing many thousands of Jews who have been reduced to living skeletons – those, that is, who have survived the murder squads. My main justification for going to war has come after firing my last shot.

Perhaps my lack of eagerness to go home has other roots. Something deep down within me demands a more dramatic finale to my war. There is the knowledge that I have never really conquered Fear. I feel guilty about that. When I see others, like Hank and Bill Fox and the Dutch doctor, walking coolly through the thickest storm of battle, I feel ashamed of the fear still hidden away in my own mind.

Perhaps the greatest resentment is my failure to resolve my personal quarrel with Death. I remember that pale-faced reinforcement Trooper of yesterday, or was it the day before? A lad doubly pale from lack of exposure and from paralytic horror. I know why and how he could stand out in the road, battered by the shell-racked air, and still be more afraid of going into the burning house to handle the gruesome remains, dead or wounded, of a comrade. I share his disgust at death and his horror of blood. It could have been *me* put under arrest by the newly bathed and powdered Major.

That was a battle I never won, even when I had to tend my own mate, his head and chest half torn away like a surgical school model, the meat within him still raw and bleeding. I envisaged myself sitting there in his place, a gruesome cadaver. I saw myself dead. And was disgusted. Terrorized. And went away calling myself a coward. Now it is too late for last heroics. What was not done in those Normandy lanes and Dutch streets may be left undone for ever. I am for Blighty. Labelled, finally and fatefully, 'UK'. Like a prize Hereford bull labelled for export.

At the end of my journey from Hereford to Aberdeen and Catterick, Salisbury Plain, Normandy, the Netherlands, I hold my own inquest. Since those far-away tough but kindly gamekeepers at the Gordon Barracks went to work on my frail civilian physique, I have grown a full inch taller, put on pounds in weight, squared an inch at the shoulders and knocked several seconds off the time for the quarter-mile. I react faster to the bullet and the bomb. I am bigger and tougher and older and wiser. Yet here, as the evening mists rise, I feel something evaporating from my being, an essence of loyalty and comradeship. A vital spirit divorcing itself from my body and returning to the Regiment where it belongs.

If the Genie of the Lamp appeared now with all the promises of Arabia, I would barter my soul to be allowed to go back up the Vught road and report to Hank. Or fly back to be with Corporal Ken and Rex and Tommy and Hickey in that tank on the Night March at St-Aignan. Or perhaps even farther, with a second wish, to stand again with Michael Hunt at Jérusalem crossroads and hear Michael say that it was all a mistake, a bad dream, that Frank Hickson and Tommy Madelaine and George Valentine and the rest were not dead . . .

I wriggle down into the unfamiliar blankets borrowed from an RAMC store. But if *they* – Frank and Tommy, George and so many – had not died, those of us who remained would not have crowded together for comfort and safety, would not have grown together in such mutual understanding and comradeship . . . had it not been for those friends, each at his own uncharted little Calvary . . . laughing, cursing, vibrant, inappropriate Christs . . . paying the price of our new knowledge and kinship.

Above the runway the white mists slowly thicken into the darker fog of tremulous sleep.

28 OCTOBER 1944 – SATURDAY – D + 144:

The mists are still with us. The far wall of black pines is almost invisible beyond the airstrip. But we are rescued by

a Squadron Leader who is the epitome of the cinema-
screen RAF officer: dashing, handsome, elegant, in a
smartly pressed tunic garnished by bright medal ribbons
with diagonal stripes; he sports the typical huge mousta-
chios and lards every sentence with 'wizard' and 'prang'
and 'gung-ho'. He addresses us as though he were Mark
Antony at the funeral of Caesar and even calls us 'Friends,
Romans and Countrymen'. Though visibility is below the
accepted minimum, his boys will take us up and home, 'if
you're willing to take the risk, me lads?'

We are lifted into the long, cavernous box of aeroplane
with double-tier beds slung from the walls all the way along
the fuselage. As a 'walking wounded' I am asked to watch
the plasma bottle mounted above a badly mutilated
Durham Light Infantryman. I ask an RAF medical attend-
ant about the flight arrangements.

'Where do I sit?'

'You don't!'

'Where do I find my parachute?'

'You don't!'

'What do I do if we get shot down over the sea?'

'You don't!'

End of arrangements. In spite of his weakness, the
Durham man manages a smile. 'Squat on the edge of my
bunk, Geordie,' he suggests.

Engines boom like a full Troop of tanks. Thin fuselage
walls shudder and stretch as we begin to move. A wide-
open door in one wall offers an opportunity for any
aerophobes to jump out at the last moment. Or for anyone
of more suicidal tendencies to take a high dive in mid-
ocean. The plane lifts off with all the resilience of an old
bucket with a hole in the bottom.

Now in the sky an unspoken hierarchy of suffering takes
effect. Those of us with plebeian ailments, like stomach
ulcers or appendicitis or my splintered leg, gather round

and minister to the real aristocracy of pain – the engineer with two legs missing, the Highlander with shot lungs and double pneumonia, the artilleryman with half a face blown away and half a brain showing, my own light infantryman with blood still staining his bandages. They have come so far. Death leaped upon them, savaged them, raked them tooth and claw. Almost drank the life-blood out of their veins. But they fought back. On the bumping stretcher as their clumsy pals carried them delicately back to the aid post; in the churning, clashing medical half-track blundering across country; through the hospital bed and the operating theatre and the surgeon's kind but torturing fingers; loaded into a rocking, juddering ambulance again; exposed to the weather this last lethal night on a stretcher by the runway; finally bundled awkwardly into a chilly, thundering plane.

Now there is the altitude. And the cold. And the swaying. And the diabolical noise. And the smell of other men's decay and degeneration. And the vast distances before we again come to earth. The ease with which the spirit might lift from this altitude into the farthest skies, through the clouds to the peace – beyond the pain and beyond the noise and beyond the terror of war.

So we, who sense the inferiority of our suffering and the hypocrisy of our flight back to Blighty, we serve them and encourage them and woo them towards the place where the surgeons and nurses may again impose their healing will. We watch them and we touch them gently and we breathe the very breath for them, holding them close in the on-going rhythm of life.

Then the cold, grey sea is behind us. And the green fields of England smile up at us in a resurrected sun. And London sprawls smoking away to the south. And soon the golden towers of Oxford send their ancient radiant greetings up towards us as the plane dips and the booming engines hiss into quietness and the clumsy flying box becomes a graceful, gliding bird, lifting swiftly over the Oxford hills and down among the tree-tops and flattening along a lush, green, unending meadow as though the soft, spinning tyres hesitate to bruise those butter-rich wild flowers strewn across our triumphal path.

Down. Thump. Rattle. Squeal. And all our aristocracy of pain are alive and lifting themselves painfully to look with misting eyes at the soil, the bracken, the greenwood of Blighty.

Another ambulance. I sit up front with the talkative girl driver. A plain, stubby country girl in khaki, for me she is a welcoming angel. I ask her the name of the airfield but I am so bemused with the green serenity of England that I have no memory of what she says, even seconds after she says it. Only the merry tinkling, that might be cascading fountains or falling raindrops or the irrelevant chatter of a plain, stubby country girl in khaki.

The railway station sign says SHRIVENHAM in letters too large and important to ignore. And in Shrivenham station a GWR train is drawn up. Volunteers in uniforms of WVS and Red Cross and St John Ambulance, or just plain Wilts or Oxon country plaid, swarm around the ambulances and across the platform and into the train. Welcoming us home. Bumptious, proper county ladies, softening their aggressive accents, fuss over us. Anxious, reticent countrymen carry urns of tea and ease stretchers into place. We are even given an apple, a ham sandwich and a sugary doughnut. Food of the gods, for those able to manipulate sandwiches and cakes. Solicitous WVS workers hold sandwiches to the mouths of those too ill to raise a hand. Endless cups of tea slop on the carriage floors.

I ask a St John sergeant where the train will be headed. 'Us don' know, do us, son,' he replies. 'They don' tell us. Some trains 'as gone all the ways to Scotland. Or p'raps

Dev'n. Or the Midlands. Or up Manchister, Liverpool, Wales. Only one thing certain. Us be pointed westwards so 't won' be Lon'on. Where d'you come from? You West Country yourselve?'

'Strange they don't tell you,' I insist, 'where we are going.'

'War secrets, en' it, like? Ol' 'itler might find out where you was 'eaded. Then where would we be? Better for us not to know these things, hey?'

It is dark before the train pulls out. As we pass little country stations, barely seventy miles from my home, I recognize some of them in the low glow of their tiny war lamps. Quiet rural stations trending ever nearer home.

At least if our train is headed for Scotland or 'Manchister' I shall have breathed the air of my home counties on this long and unexpected journey from Holland. Home-sickness and excitement drive me again and again to the window to identify woods and hills which, to my travelling companions, are merely meaningless blurs against a darkening sky. As the hills grow higher and the woods crowd more thickly, a callow, home-loving youth, the civilian me, begins to take control, and my *doppelganger*, my other self, the hardened military Yeoman, drifts away into the distances behind the chugging train.

I recognize Worcester and strain out of the windows to catch the familiar sights in the blackened-out darkness of war-time. The cathedral, the county cricket ground, the well-known streets. And leaning thus out of the window I hear the cry of 'All change!'

'All walking wounded off the train, please. You will proceed in buses. Stretcher cases stay put for now. You will be going in ambulances to local hospitals. Watch your step in the dark, lads.'

We climb gingerly down into forests of waiting hands which guide us in the shaded glim of one dim electric bulb across the crowded station yard towards waiting buses. Arms support me, pat me, sustain me, caress me. I can hardly see the faces. But the arms are firm and gentle. And I hear the applauding, welcoming West Midland voices. Somewhere on the fringes of the crowd I seem to see my other self in black beret and with sad eyes, scorning my eagerness to be home. Looking as Jesus must have looked from the fringes of another crowd as Peter, anxious to be popular in an alien company, hotly denied his holy allegiance.

The buses are half empty and we have double seats to ourselves. Destination still unknown. (Hitler might find out!) Worcester is only thirty miles from home, and anywhere within bus range of Worcester is good enough for me. But we turn westwards, ever westwards. Soon the midnight road rises to the giddy, twisting heights of the Malvern Hills. Twenty miles from home.

Passing through Ledbury's empty streets of black-and-white houses, the Orderly Sergeant comes along with a clipboard, checking everybody's name, number and religion. I summon up courage to ask the question.

'Are we, by any remote chance, heading for Hereford, Sarge?'

'That's our destination.'

'The General Hospital?'

'Know it?'

'Born and bred in the city.'

'Then you effing-well drew the ace in today's shuffle, laddie. Most of the wounded on this convoy are Geordies or Jocks.'

29 OCTOBER 1944 – SUNDAY – D + 145:

01.00 hours. Ledbury, Stoke Edith, Ludwardine, Tupsley: the very names are like long-lost lovers embracing me as I pass by. Names of villages change into names of streets:

Ledbury Road, St James's Road, Green Street. The shape of the hospital roof.

Open gates. Dimly lit courtyard. People. And a silvery moon glints on the river down the garden slopes.

Again the extended, eager hands as the first walking wounded slowly descend. Excited, babbling 'Ereeful' voices. I stand at the top of the bus steps, tired, dirty, hungry, battle-shocked, alien, frightened of these solicitous civilians. My battledress collar still scorched from a turret fire. My trousers stained with oil from a Sherman gun. My socks matted with dirt from the camping ground at Eindhoven airfield. My face scored deep with fear-furrows. The very antithesis of the conquering hero or the gallant Liberator returning.

A deflated, juvenile St Michael with extinguished sword and shoddy armour. Two campaign ribbons on my chest, one stripe on my sleeve, a tiny red-and-blue HD sign on one arm, and six revolver bullets in my pocket.

Hands lift me down the steps. I hardly touch the floor. A civilian lifts me at one side, and a St John man at the other. Two nurses hover in angelic attendance. They will not listen to my protests that I can walk. Not until we pass into the more brightly lit hospital entrance.

The St John man looks at me in the new light. Stares. Blinks. Opens his eyes wider. 'Here! Your face be familiar, young boy. I really think I ought to know you. You don't come from Hereford by any blimmin' stroke of luck?' I nod dumbly. He turns and shouts, 'Hey! *Hereford Times*! Over yer. There's one of our own boys yer! Now wait a minute . . . You gotta be young Tout. Are you? Jack Tout's boy?' I nod again, my capacity for stirring, heroic speeches totally dried up. No Shakespearian climax to this sordid little war story.

'You remember me, young 'un? I'm Mr Philips from down Portland Street. Just roun' the corner from you. I 'elps out with the convoys when they comes in. Additional to normal St John duties.'

'Yes, I remember you.'

The early morning hour blurs into a barrage of words like machine-gun bullets, and laughter like bomb-bursts, and back-slapping like the battering of gun blasts. And the weariness of months of battle. And the agonizing of cramped leg muscles.

And almost like Hank's voice speaking coolly over the air and dispelling the chaotic misapprehensions of battle, I hear the Sister say, 'Come along and let that boy get to bed. He's tired. He's ill. He deserves to sleep. This is not a victory parade. Clear the ward, please. Quickly now!'

THIS IS NOT A VICTORY PARADE. This is not a victory parade. This-is-not-a-victory-parade-thisisnota . . .

The Sister and the St John man from Portland Street pull off my shoes and socks and trousers and battledress blouse and roll me into bed partially clothed as I am for this is not a . . . not a . . . not a . . .

The St John Mr Portland Street Philips leans over my bed and whispers, 'I'll go roun' now to your 'ouse. Wake your folk. Throw stones at their window. Tell 'em you're 'ome. Tell 'em you blimmin' well finished with that there war . . . Tell 'em . . .'

In the dim doorway a still dimmer and dimming figure in oily denims and black beret seems to beckon . . . blowing a silver trumpet . . . sounding the 'Rally!' . . .

But I shake my head . . . my denial is complete. I want to go home.

True war – now available in paperback from
Grafton Books

To order direct from the publisher just tick the titles you want
and fill in the order form.

True war – now available in paperback from Grafton Books

Len Deighton

Fighter	£2.95	☐
Blitzkrieg	£2.50	☐

Tim O'Brien

If I Die in a Combat Zone	£1.95	☐

Edward Young

One of Our Submarines	£2.50	☐

G S Graber

The History of the SS (illustrated)	£2.50	☐

William Manchester

Goodbye, Darkness	£2.95	☐

Peter Shankland and Anthony Hunter

Dardanelles Patrol	£1.50	☐

Kitty Hart

Return to Auschwitz (illustrated)	£1.95	☐

Angus Calder

The People's War (illustrated)	£3.95	☐

Wolf Heckmann

Rommel's War in Africa (illustrated)	£2.95	☐

Viktor Suvorov

Inside the Soviet Army (illustrated)	£3.50	☐
Soviet Military Intelligence	£2.95	☐

John Winton

The Death of the Scharnhorst (illustrated)	£2.50	☐

Wing Commander H R Allen

Fighter Station Supreme: RAF Tangmere (illustrated)	£2.50	☐

Peter Cremer

U333: The Story of a U-Boat Ace (illustrated)	£2.95	☐

To order direct from the publisher just tick the titles you want
and fill in the order form.   GF2081

True war – now available in paperback from Grafton Books

Alexander Baron
From the City, From the Plough   £1.95 ☐

C S Forester
Hunting the Bismarck   £1.50 ☐

Ka-Tzetnik
House of Dolls   £2.50 ☐

Olga Lengyel
Five Chimneys   £1.95 ☐

Dr Miklos Nyiszli
Auschwitz   £1.95 ☐

Alexander McKee
Dresden 1945 (illustrated)   £2.50 ☐

F Spencer-Chapman
The Jungle is Neutral [illustrated]   £2.50 ☐

Bryan Perrett
Lightning War: A History of Blitzkrieg (illustrated)   £2.95 ☐

Leonce Péillard
Sink the Tirpitz!   £1.95 ☐

Richard Pape
Boldness Be My Friend (illustrated)   £2.50 ☐

Baron Burkhard von Mullenheim-Rechberg
Battleship Bismarck (illustrated)   £3.50 ☐

Livia E Bitton Jackson
Elli: Coming of Age in the Holocaust   £2.50 ☐

Charles Whiting
Siegfried: The Nazis' Last Stand (illustrated)   £2.50 ☐
First Blood: The Battle of the Kasserine Pass 1943
  (illustrated)   £2.50 ☐

To order direct from the publisher just tick the titles you want
and fill in the order form.   **GF2181**

All these books are available at your local bookshop or newsagent, or can be ordered direct from the publisher.

To order direct from the publishers just tick the titles you want and fill in the form below.

Name _____

Address _____

_____

Send to:
Grafton Cash Sales
PO Box 11, Falmouth, Cornwall TR10 9EN.

Please enclose remittance to the value of the cover price plus:

UK 60p for the first book, 25p for the second book plus 15p per copy for each additional book ordered to a maximum charge of £1.90.

BFPO 60p for the first book, 25p for the second book plus 15p per copy for the next 7 books, thereafter 9p per book.

Overseas including Eire £1.25 for the first book, 75p for second book and 28p for each additional book.

Grafton Books reserve the right to show new retail prices on covers, which may differ from those previously advertised in the text or elsewhere.